# STAR WARS
# KNIGHT ERRANT

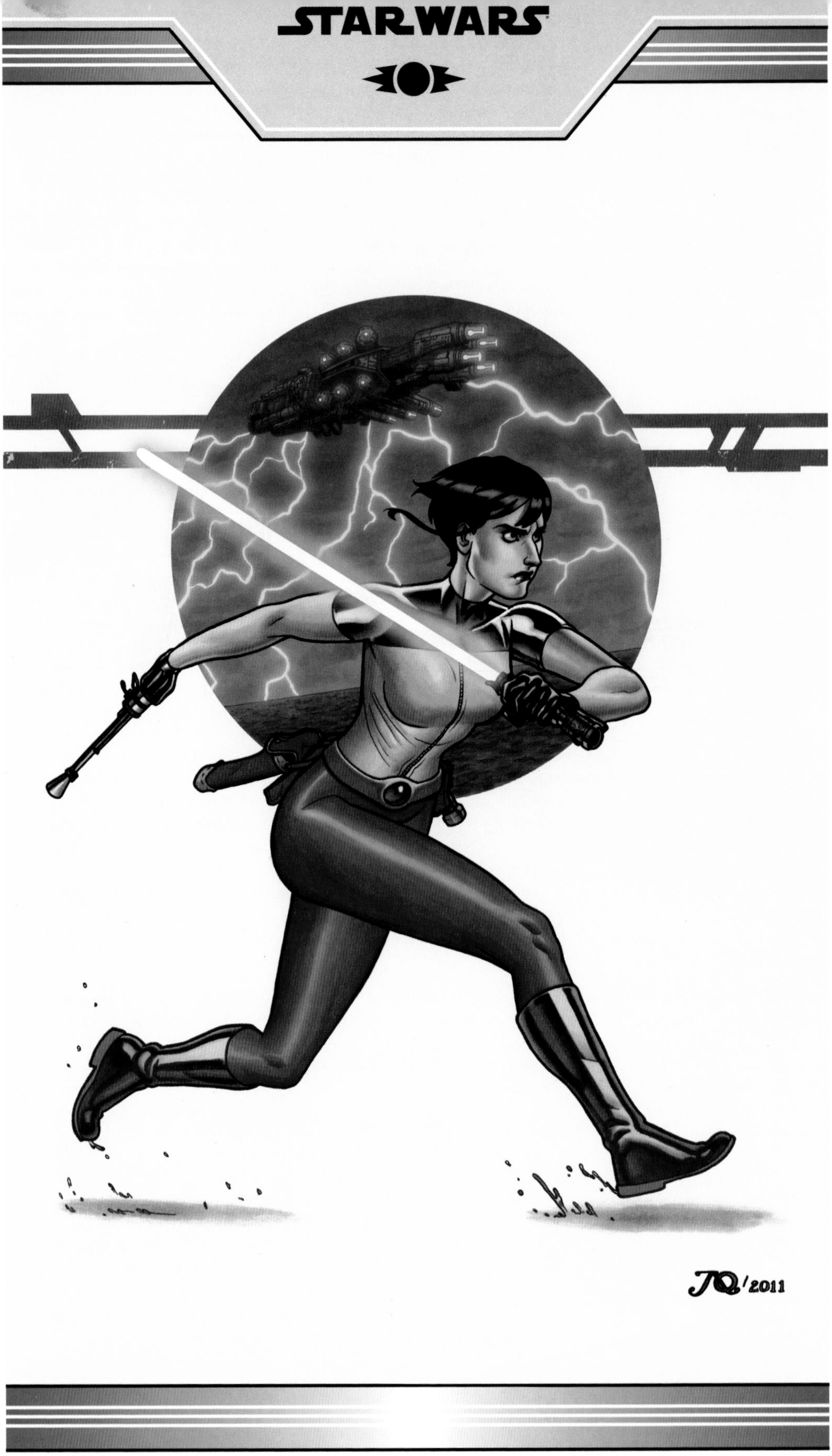
STAR WARS
JQ/2011

ILLUSTRATION BY JOE QUINONES

# STAR WARS®
# KNIGHT ERRANT

## VOLUME TWO
## DELUGE

Script
**JOHN JACKSON MILLER**

Pencils
**IVAN RODRIGUEZ**
**IBAN COELLO**
**DAVID DAZA**

Inks
**IVAN RODRIGUEZ**
**SERGIO ABAD**

Colors
**MICHAEL ATIYEH**

Letters
**MICHAEL HEISLER**

Cover Art
**JOE QUINONES**

DARK HORSE BOOKS

## THE OLD REPUBLIC
(25,000–1,000 years before the Battle of Yavin)

The Old Republic was the legendary government that united a galaxy under the rule of the Senate. In this era, the Jedi are numerous, and serve as guardians of peace and justice. The *Tales of the Jedi* comics series takes place in this era, chronicling the immense wars fought by the Jedi of old, and the ancient Sith.

This story takes place approximately 1,032 years before the Battle of Yavin.

President and Publisher
**MIKE RICHARDSON**

Collection Designer
**KAT LARSON**

Editor
**DAVE MARSHALL**

Assistant Editor
**FREDDYE LINS**

NEIL HANKERSON Executive Vice President TOM WEDDLE Chief Financial Officer RANDY STRADLEY Vice President of Publishing MICHAEL MARTENS Vice President of Book Trade Sales ANITA NELSON Vice President of Business Affairs MICHA HERSHMAN Vice President of Marketing DAVID SCROGGY Vice President of Product Development DALE LAFOUNTAIN Vice President of Information Technology DARLENE VOGEL Senior Director of Print, Design, and Production KEN LIZZI General Counsel DAVEY ESTRADA Editorial Director SCOTT ALLIE Senior Managing Editor CHRIS WARNER Senior Books Editor DIANA SCHUTZ Executive Editor CARY GRAZZINI Director of Print and Development LIA RIBACCHI Art Director CARA NIECE Director of Scheduling

Special thanks to Jennifer Heddle, Leland Chee, Troy Alders, Carol Roeder, Jann Moorhead, and David Anderman at Lucas Licensing.

STAR WARS: KNIGHT ERRANT—DELUGE

This volume collects issues #1–#5 of the Dark Horse comic-book series *Star Wars: Knight Errant—Deluge*.

Published by
Dark Horse Books
A division of Dark Horse Comics, Inc.
10956 SE Main Street
Milwaukie, OR 97222

DarkHorse.com
StarWars.com

To find a comics shop in your area, call the Comic Shop Locator Service toll-free at 1-888-266-4226

First edition: June 2012
ISBN 978-1-59582-638-1

1 3 5 7 9 10 8 6 4 2
Printed at Midas Printing International, Ltd., Huizhou, China

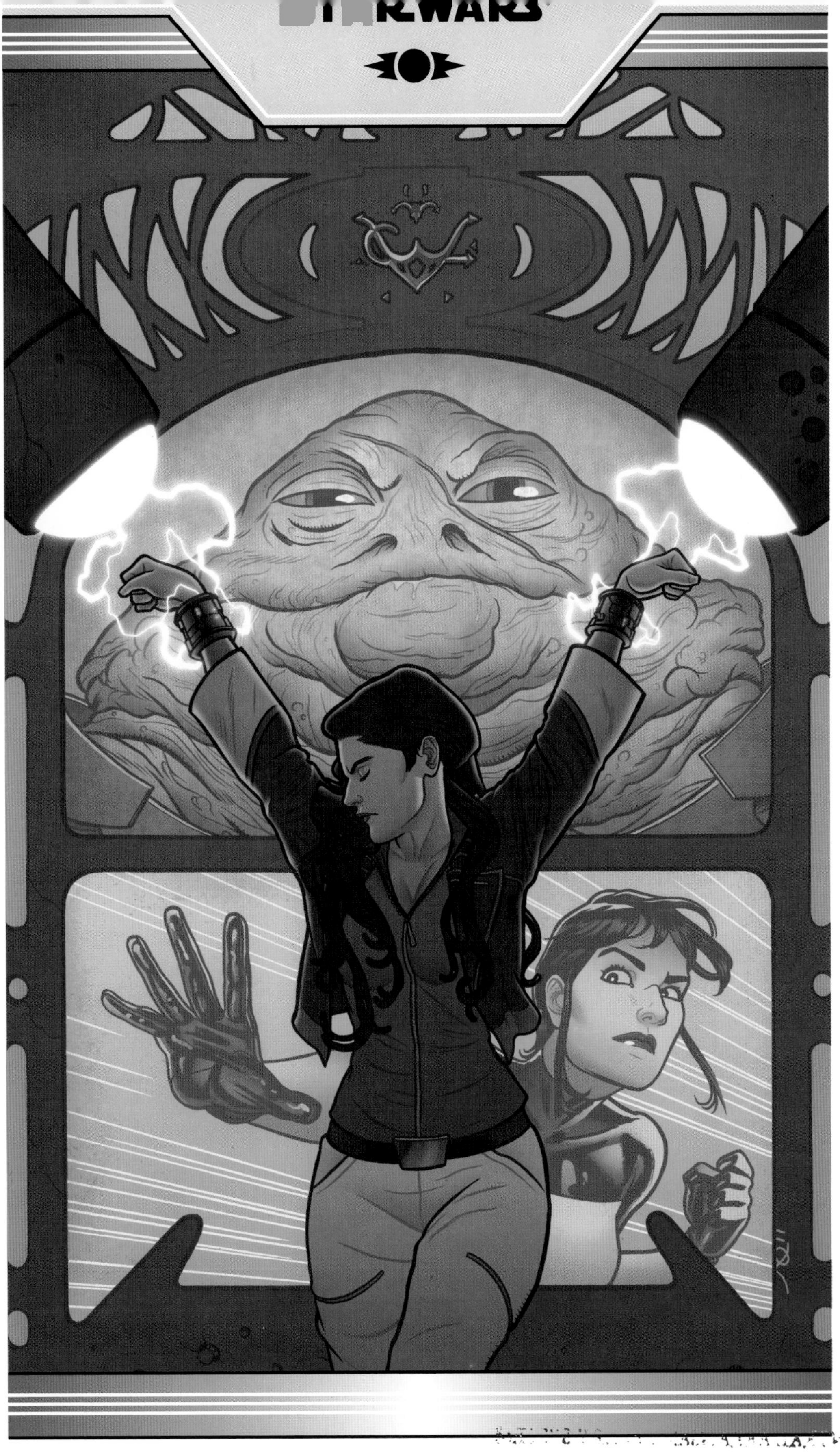

ILLUSTRATION BY JOE QUINONES

# DELUGE

Great civilizations lie in ruins. Sith Lords battle one another for dominance across vast regions abandoned by the Republic. Crushed underfoot are the teeming billions of the forgotten, those enslaved beings unable to fight back against the evil that surrounds them.

Now, a new hope has entered this benighted region. Remaining in Sith space after a failed raid, Kerra Holt, a young Jedi Knight, makes protecting the downtrodden her personal cause. Through acts of sabotage and selfless heroics, Kerra launches a campaign to rescue as many refugees as she possibly can.

Answering another call for help, Kerra returns to the planet she once called home—the idyllic ocean world of Aquilaris, currently held by Sith Lord Daiman. But Kerra is not the only one who sees an opportunity on Aquilaris. And, as she is about to learn, not all evil in the galaxy is Sith . . .

This story takes place approximately 1,032 years before the Battle of Yavin.

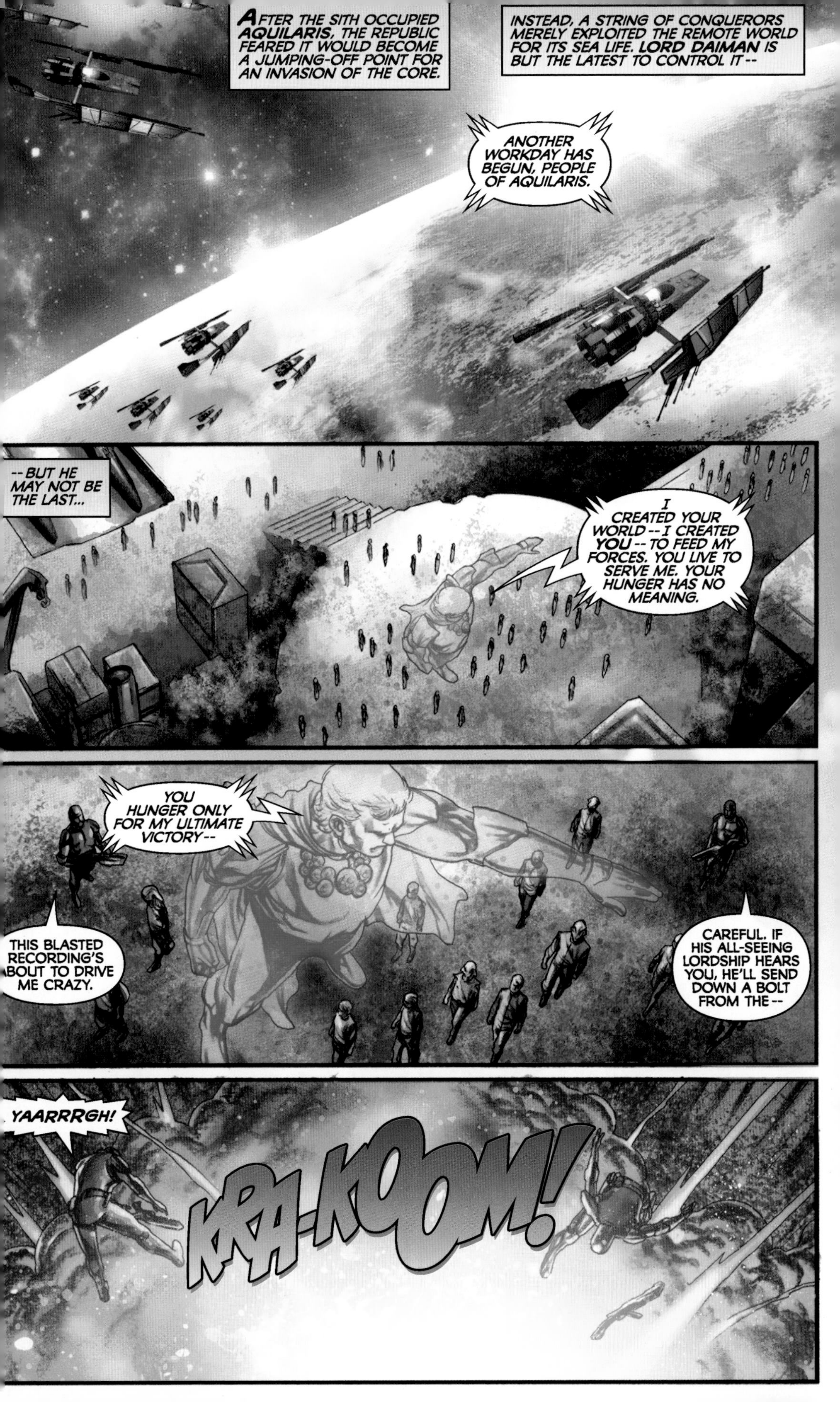
AFTER THE SITH OCCUPIED AQUILARIS, THE REPUBLIC FEARED IT WOULD BECOME A JUMPING-OFF POINT FOR AN INVASION OF THE CORE.
INSTEAD, A STRING OF CONQUERORS MERELY EXPLOITED THE REMOTE WORLD FOR ITS SEA LIFE. LORD DAIMAN IS BUT THE LATEST TO CONTROL IT --
ANOTHER WORKDAY HAS BEGUN, PEOPLE OF AQUILARIS.
-- BUT HE MAY NOT BE THE LAST...
I CREATED YOUR WORLD -- I CREATED YOU -- TO FEED MY FORCES. YOU LIVE TO SERVE ME. YOUR HUNGER HAS NO MEANING.
YOU HUNGER ONLY FOR MY ULTIMATE VICTORY --
THIS BLASTED RECORDING'S 'BOUT TO DRIVE ME CRAZY.
CAREFUL. IF HIS ALL-SEEING LORDSHIP HEARS YOU, HE'LL SEND DOWN A BOLT FROM THE --
YAARRRGH!
KRA-KOOM!

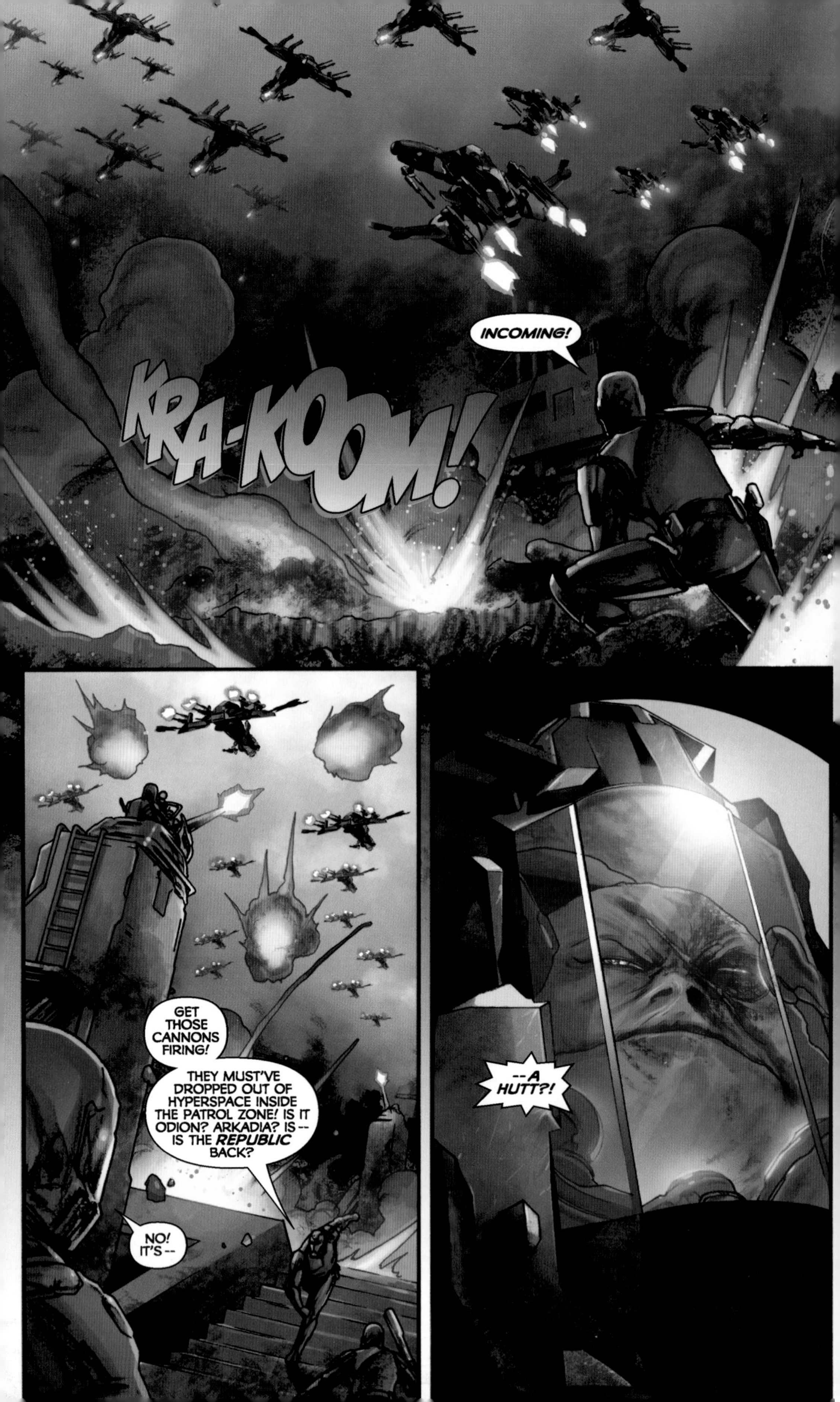
INCOMING!
KRA-KOOM!
GET THOSE CANNONS FIRING!
THEY MUST'VE DROPPED OUT OF HYPERSPACE INSIDE THE PATROL ZONE! IS IT ODION? ARKADIA? IS -- IS THE *REPUBLIC* BACK?
NO! IT'S --
-- A HUTT?!

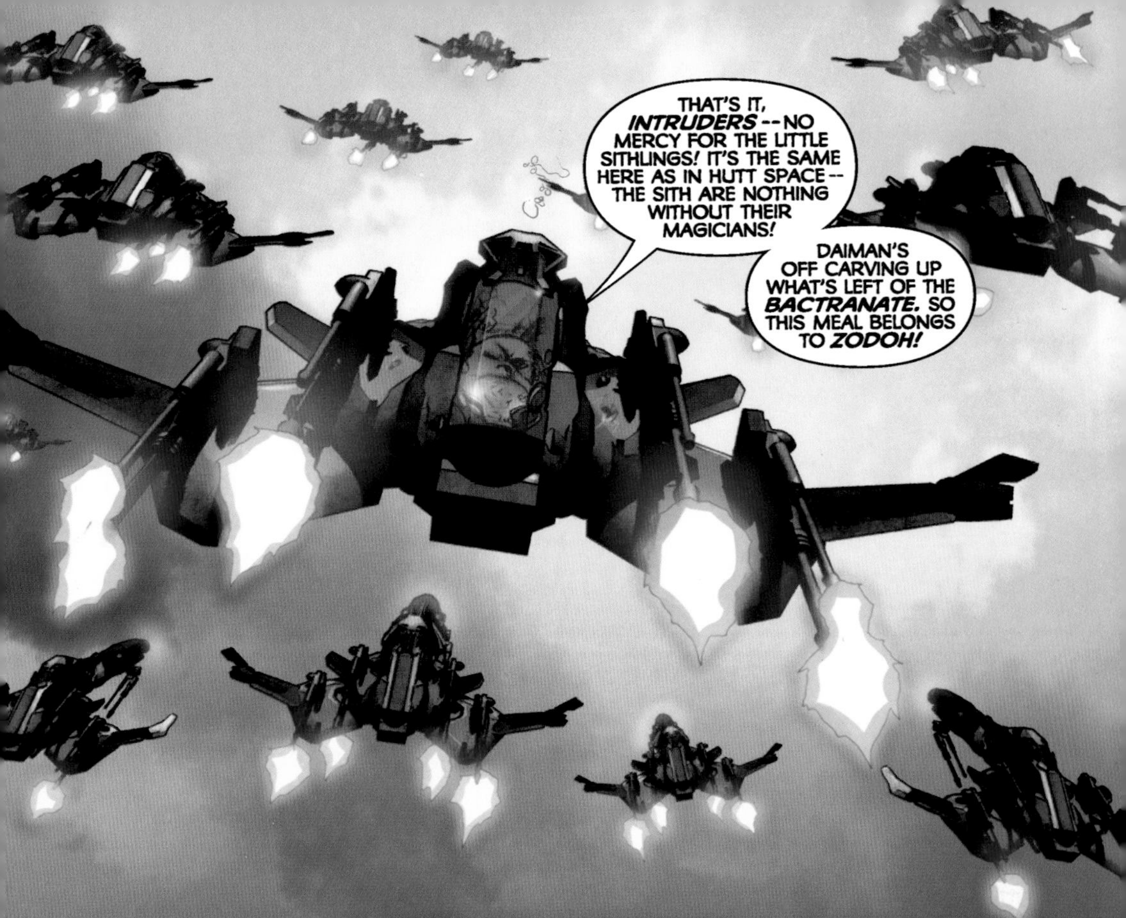

THAT'S IT, INTRUDERS--NO MERCY FOR THE LITTLE SITHLINGS! IT'S THE SAME HERE AS IN HUTT SPACE--THE SITH ARE NOTHING WITHOUT THEIR MAGICIANS!
DAIMAN'S OFF CARVING UP WHAT'S LEFT OF THE BACTRANATE. SO THIS MEAL BELONGS TO ZODOH!

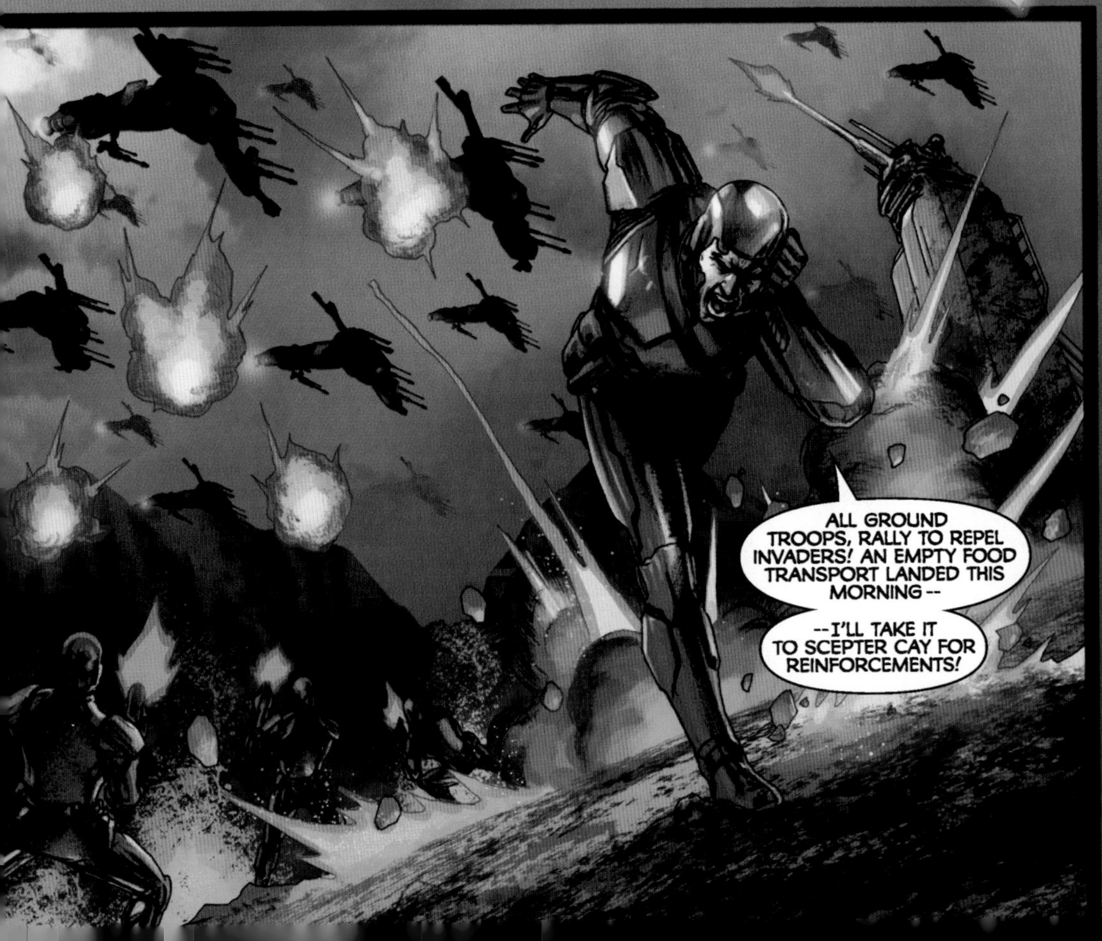

ALL GROUND TROOPS, RALLY TO REPEL INVADERS! AN EMPTY FOOD TRANSPORT LANDED THIS MORNING--
--I'LL TAKE IT TO SCEPTER CAY FOR REINFORCEMENTS!

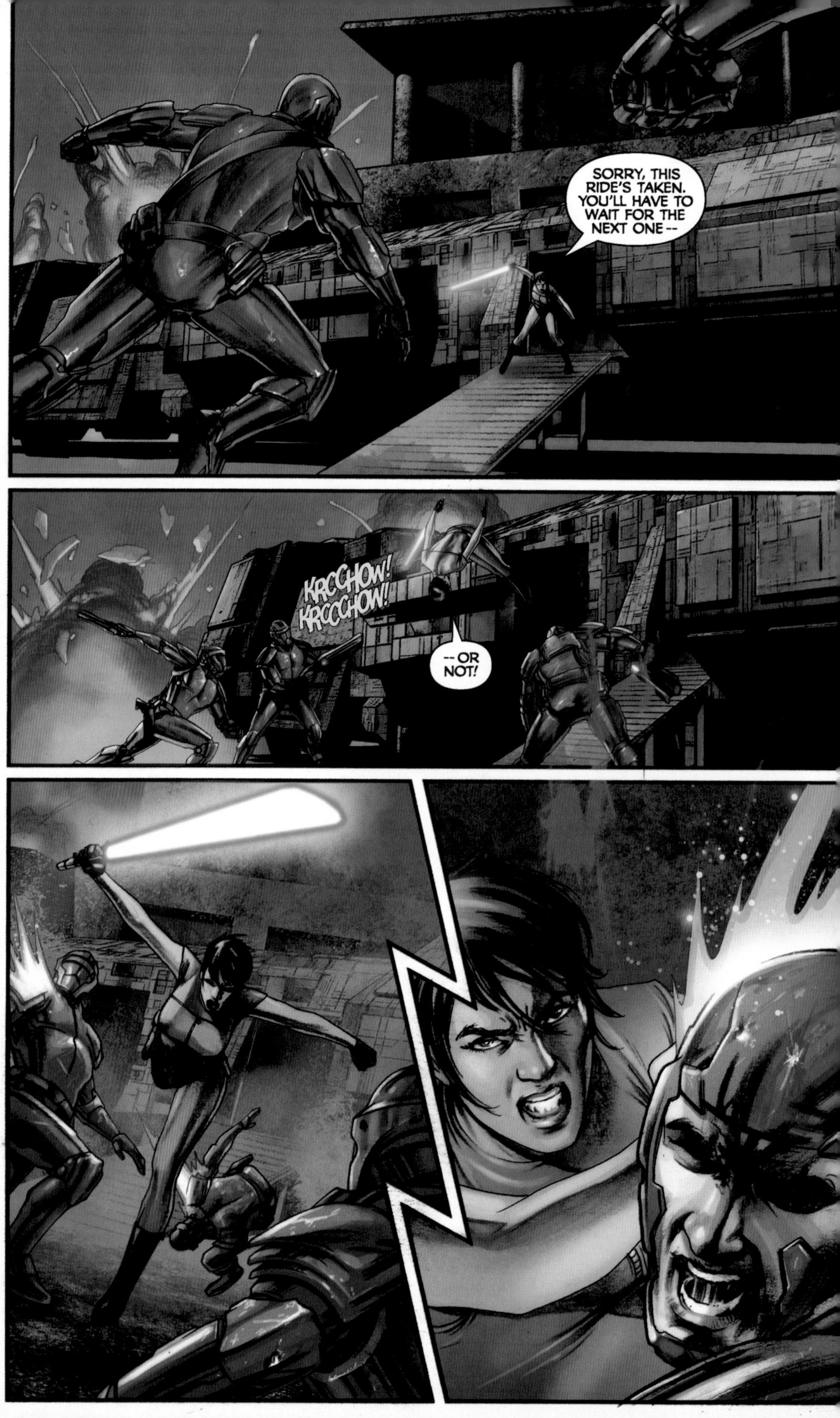
SORRY, THIS RIDE'S TAKEN. YOU'LL HAVE TO WAIT FOR THE NEXT ONE--
KRCCHOW! KRCCCHOW!
--OR NOT!

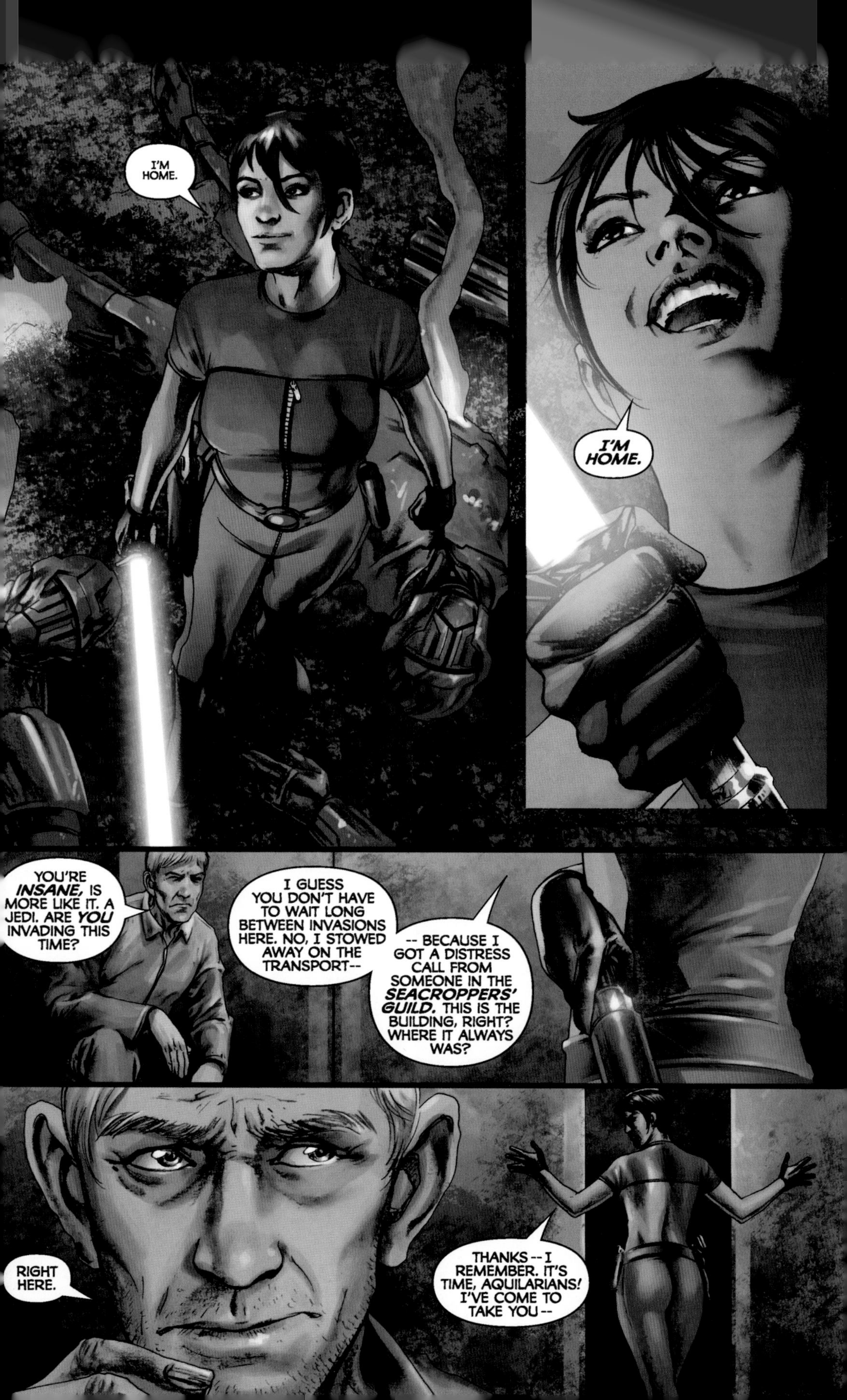
I'M HOME.
I'M HOME.
YOU'RE INSANE, IS MORE LIKE IT. A JEDI. ARE YOU INVADING THIS TIME?
I GUESS YOU DON'T HAVE TO WAIT LONG BETWEEN INVASIONS HERE. NO, I STOWED AWAY ON THE TRANSPORT--
-- BECAUSE I GOT A DISTRESS CALL FROM SOMEONE IN THE SEACROPPERS' GUILD. THIS IS THE BUILDING, RIGHT? WHERE IT ALWAYS WAS?
RIGHT HERE.
THANKS -- I REMEMBER. IT'S TIME, AQUILARIANS! I'VE COME TO TAKE YOU --

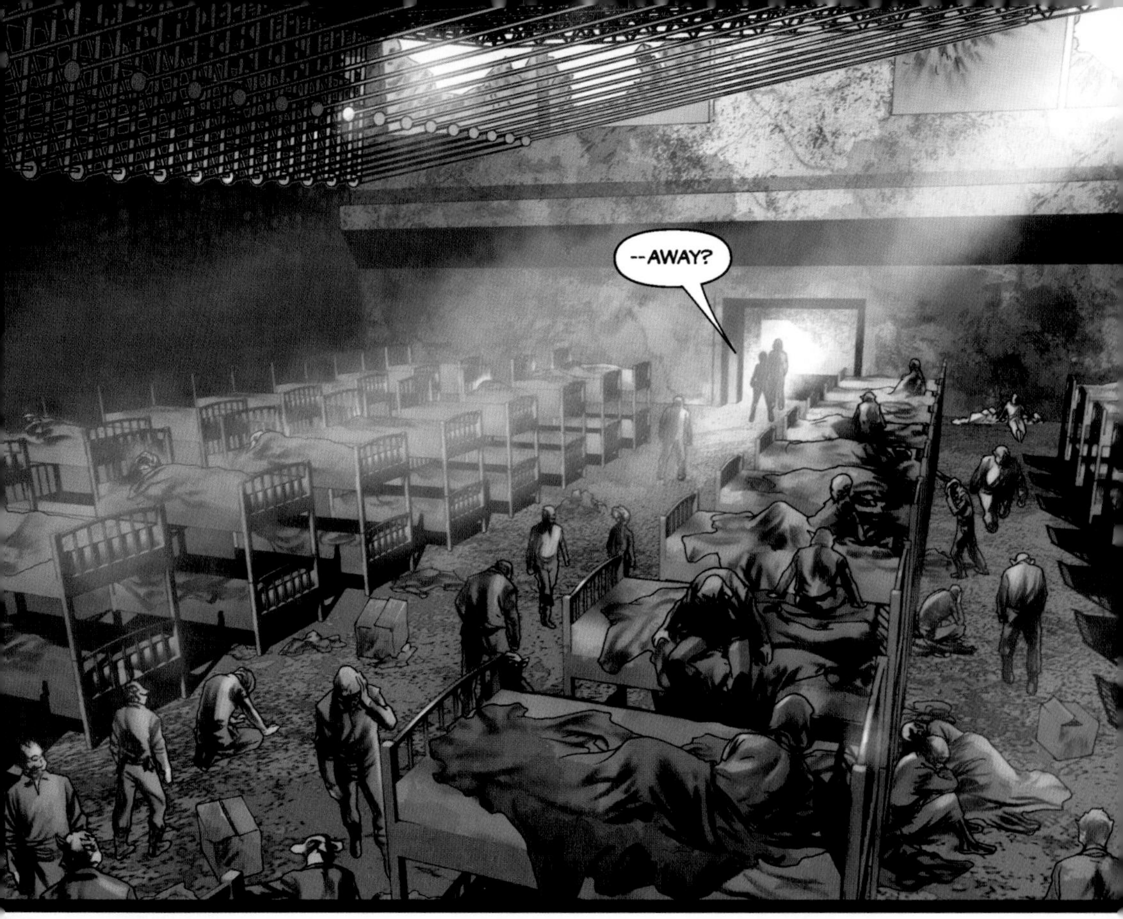
--AWAY?

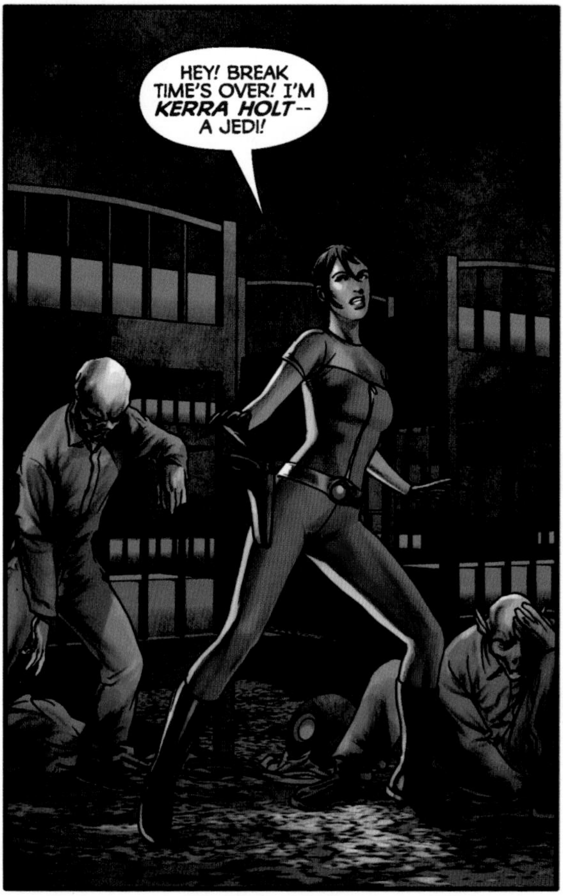
HEY! BREAK TIME'S OVER! I'M *KERRA HOLT*-- A JEDI!

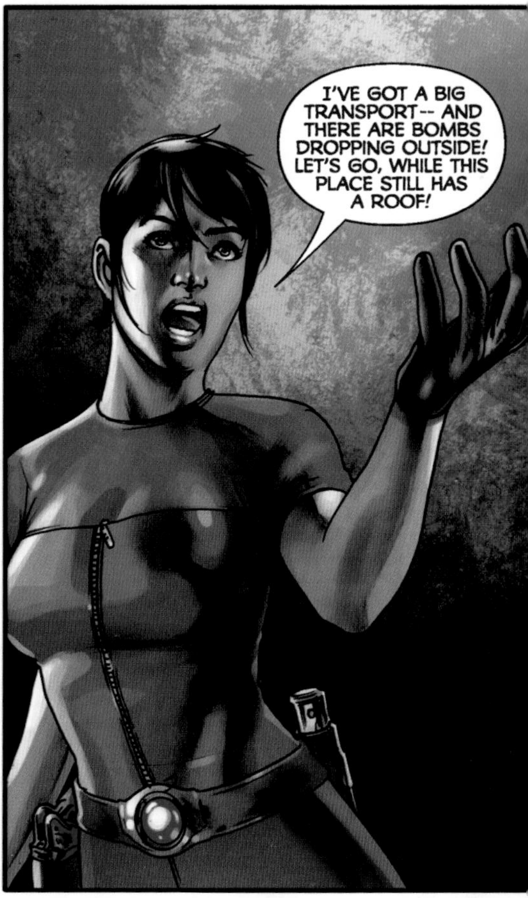
I'VE GOT A BIG TRANSPORT-- AND THERE ARE BOMBS DROPPING OUTSIDE! LET'S GO, WHILE THIS PLACE STILL HAS A ROOF!

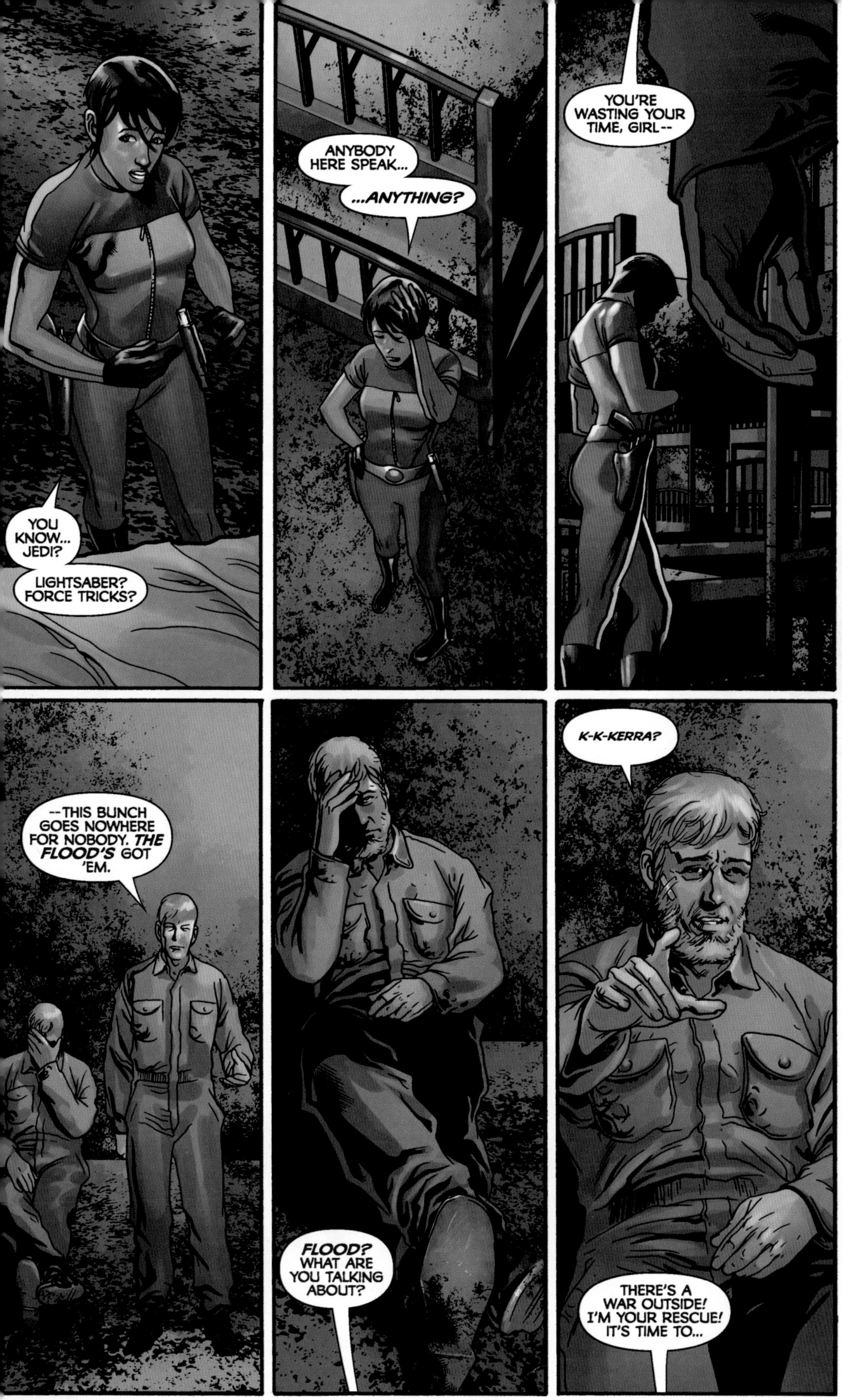
YOU KNOW... JEDI?
LIGHTSABER? FORCE TRICKS?
ANYBODY HERE SPEAK...
...ANYTHING?
YOU'RE WASTING YOUR TIME, GIRL--
--THIS BUNCH GOES NOWHERE FOR NOBODY. THE FLOOD'S GOT 'EM.
FLOOD? WHAT ARE YOU TALKING ABOUT?
K-K-KERRA?
THERE'S A WAR OUTSIDE! I'M YOUR RESCUE! IT'S TIME TO...

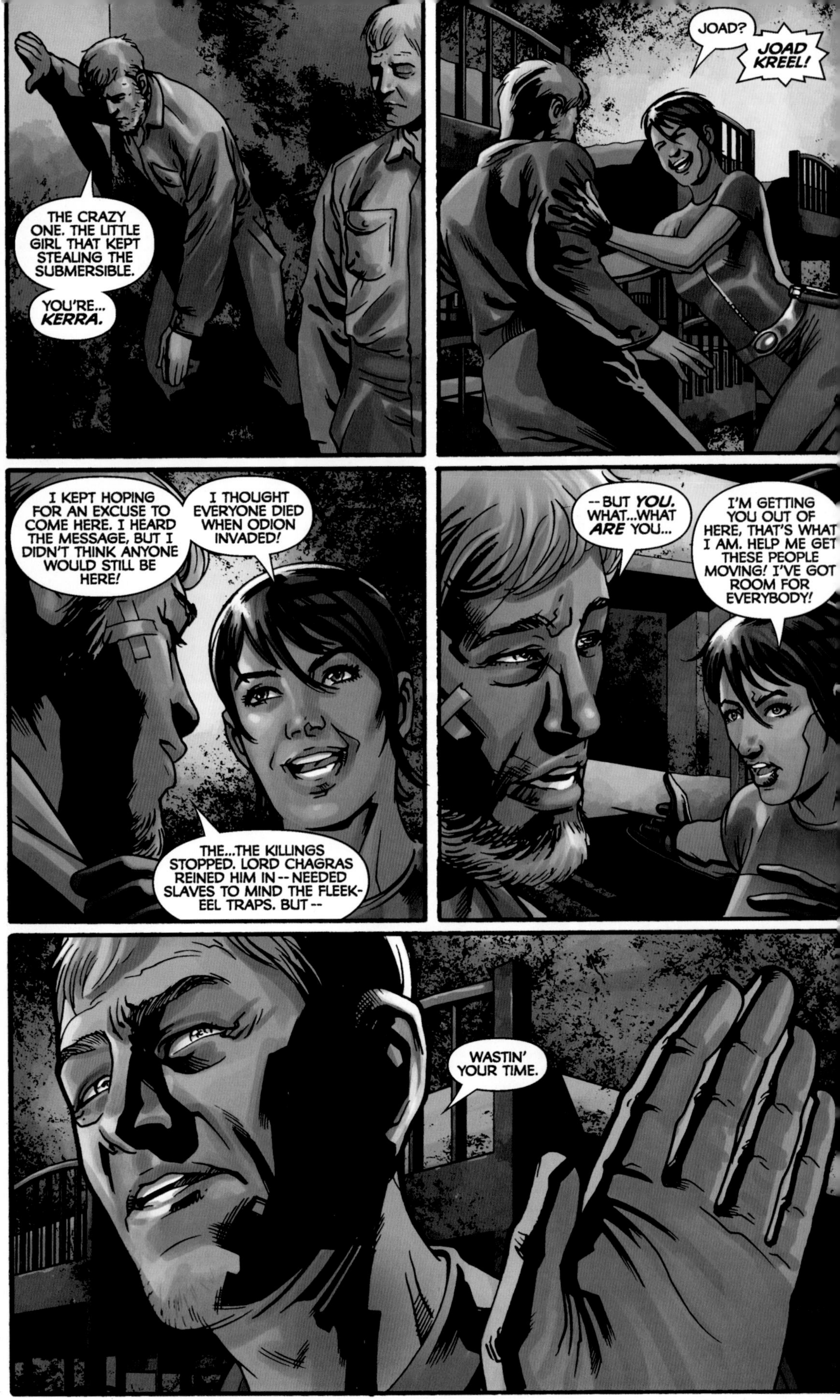
THE CRAZY ONE. THE LITTLE GIRL THAT KEPT STEALING THE SUBMERSIBLE.
YOU'RE... KERRA.
JOAD?
JOAD KREEL!
I KEPT HOPING FOR AN EXCUSE TO COME HERE. I HEARD THE MESSAGE, BUT I DIDN'T THINK ANYONE WOULD STILL BE HERE!
I THOUGHT EVERYONE DIED WHEN ODION INVADED!
THE...THE KILLINGS STOPPED. LORD CHAGRAS REINED HIM IN--NEEDED SLAVES TO MIND THE FLEEK-EEL TRAPS. BUT--
--BUT YOU. WHAT...WHAT ARE YOU...
I'M GETTING YOU OUT OF HERE, THAT'S WHAT I AM. HELP ME GET THESE PEOPLE MOVING! I'VE GOT ROOM FOR EVERYBODY!
WASTIN' YOUR TIME.

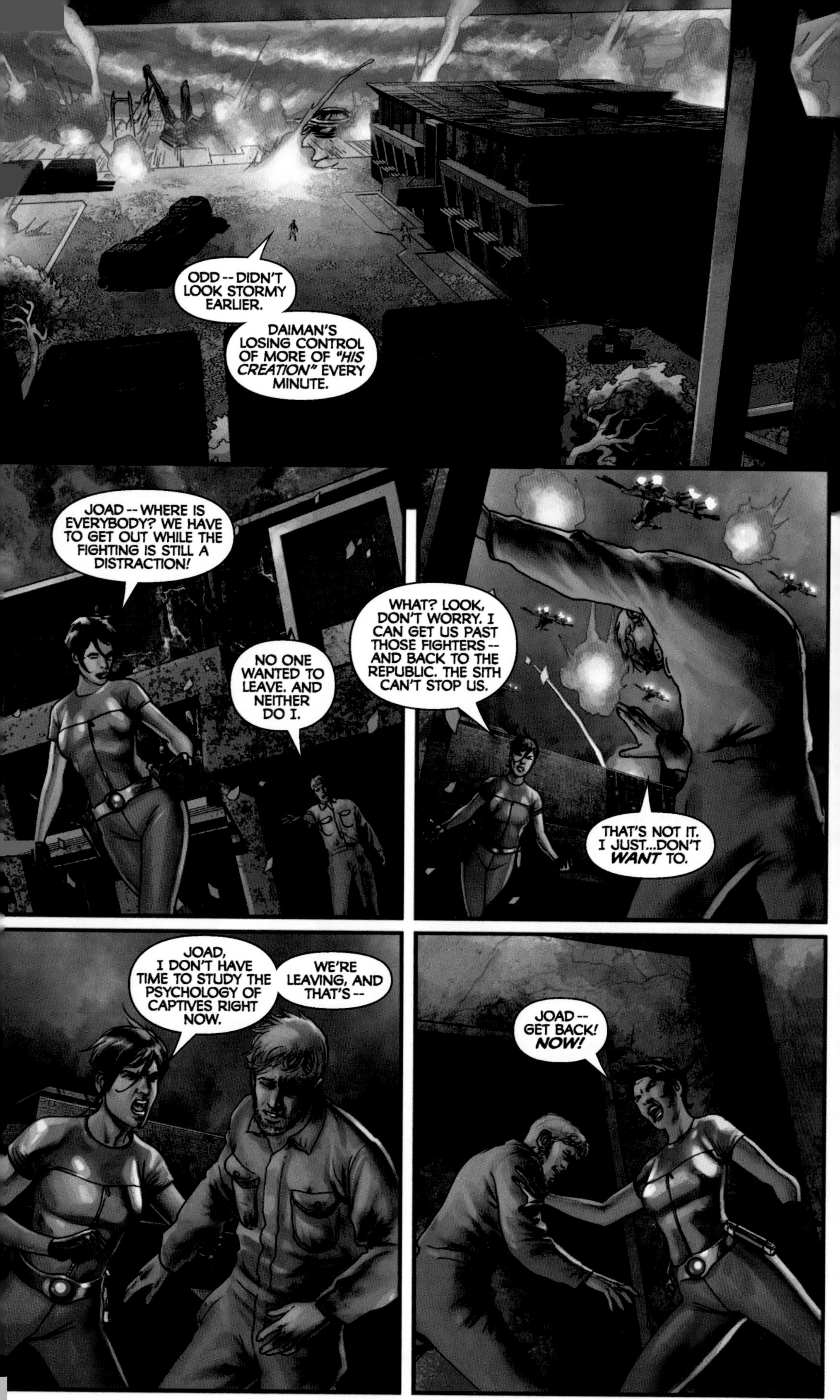
ODD -- DIDN'T LOOK STORMY EARLIER.
DAIMAN'S LOSING CONTROL OF MORE OF *"HIS CREATION"* EVERY MINUTE.
JOAD -- WHERE IS EVERYBODY? WE HAVE TO GET OUT WHILE THE FIGHTING IS STILL A DISTRACTION!
NO ONE WANTED TO LEAVE. AND NEITHER DO I.
WHAT? LOOK, DON'T WORRY. I CAN GET US PAST THOSE FIGHTERS -- AND BACK TO THE REPUBLIC. THE SITH CAN'T STOP US.
THAT'S NOT IT. I JUST...DON'T ***WANT*** TO.
JOAD, I DON'T HAVE TIME TO STUDY THE PSYCHOLOGY OF CAPTIVES RIGHT NOW.
WE'RE LEAVING, AND THAT'S --
JOAD -- GET BACK! ***NOW!***

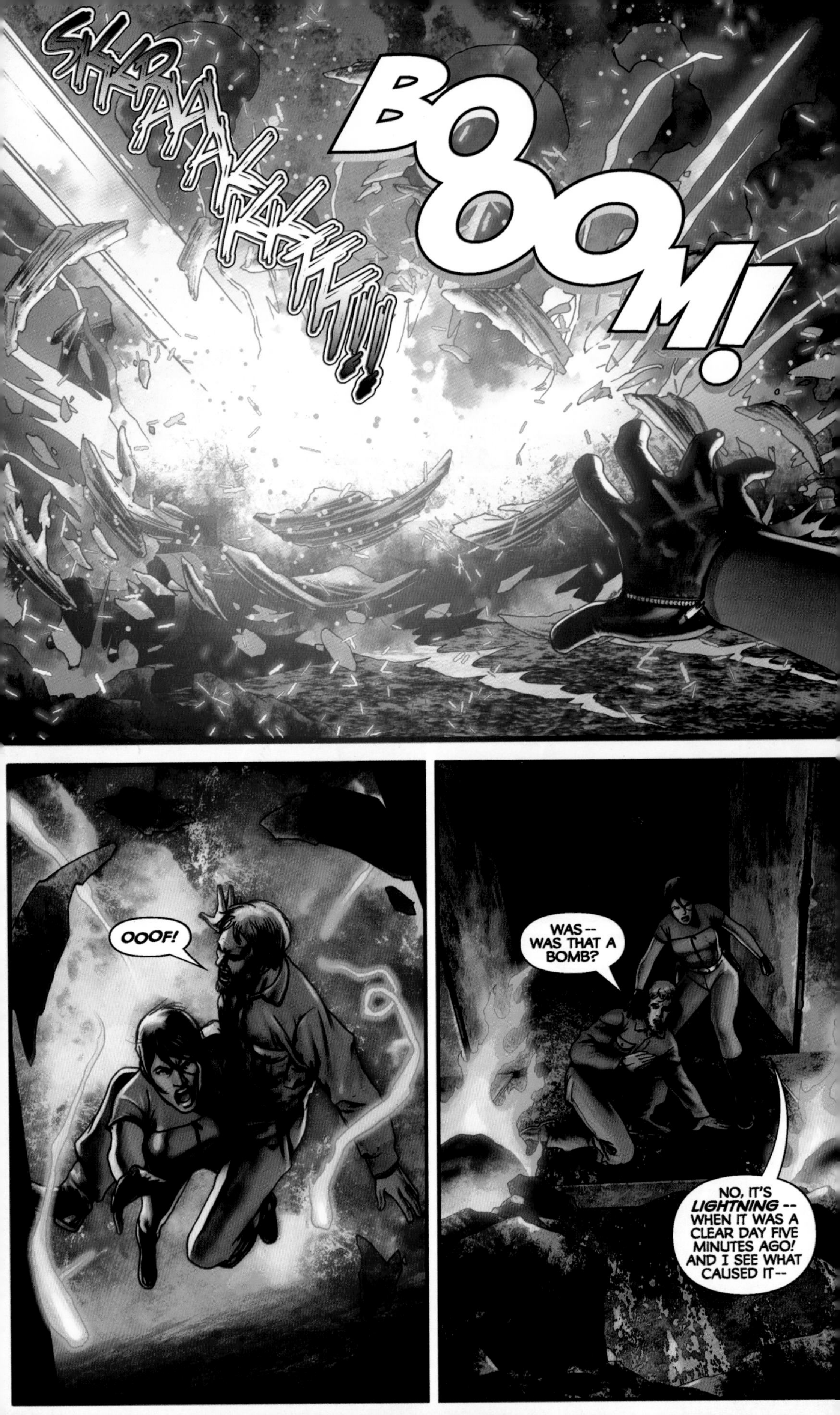
BOOOM!
OOOF!
WAS -- WAS THAT A BOMB?
NO, IT'S *LIGHTNING* -- WHEN IT WAS A CLEAR DAY FIVE MINUTES AGO! AND I SEE WHAT CAUSED IT --

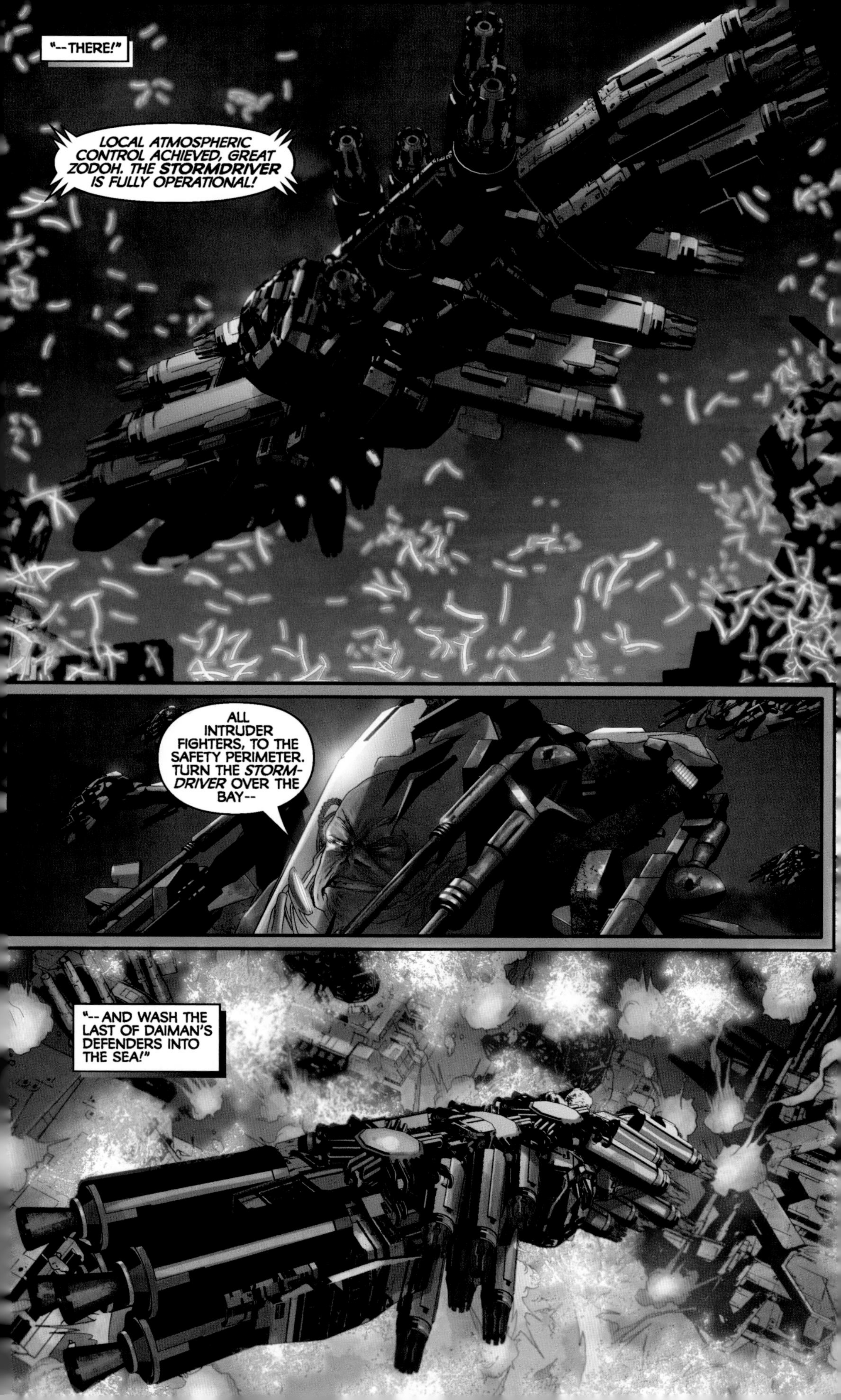
"--THERE!"
LOCAL ATMOSPHERIC CONTROL ACHIEVED, GREAT ZODOH. THE STORMDRIVER IS FULLY OPERATIONAL!
ALL INTRUDER FIGHTERS, TO THE SAFETY PERIMETER. TURN THE STORM-DRIVER OVER THE BAY--
"--AND WASH THE LAST OF DAIMAN'S DEFENDERS INTO THE SEA!"

THEY'VE WEAPONIZED -- *VAPORATORS?* IS EVERYONE HERE INSANE?

YEAH --

-- AND YOU ARE, TOO, IF YOU THINK YOU'RE GONNA GET THESE PEOPLE TO GIVE A CARE FOR THEIR OWN SKINS.

YOU LISTEN TO *OLD PADGETT* THIS TIME. I TOLD YOU, THE *FLOOD'S* GOT 'EM.

SPICE?

SPECIAL KIND -- DELUGE. WORK CREW BROUGHT SOME IN. BOOSTS THE EFFECTS OF EATING, SO EVEN ON SLAVE RATIONS YOU THINK YOU'RE SATISFIED.

"BUT IT'S TOO STRONG. SOON, YOU DON'T WANT *ANYTHING.* WE'RE BARELY ABLE TO GET OUR WORK QUOTA DONE --

"-- BECAUSE THIS BUNCH WON'T EVEN COME IN OUTTA THE RAIN!"

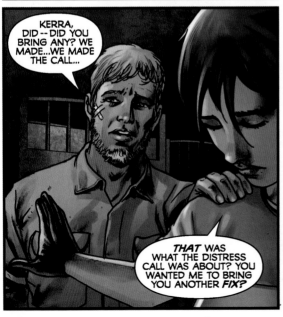

KERRA, DID -- DID YOU BRING ANY? WE MADE...WE MADE THE CALL...

*THAT* WAS WHAT THE DISTRESS CALL WAS ABOUT? YOU WANTED ME TO BRING YOU ANOTHER *FIX?*

*HUH.* I GUESS THEY *DO* STILL WANT SOMETHING. MY MISTAKE.

FORGET IT. WHAT ABOUT THE *SUBMERSIBLE PENS?*

YOU'VE GOT TO HARVEST EELS WITH SOMETHING! WE CAN ESCAPE UNDERSEA TO BOGGINS CAY AND --

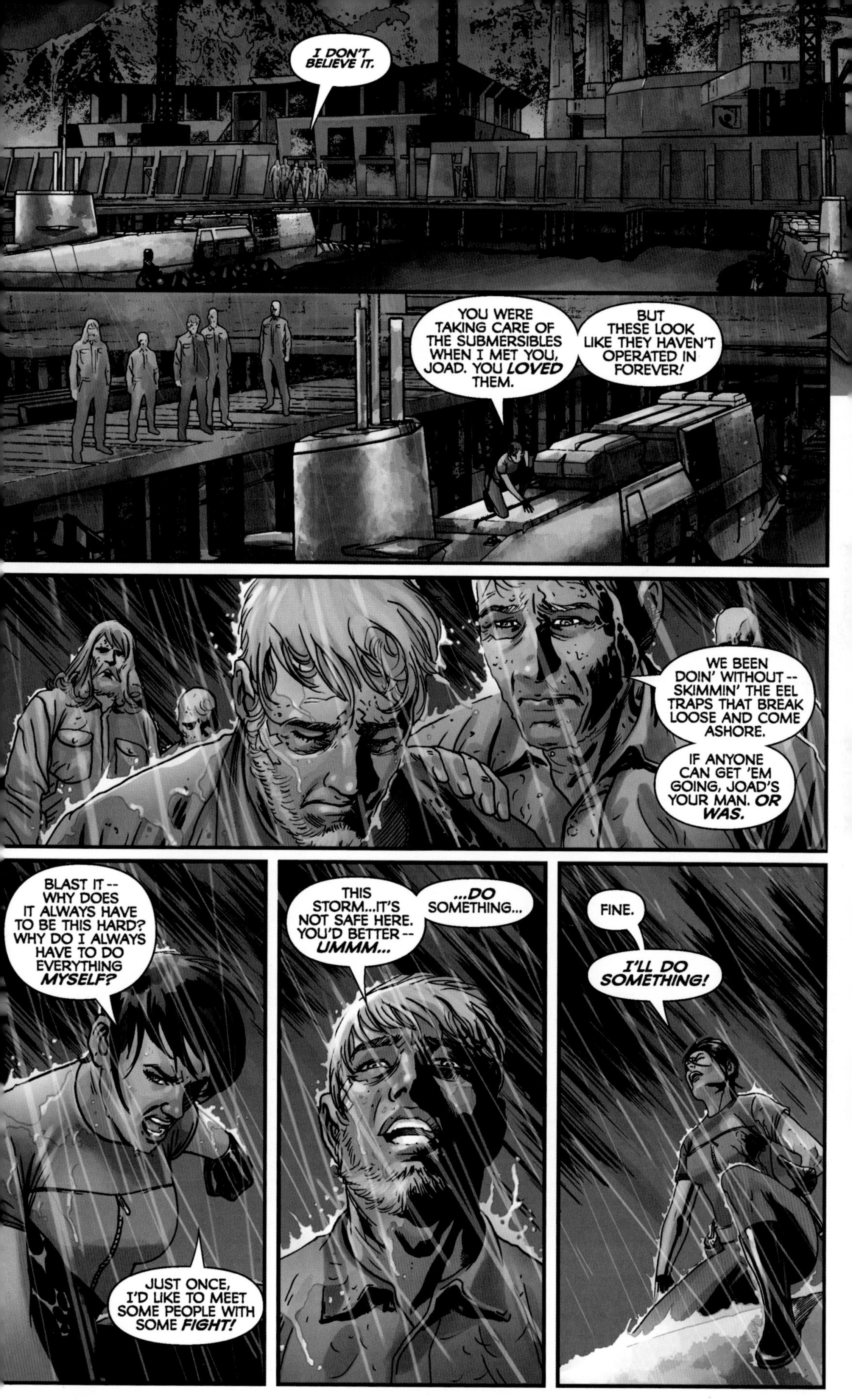
I DON'T BELIEVE IT.
YOU WERE TAKING CARE OF THE SUBMERSIBLES WHEN I MET YOU, JOAD. YOU *LOVED* THEM.
BUT THESE LOOK LIKE THEY HAVEN'T OPERATED IN FOREVER!
WE BEEN DOIN' WITHOUT -- SKIMMIN' THE EEL TRAPS THAT BREAK LOOSE AND COME ASHORE.
IF ANYONE CAN GET 'EM GOING, JOAD'S YOUR MAN. *OR WAS.*
BLAST IT -- WHY DOES IT ALWAYS HAVE TO BE THIS HARD? WHY DO I ALWAYS HAVE TO DO EVERYTHING *MYSELF?*
JUST ONCE, I'D LIKE TO MEET SOME PEOPLE WITH SOME *FIGHT!*
THIS STORM...IT'S NOT SAFE HERE. YOU'D BETTER -- *UMMM...*
*...DO* SOMETHING...
FINE.
*I'LL DO SOMETHING!*

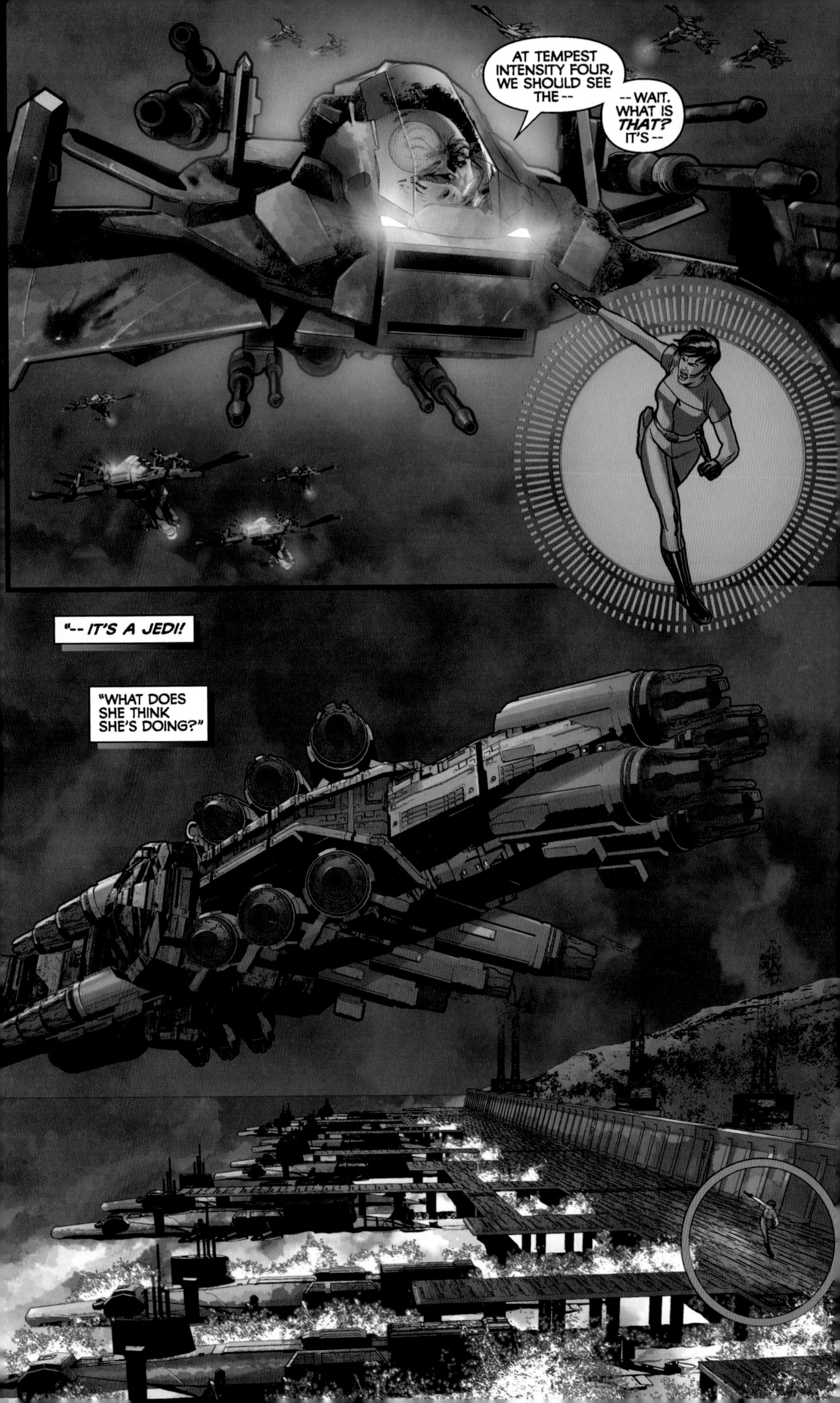
AT TEMPEST INTENSITY FOUR, WE SHOULD SEE THE --
-- WAIT. WHAT IS *THAT?* IT'S --
"-- *IT'S A JEDI!*
"WHAT DOES SHE THINK SHE'S DOING?"

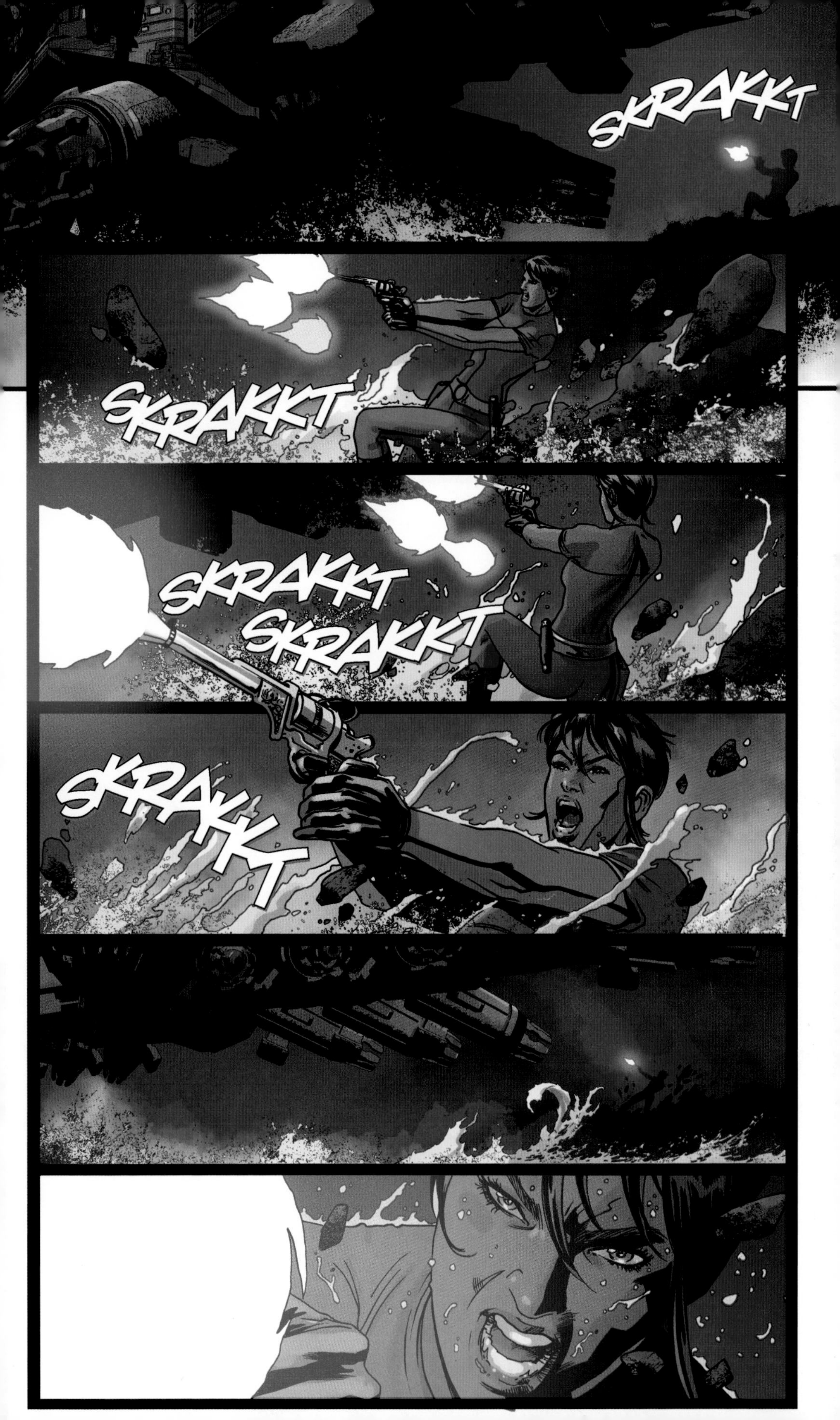
SKRAKKT
SKRAKKT
SKRAKKT
SKRAKKT
SKRAKKT

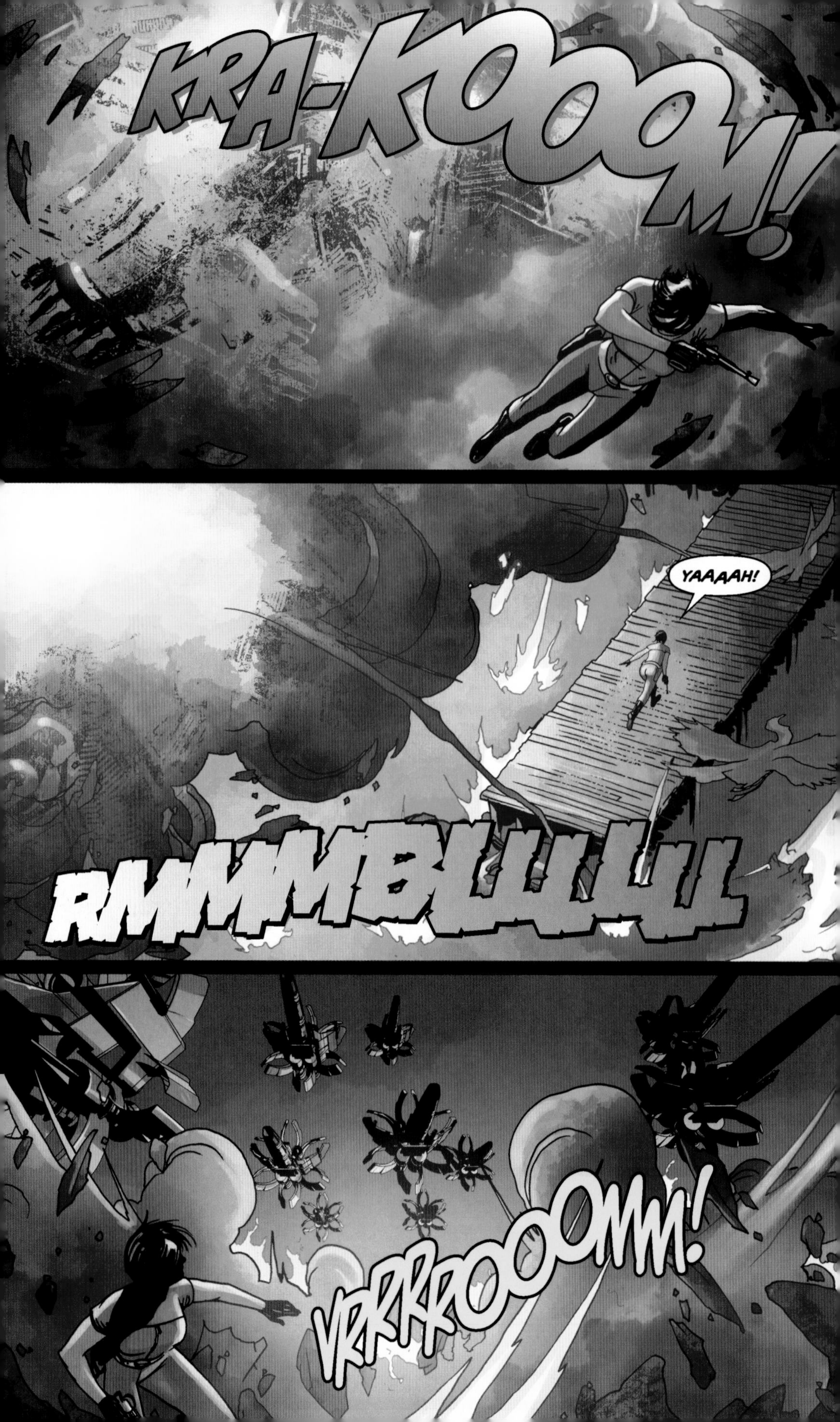
KRA-KOOOM!
YAAAAH!
RMMMMBLLLLL
VRRRROOOOMM!

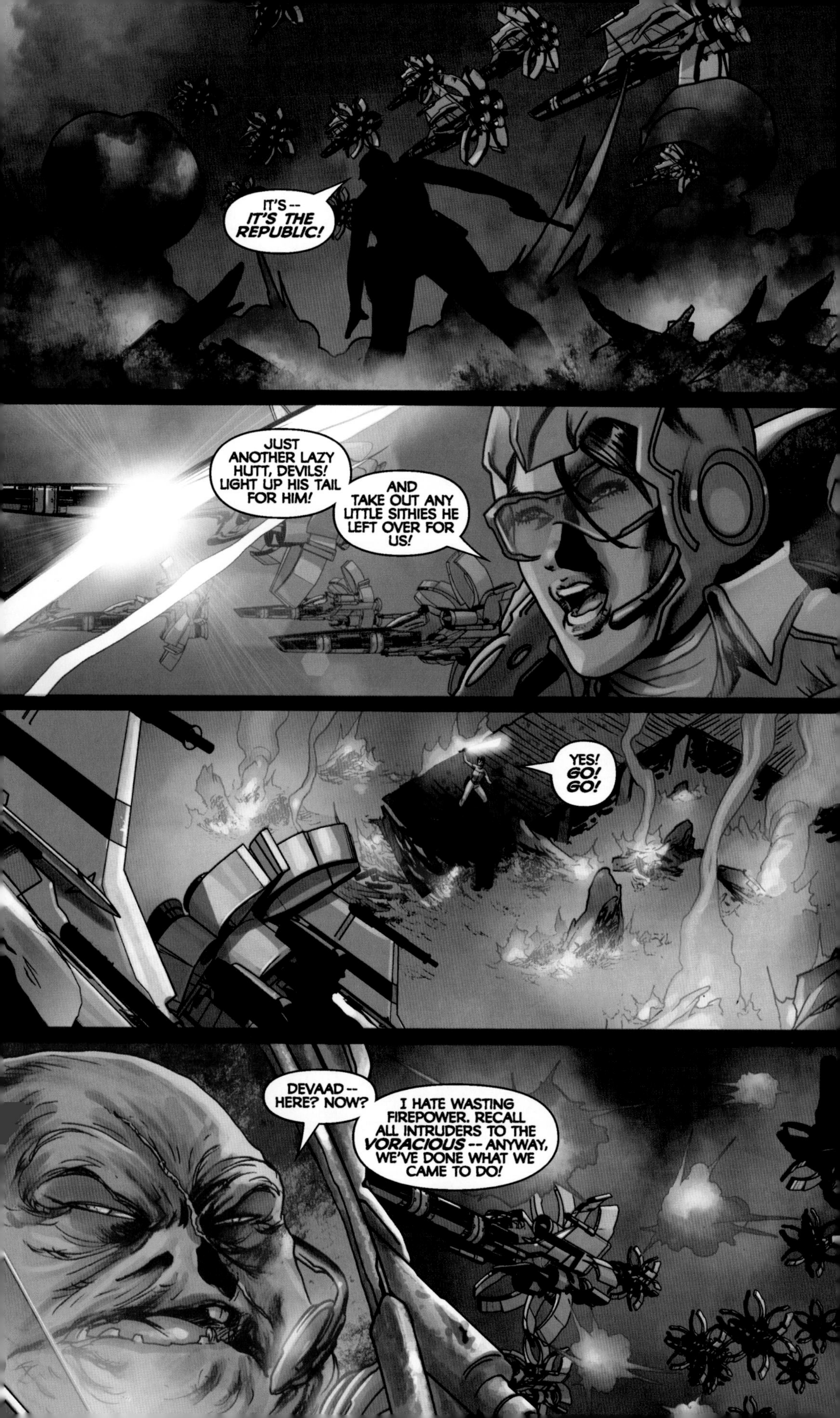
IT'S -- *IT'S THE REPUBLIC!*
JUST ANOTHER LAZY HUTT, DEVILS! LIGHT UP HIS TAIL FOR HIM!
AND TAKE OUT ANY LITTLE SITHIES HE LEFT OVER FOR US!
YES! *GO! GO!*
DEVAAD -- HERE? NOW?
I HATE WASTING FIREPOWER. RECALL ALL INTRUDERS TO THE *VORACIOUS* -- ANYWAY, WE'VE DONE WHAT WE CAME TO DO!

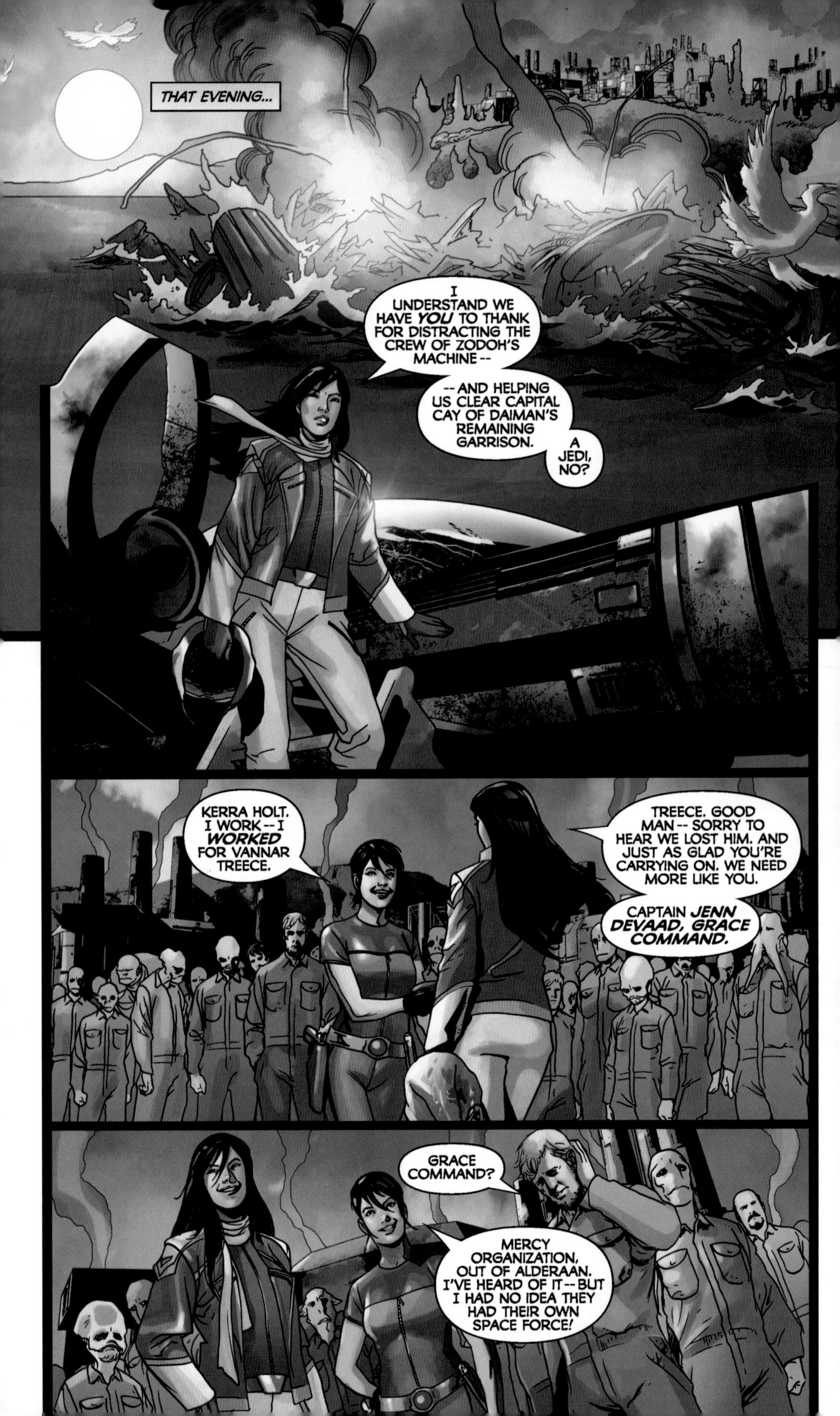
THAT EVENING...
I UNDERSTAND WE HAVE YOU TO THANK FOR DISTRACTING THE CREW OF ZODOH'S MACHINE --
-- AND HELPING US CLEAR CAPITAL CAY OF DAIMAN'S REMAINING GARRISON.
A JEDI, NO?
KERRA HOLT. I WORK -- I WORKED FOR VANNAR TREECE.
TREECE. GOOD MAN -- SORRY TO HEAR WE LOST HIM. AND JUST AS GLAD YOU'RE CARRYING ON. WE NEED MORE LIKE YOU.
CAPTAIN JENN DEVAAD, GRACE COMMAND.
GRACE COMMAND?
MERCY ORGANIZATION, OUT OF ALDERAAN. I'VE HEARD OF IT -- BUT I HAD NO IDEA THEY HAD THEIR OWN SPACE FORCE!

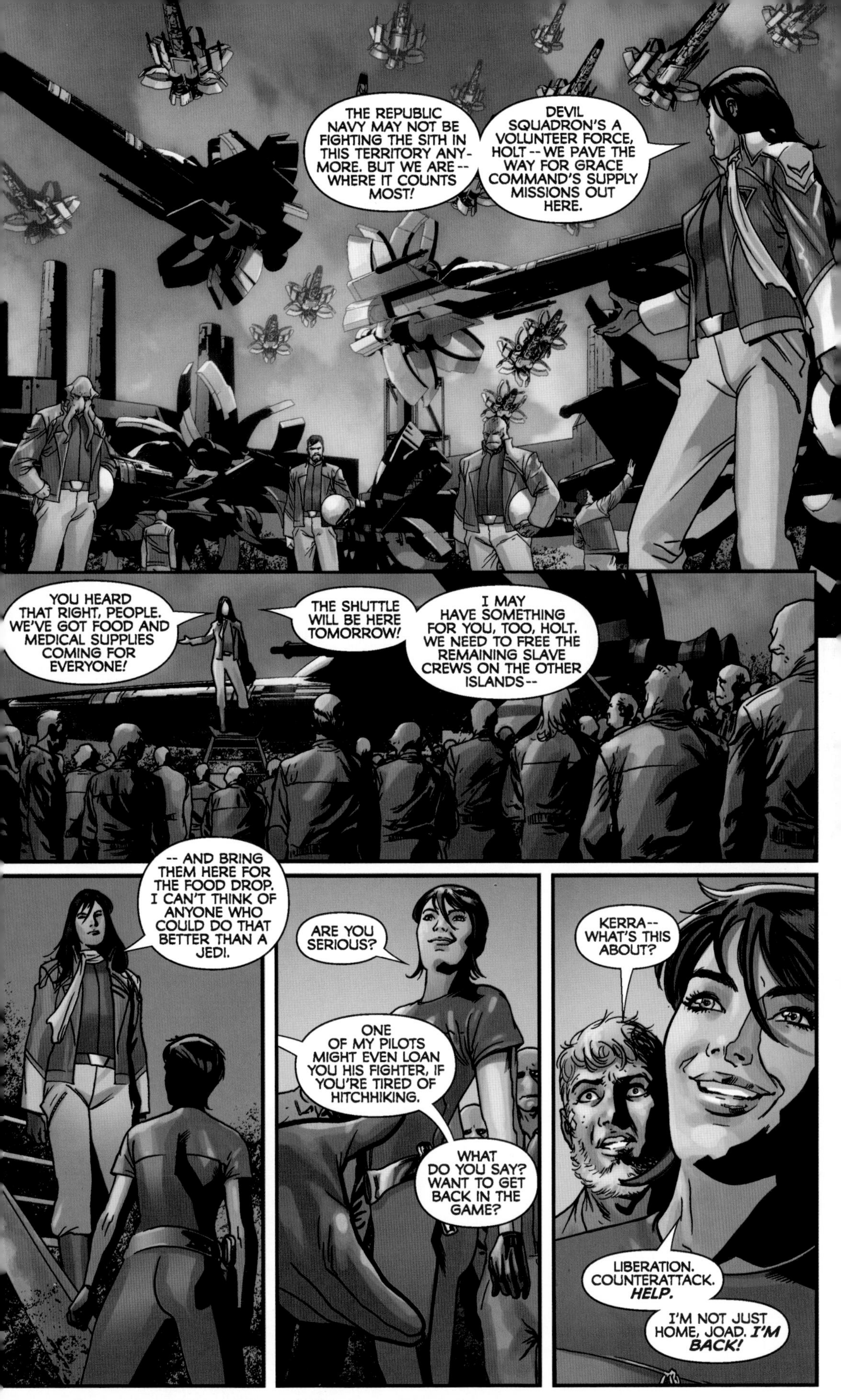
THE REPUBLIC NAVY MAY NOT BE FIGHTING THE SITH IN THIS TERRITORY ANY-MORE. BUT WE ARE-- WHERE IT COUNTS MOST!
DEVIL SQUADRON'S A VOLUNTEER FORCE, HOLT--WE PAVE THE WAY FOR GRACE COMMAND'S SUPPLY MISSIONS OUT HERE.
YOU HEARD THAT RIGHT, PEOPLE. WE'VE GOT FOOD AND MEDICAL SUPPLIES COMING FOR EVERYONE!
THE SHUTTLE WILL BE HERE TOMORROW!
I MAY HAVE SOMETHING FOR YOU, TOO, HOLT. WE NEED TO FREE THE REMAINING SLAVE CREWS ON THE OTHER ISLANDS--
-- AND BRING THEM HERE FOR THE FOOD DROP. I CAN'T THINK OF ANYONE WHO COULD DO THAT BETTER THAN A JEDI.
ARE YOU SERIOUS?
ONE OF MY PILOTS MIGHT EVEN LOAN YOU HIS FIGHTER, IF YOU'RE TIRED OF HITCHHIKING.
WHAT DO YOU SAY? WANT TO GET BACK IN THE GAME?
KERRA-- WHAT'S THIS ABOUT?
LIBERATION. COUNTERATTACK. *HELP.*
I'M NOT JUST HOME, JOAD. *I'M BACK!*

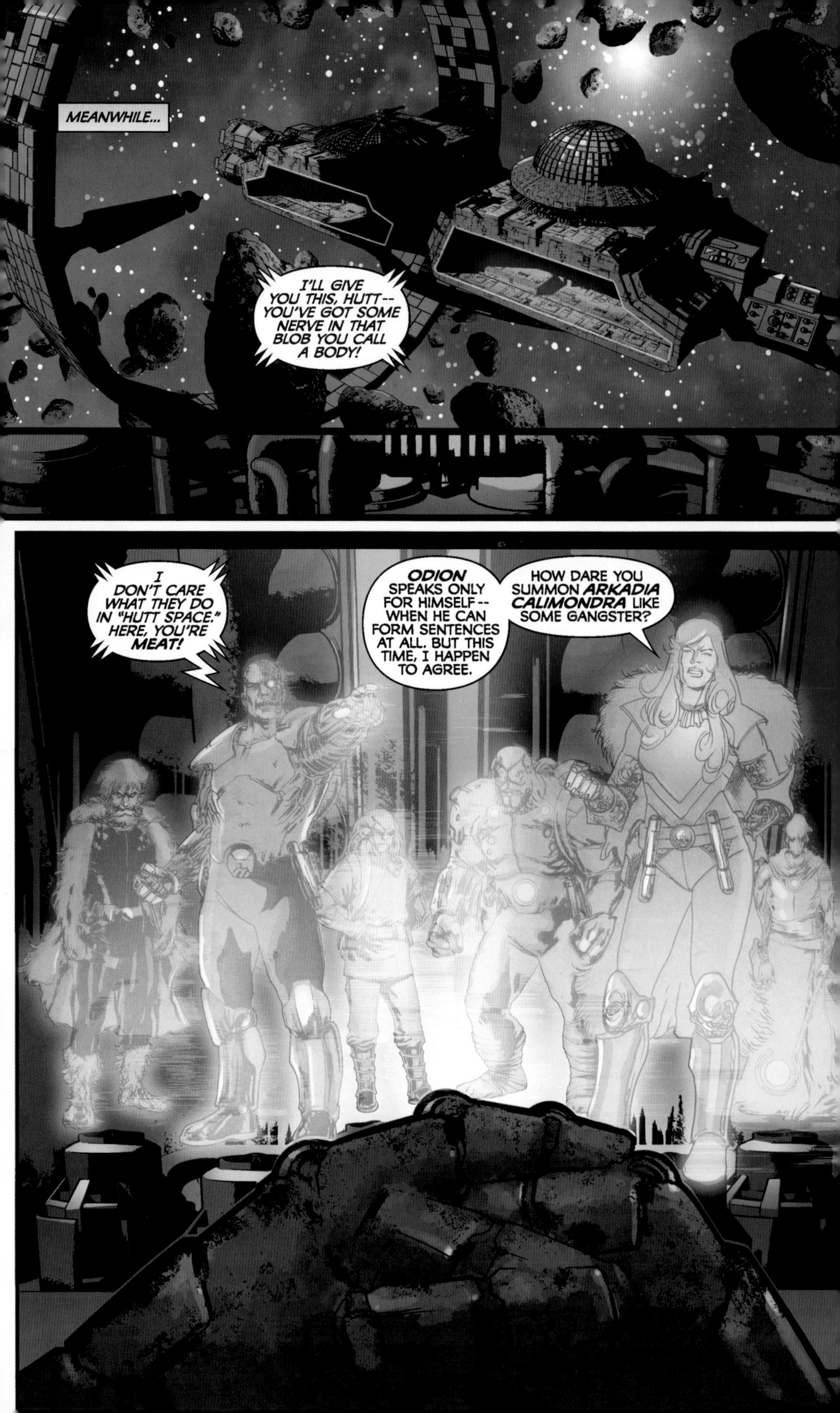
MEANWHILE...
I'LL GIVE YOU THIS, HUTT-- YOU'VE GOT SOME NERVE IN THAT BLOB YOU CALL A BODY!
I DON'T CARE WHAT THEY DO IN "HUTT SPACE." HERE, YOU'RE MEAT!
ODION SPEAKS ONLY FOR HIMSELF-- WHEN HE CAN FORM SENTENCES AT ALL. BUT THIS TIME, I HAPPEN TO AGREE.
HOW DARE YOU SUMMON ARKADIA CALIMONDRA LIKE SOME GANGSTER?

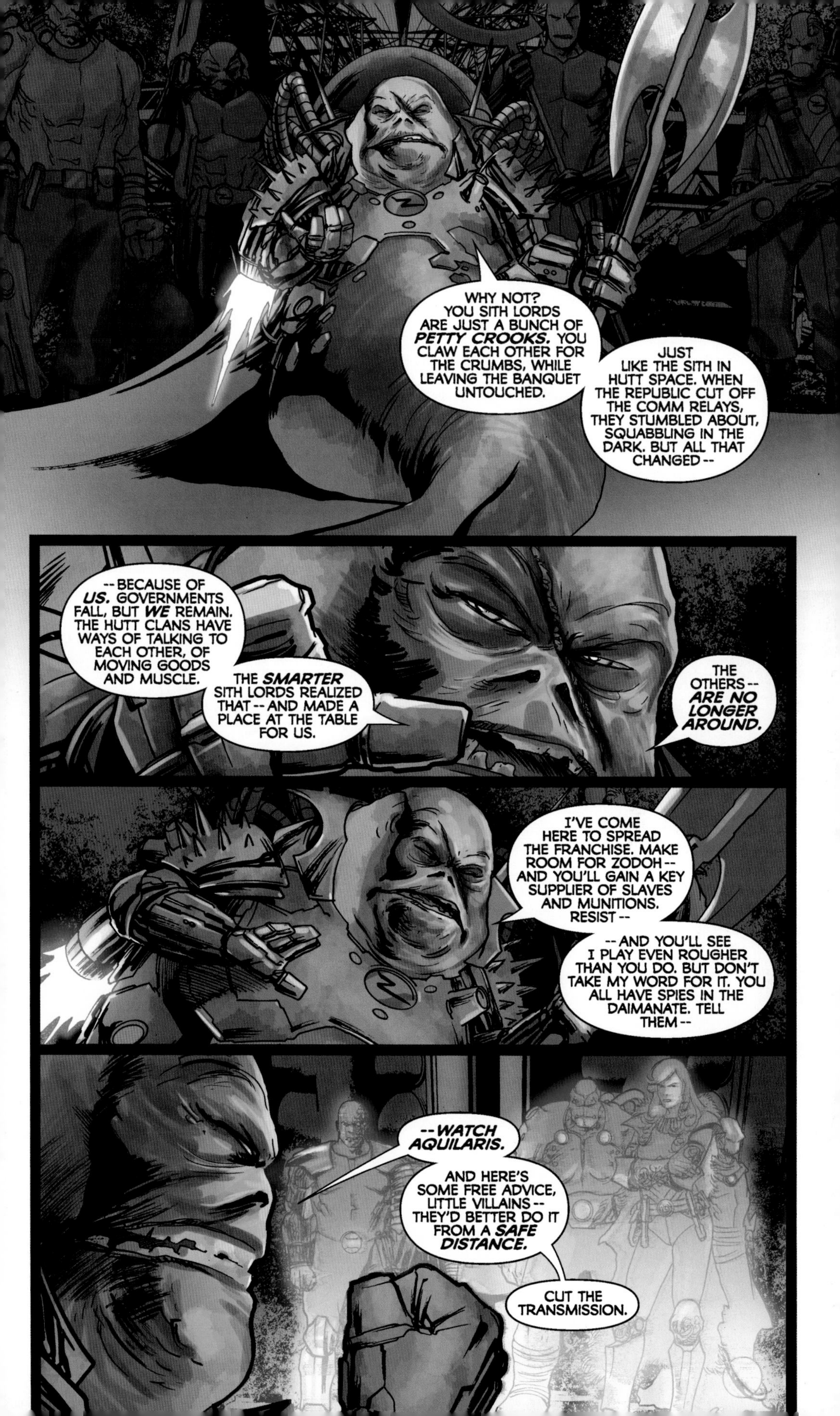

WHY NOT? YOU SITH LORDS ARE JUST A BUNCH OF *PETTY CROOKS.* YOU CLAW EACH OTHER FOR THE CRUMBS, WHILE LEAVING THE BANQUET UNTOUCHED.
JUST LIKE THE SITH IN HUTT SPACE. WHEN THE REPUBLIC CUT OFF THE COMM RELAYS, THEY STUMBLED ABOUT, SQUABBLING IN THE DARK. BUT ALL THAT CHANGED --
-- BECAUSE OF *US.* GOVERNMENTS FALL, BUT *WE* REMAIN. THE HUTT CLANS HAVE WAYS OF TALKING TO EACH OTHER, OF MOVING GOODS AND MUSCLE.
THE *SMARTER* SITH LORDS REALIZED THAT -- AND MADE A PLACE AT THE TABLE FOR US.
THE OTHERS -- *ARE NO LONGER AROUND.*
I'VE COME HERE TO SPREAD THE FRANCHISE. MAKE ROOM FOR ZODOH -- AND YOU'LL GAIN A KEY SUPPLIER OF SLAVES AND MUNITIONS. RESIST --
-- AND YOU'LL SEE I PLAY EVEN ROUGHER THAN YOU DO. BUT DON'T TAKE MY WORD FOR IT. YOU ALL HAVE SPIES IN THE DAIMANATE. TELL THEM --
-- *WATCH AQUILARIS.*
AND HERE'S SOME FREE ADVICE, LITTLE VILLAINS -- THEY'D BETTER DO IT FROM A *SAFE DISTANCE.*
CUT THE TRANSMISSION.

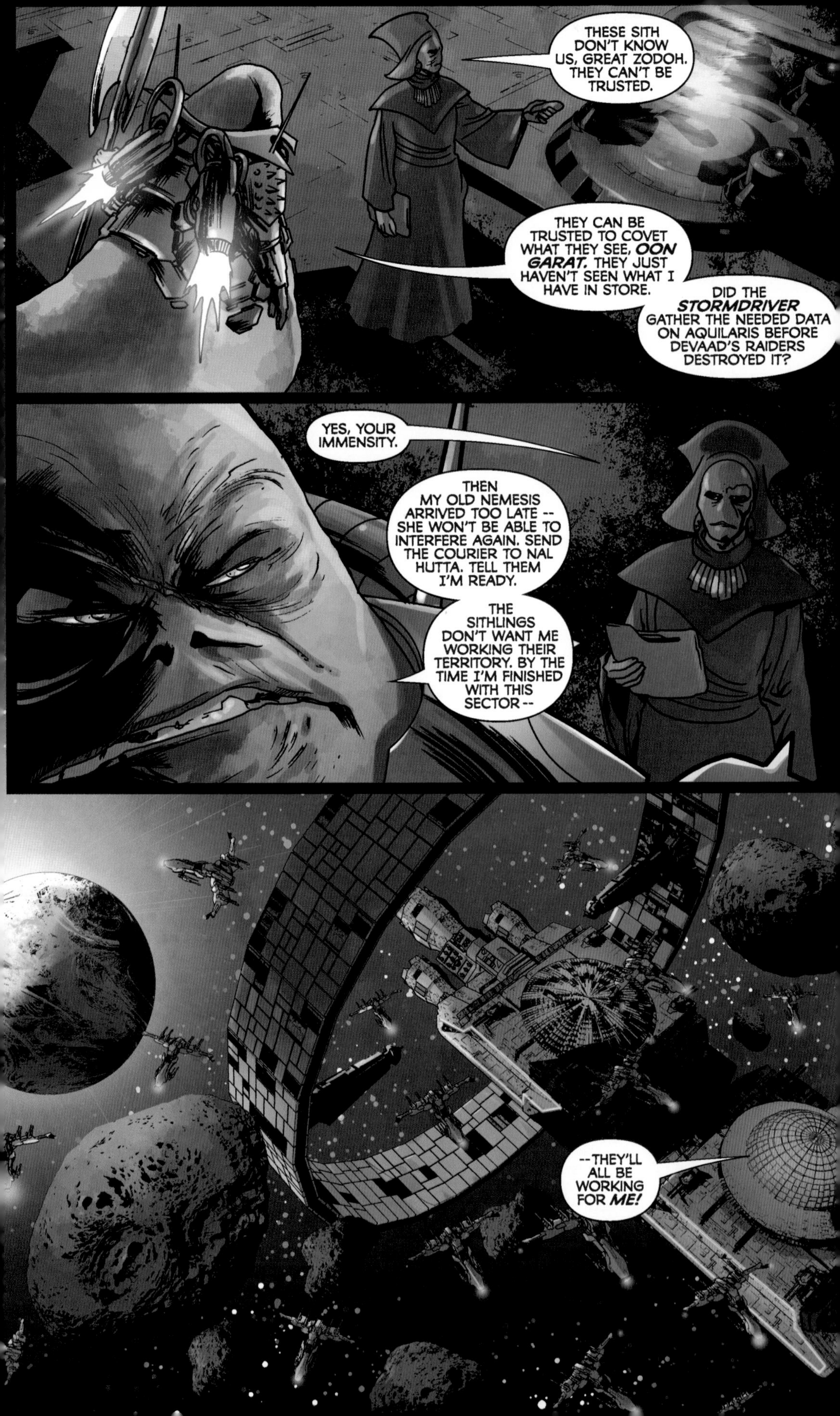
THESE SITH DON'T KNOW US, GREAT ZODOH. THEY CAN'T BE TRUSTED.
THEY CAN BE TRUSTED TO COVET WHAT THEY SEE, *OON GARAT.* THEY JUST HAVEN'T SEEN WHAT I HAVE IN STORE.
DID THE *STORMDRIVER* GATHER THE NEEDED DATA ON AQUILARIS BEFORE DEVAAD'S RAIDERS DESTROYED IT?
YES, YOUR IMMENSITY.
THEN MY OLD NEMESIS ARRIVED TOO LATE -- SHE WON'T BE ABLE TO INTERFERE AGAIN. SEND THE COURIER TO NAL HUTTA. TELL THEM I'M READY.
THE SITHLINGS DON'T WANT ME WORKING THEIR TERRITORY. BY THE TIME I'M FINISHED WITH THIS SECTOR --
--THEY'LL ALL BE WORKING FOR *ME!*

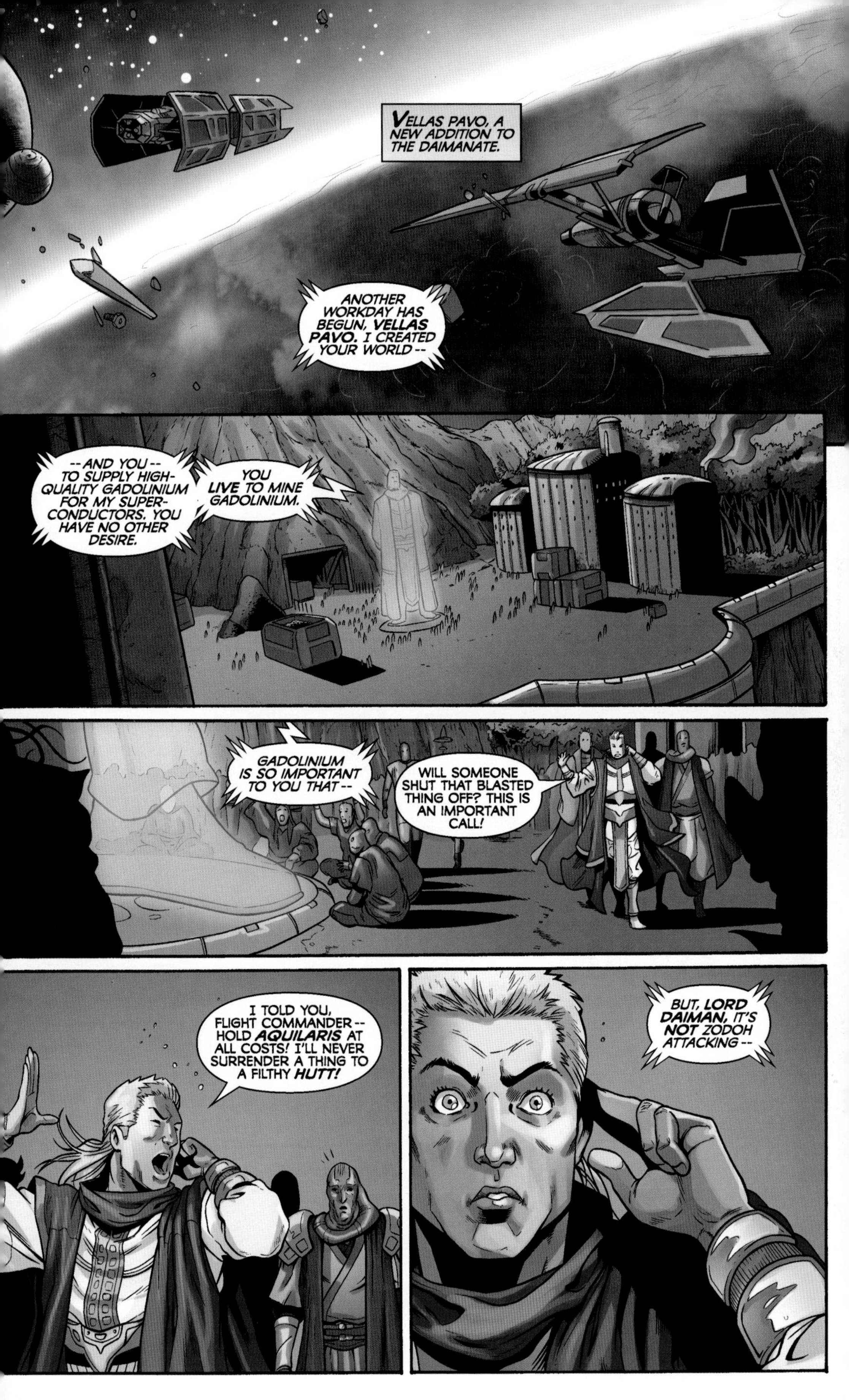
VELLAS PAVO, A NEW ADDITION TO THE DAIMANATE.
ANOTHER WORKDAY HAS BEGUN, VELLAS PAVO. I CREATED YOUR WORLD --
--AND YOU -- TO SUPPLY HIGH-QUALITY GADOLINIUM FOR MY SUPER-CONDUCTORS. YOU HAVE NO OTHER DESIRE.
YOU LIVE TO MINE GADOLINIUM.
GADOLINIUM IS SO IMPORTANT TO YOU THAT --
WILL SOMEONE SHUT THAT BLASTED THING OFF? THIS IS AN IMPORTANT CALL!
I TOLD YOU, FLIGHT COMMANDER -- HOLD AQUILARIS AT ALL COSTS! I'LL NEVER SURRENDER A THING TO A FILTHY HUTT!
BUT, LORD DAIMAN, IT'S NOT ZODOH ATTACKING --

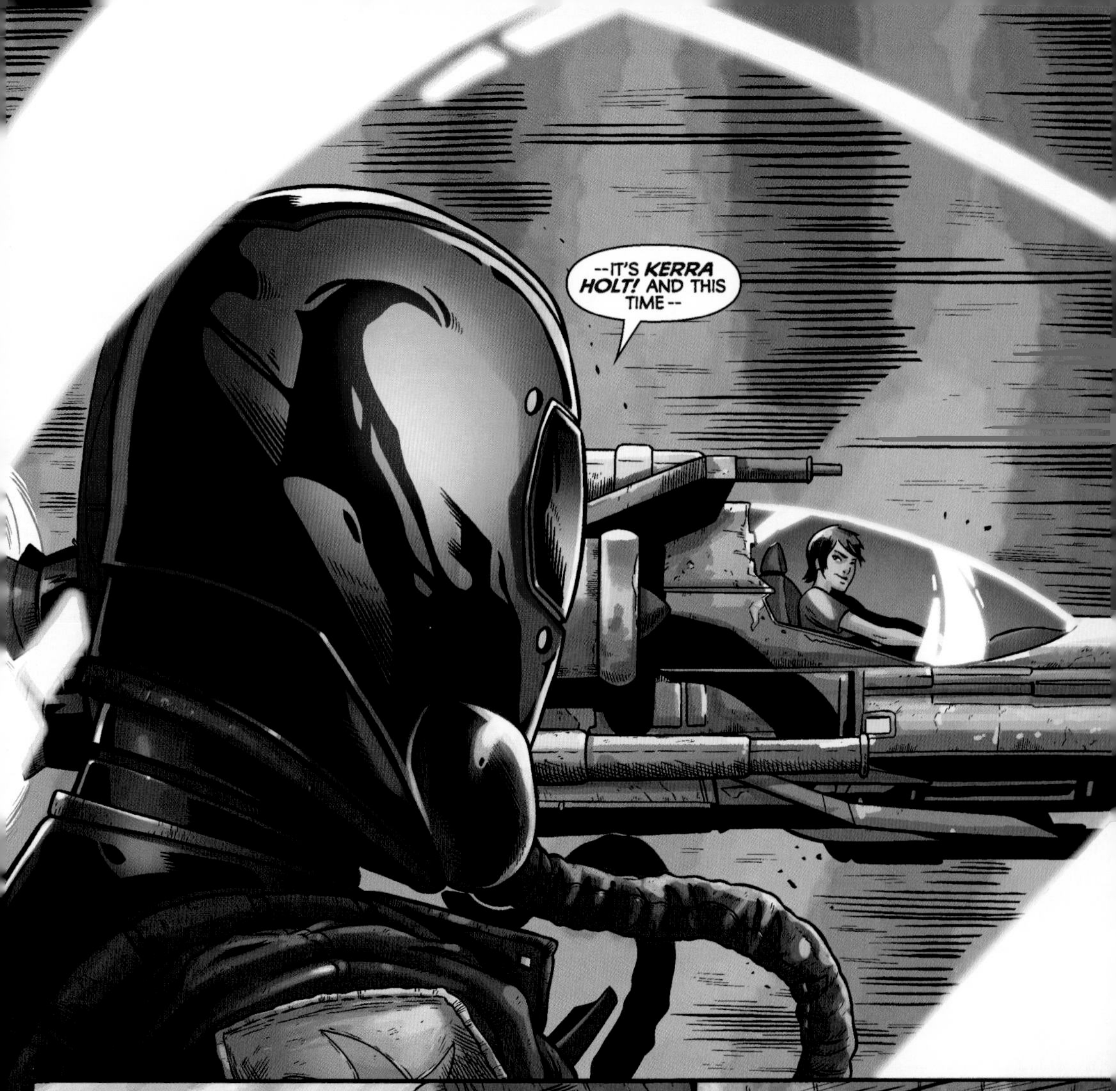
--IT'S KERRA HOLT! AND THIS TIME--

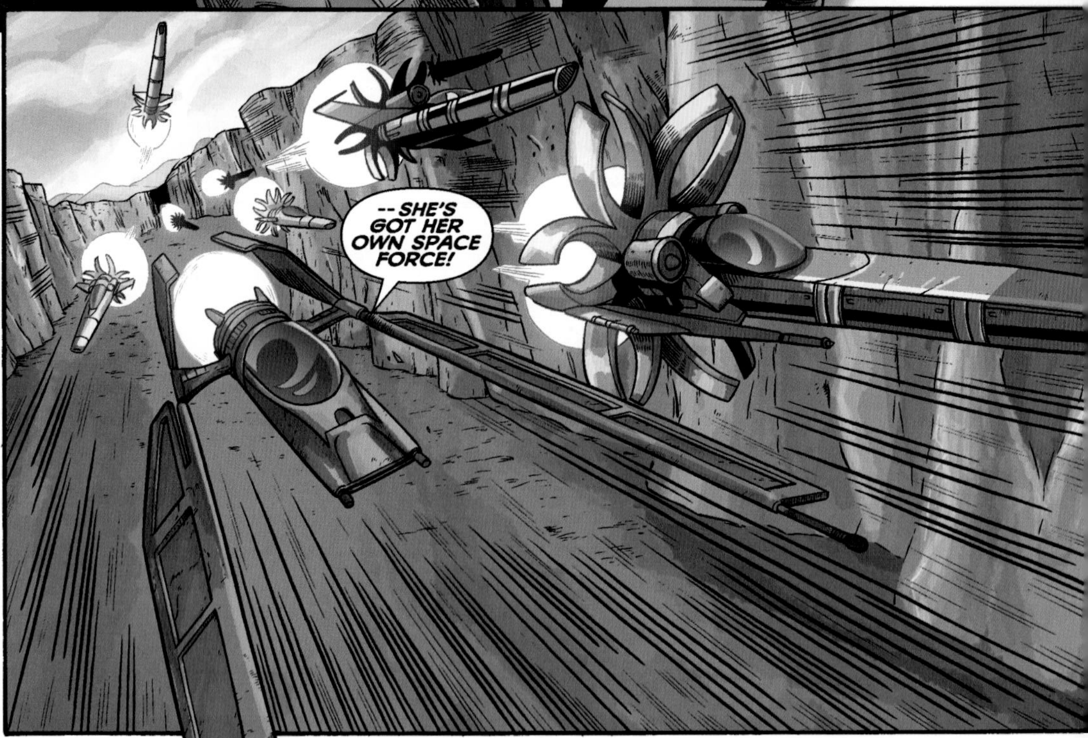
--SHE'S GOT HER OWN SPACE FORCE!

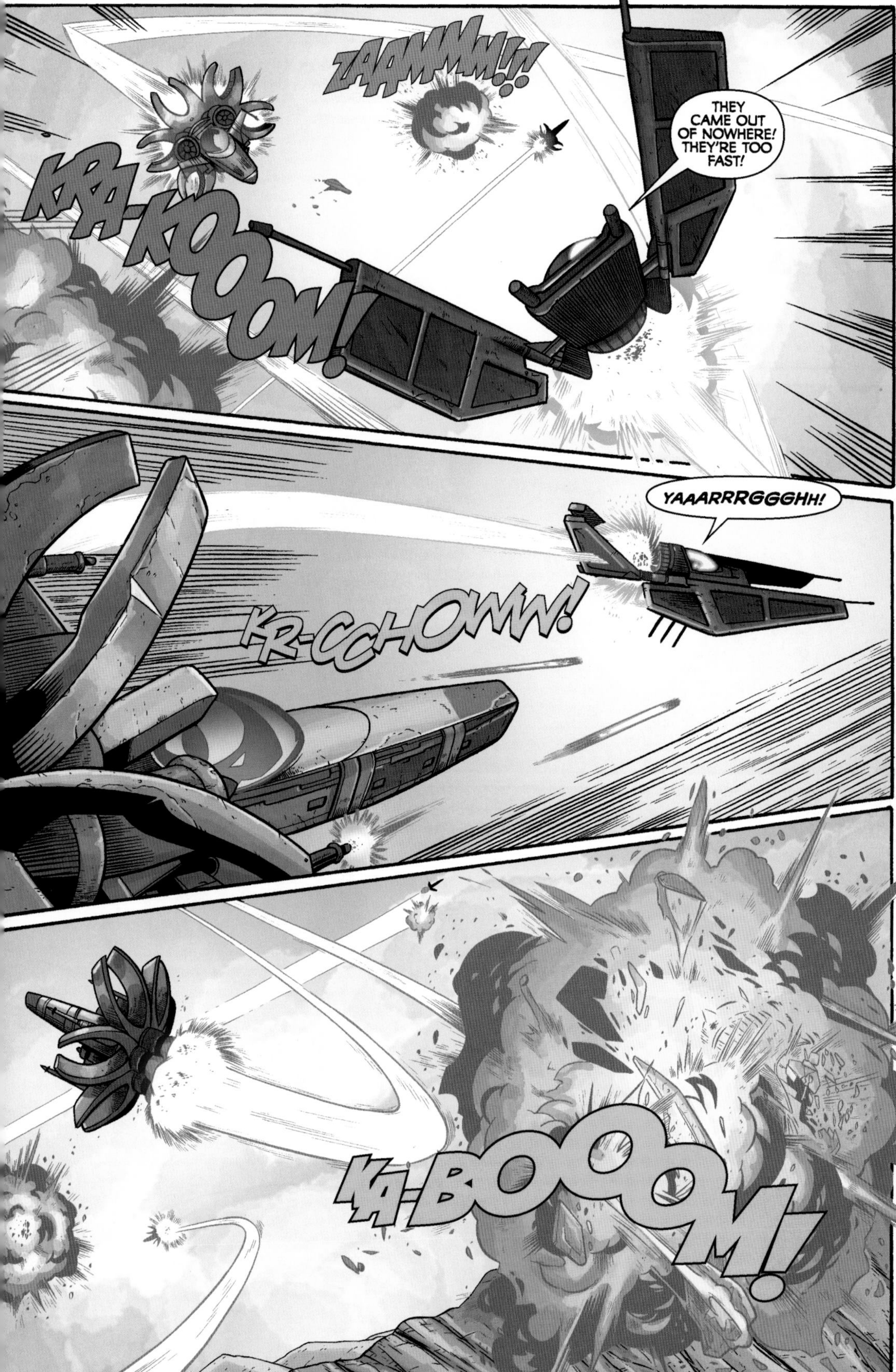
ZAAMMM!!!
THEY CAME OUT OF NOWHERE! THEY'RE TOO FAST!
KRA-KOOOOM!
YAAARRRGGGHH!
KR-CCHOWW!
KA-BOOOOM!

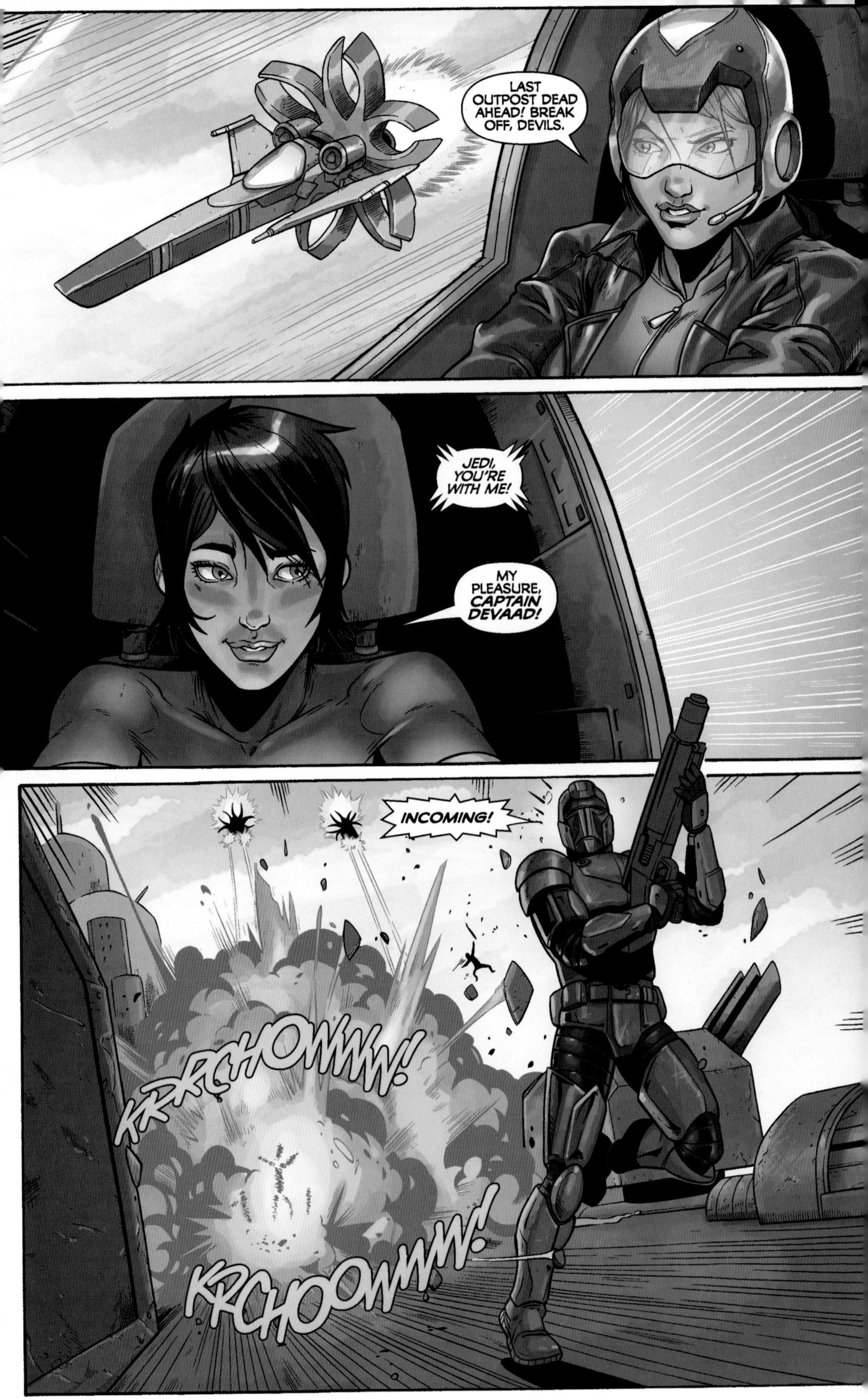
LAST OUTPOST DEAD AHEAD! BREAK OFF, DEVILS.
JEDI, YOU'RE WITH ME!
MY PLEASURE, CAPTAIN DEVAAD!
INCOMING!
KRRCHOWWW!
KRCHOOWWW!

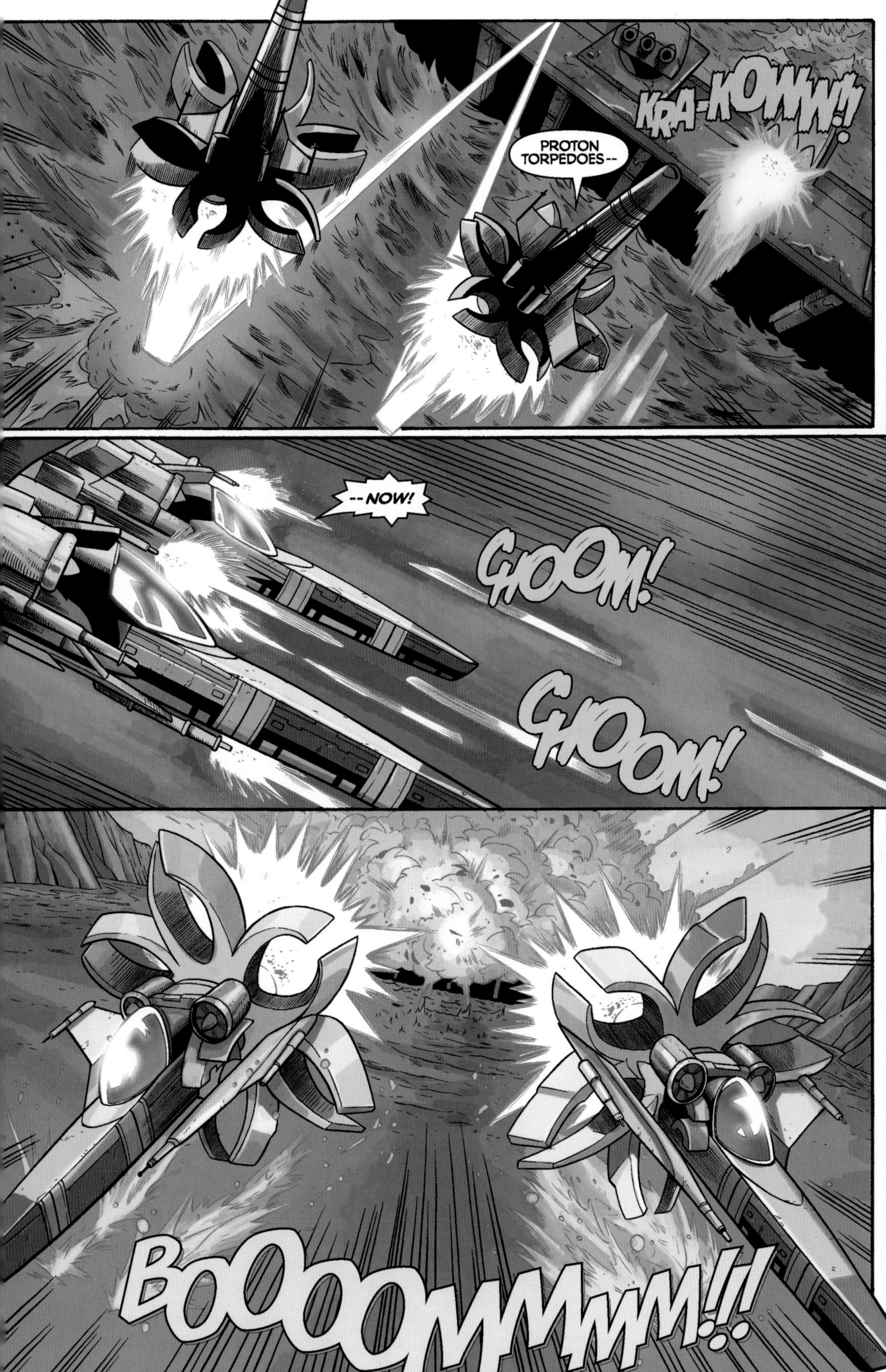
KRA-KOWW!!
PROTON TORPEDOES--
--NOW!
GHOOM!
GHOOM!
BOOOOMMMM!!!

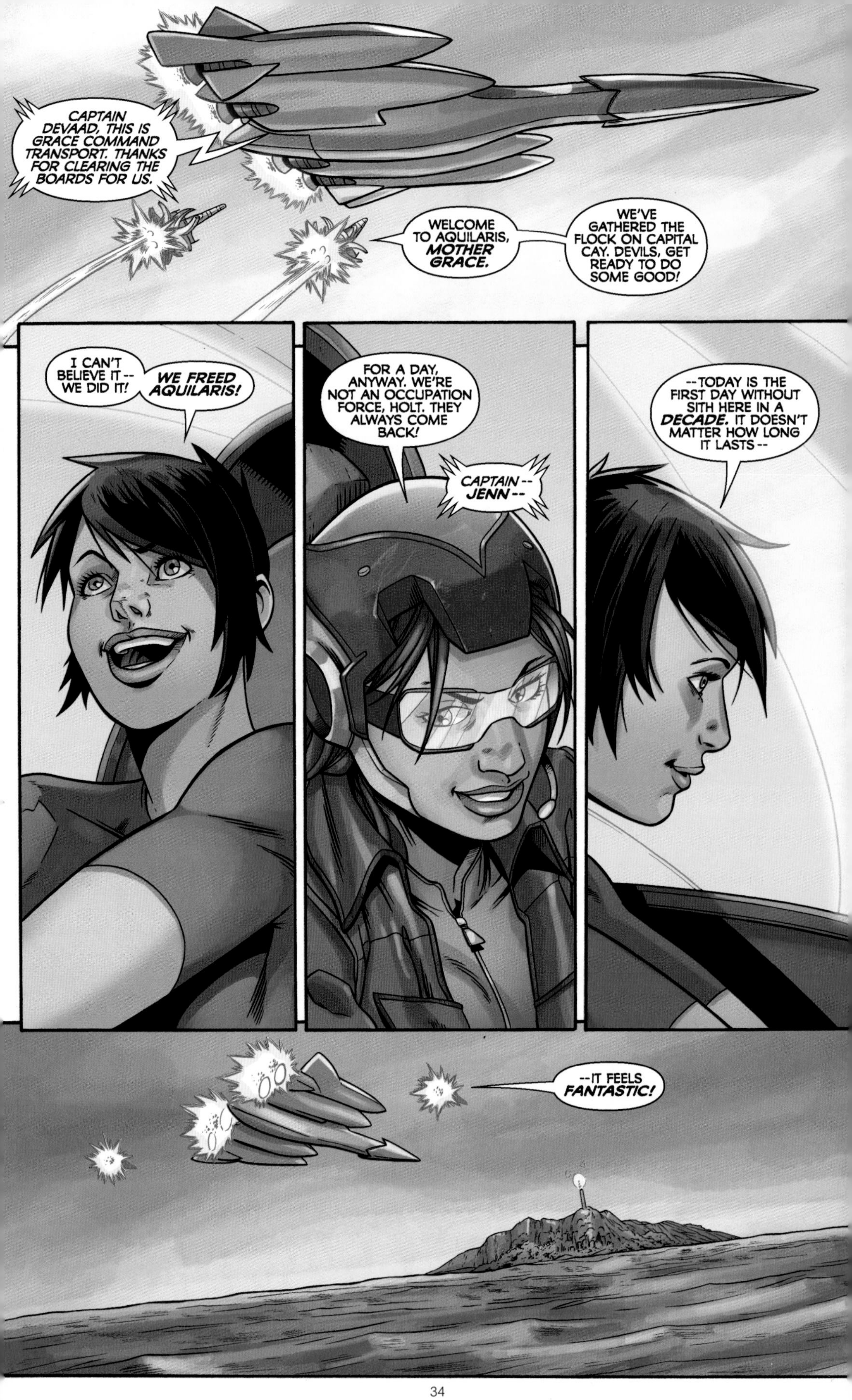
CAPTAIN DEVAAD, THIS IS GRACE COMMAND TRANSPORT. THANKS FOR CLEARING THE BOARDS FOR US.
WELCOME TO AQUILARIS, MOTHER GRACE.
WE'VE GATHERED THE FLOCK ON CAPITAL CAY. DEVILS, GET READY TO DO SOME GOOD!
I CAN'T BELIEVE IT -- WE DID IT!
WE FREED AQUILARIS!
FOR A DAY, ANYWAY. WE'RE NOT AN OCCUPATION FORCE, HOLT. THEY ALWAYS COME BACK!
CAPTAIN -- JENN --
--TODAY IS THE FIRST DAY WITHOUT SITH HERE IN A DECADE. IT DOESN'T MATTER HOW LONG IT LASTS --
--IT FEELS FANTASTIC!

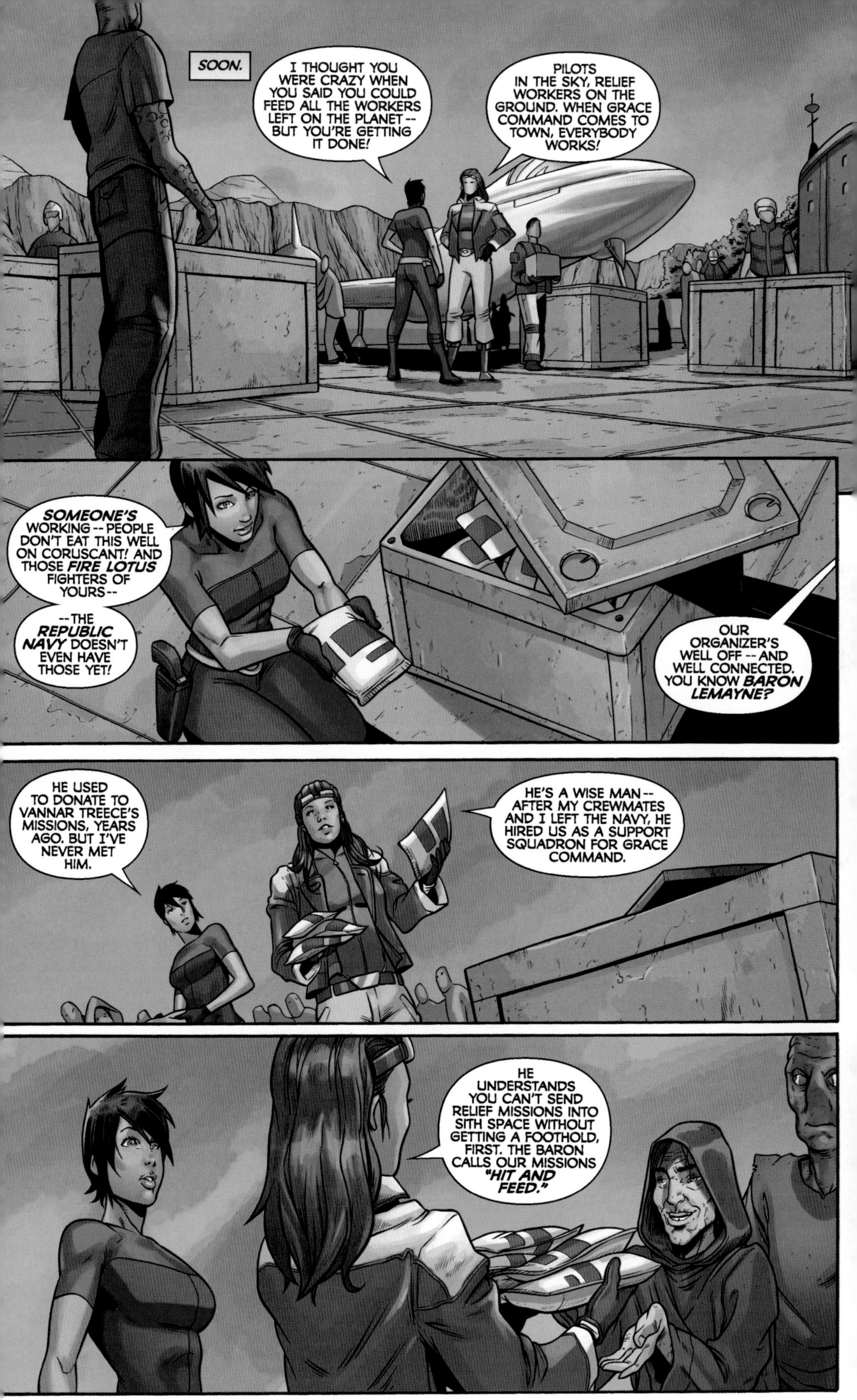
SOON.
I THOUGHT YOU WERE CRAZY WHEN YOU SAID YOU COULD FEED ALL THE WORKERS LEFT ON THE PLANET -- BUT YOU'RE GETTING IT DONE!
PILOTS IN THE SKY, RELIEF WORKERS ON THE GROUND. WHEN GRACE COMMAND COMES TO TOWN, EVERYBODY WORKS!
SOMEONE'S WORKING -- PEOPLE DON'T EAT THIS WELL ON CORUSCANT! AND THOSE FIRE LOTUS FIGHTERS OF YOURS--
--THE REPUBLIC NAVY DOESN'T EVEN HAVE THOSE YET!
OUR ORGANIZER'S WELL OFF -- AND WELL CONNECTED. YOU KNOW BARON LEMAYNE?
HE USED TO DONATE TO VANNAR TREECE'S MISSIONS, YEARS AGO. BUT I'VE NEVER MET HIM.
HE'S A WISE MAN -- AFTER MY CREWMATES AND I LEFT THE NAVY, HE HIRED US AS A SUPPORT SQUADRON FOR GRACE COMMAND.
HE UNDERSTANDS YOU CAN'T SEND RELIEF MISSIONS INTO SITH SPACE WITHOUT GETTING A FOOTHOLD, FIRST. THE BARON CALLS OUR MISSIONS "HIT AND FEED."

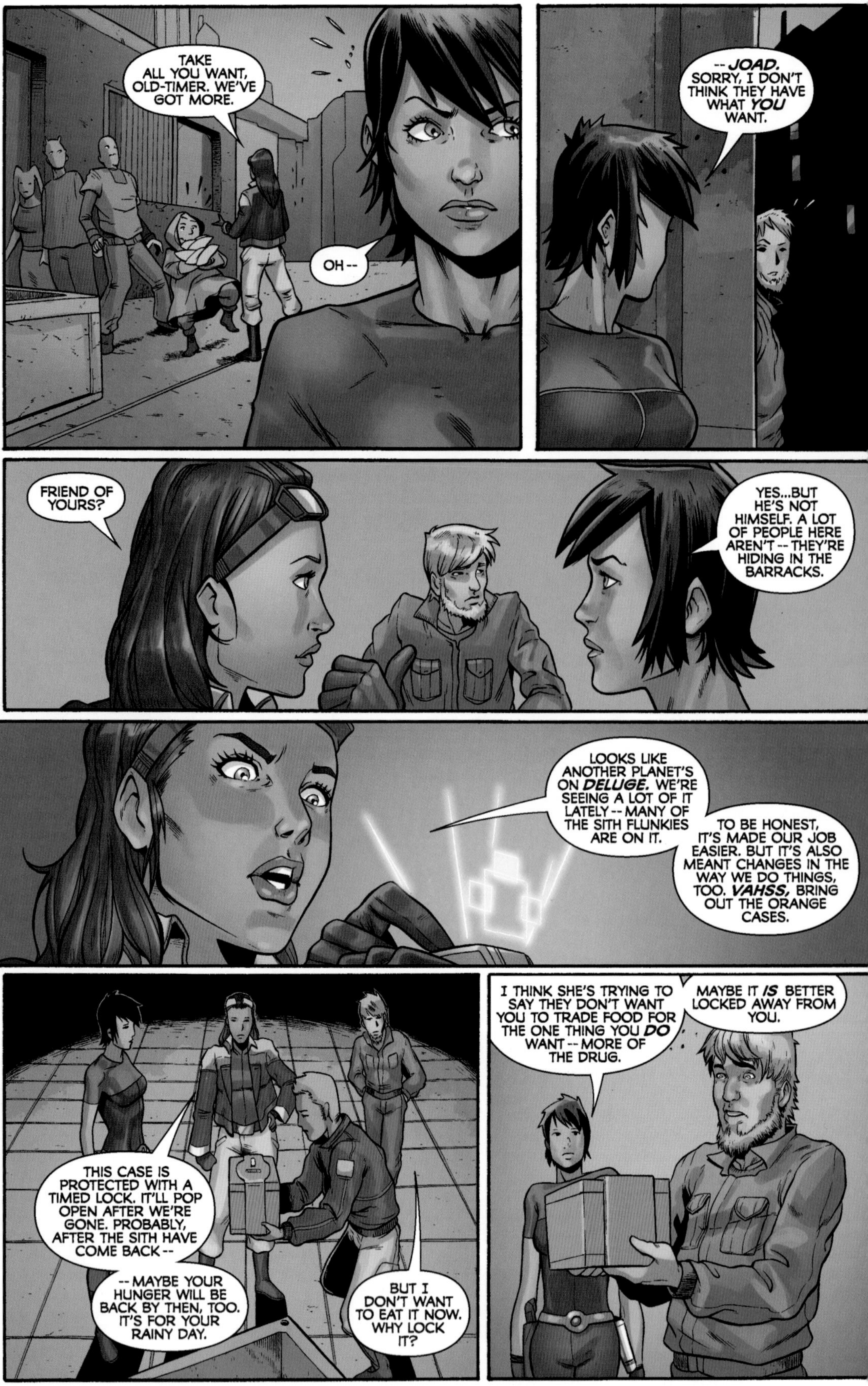
TAKE ALL YOU WANT, OLD-TIMER. WE'VE GOT MORE.
OH --
-- JOAD. SORRY, I DON'T THINK THEY HAVE WHAT YOU WANT.
FRIEND OF YOURS?
YES...BUT HE'S NOT HIMSELF. A LOT OF PEOPLE HERE AREN'T -- THEY'RE HIDING IN THE BARRACKS.
LOOKS LIKE ANOTHER PLANET'S ON DELUGE. WE'RE SEEING A LOT OF IT LATELY -- MANY OF THE SITH FLUNKIES ARE ON IT.
TO BE HONEST, IT'S MADE OUR JOB EASIER. BUT IT'S ALSO MEANT CHANGES IN THE WAY WE DO THINGS, TOO. VAHSS, BRING OUT THE ORANGE CASES.
THIS CASE IS PROTECTED WITH A TIMED LOCK. IT'LL POP OPEN AFTER WE'RE GONE. PROBABLY, AFTER THE SITH HAVE COME BACK --
-- MAYBE YOUR HUNGER WILL BE BACK BY THEN, TOO. IT'S FOR YOUR RAINY DAY.
BUT I DON'T WANT TO EAT IT NOW. WHY LOCK IT?
I THINK SHE'S TRYING TO SAY THEY DON'T WANT YOU TO TRADE FOOD FOR THE ONE THING YOU DO WANT -- MORE OF THE DRUG.
MAYBE IT IS BETTER LOCKED AWAY FROM YOU.

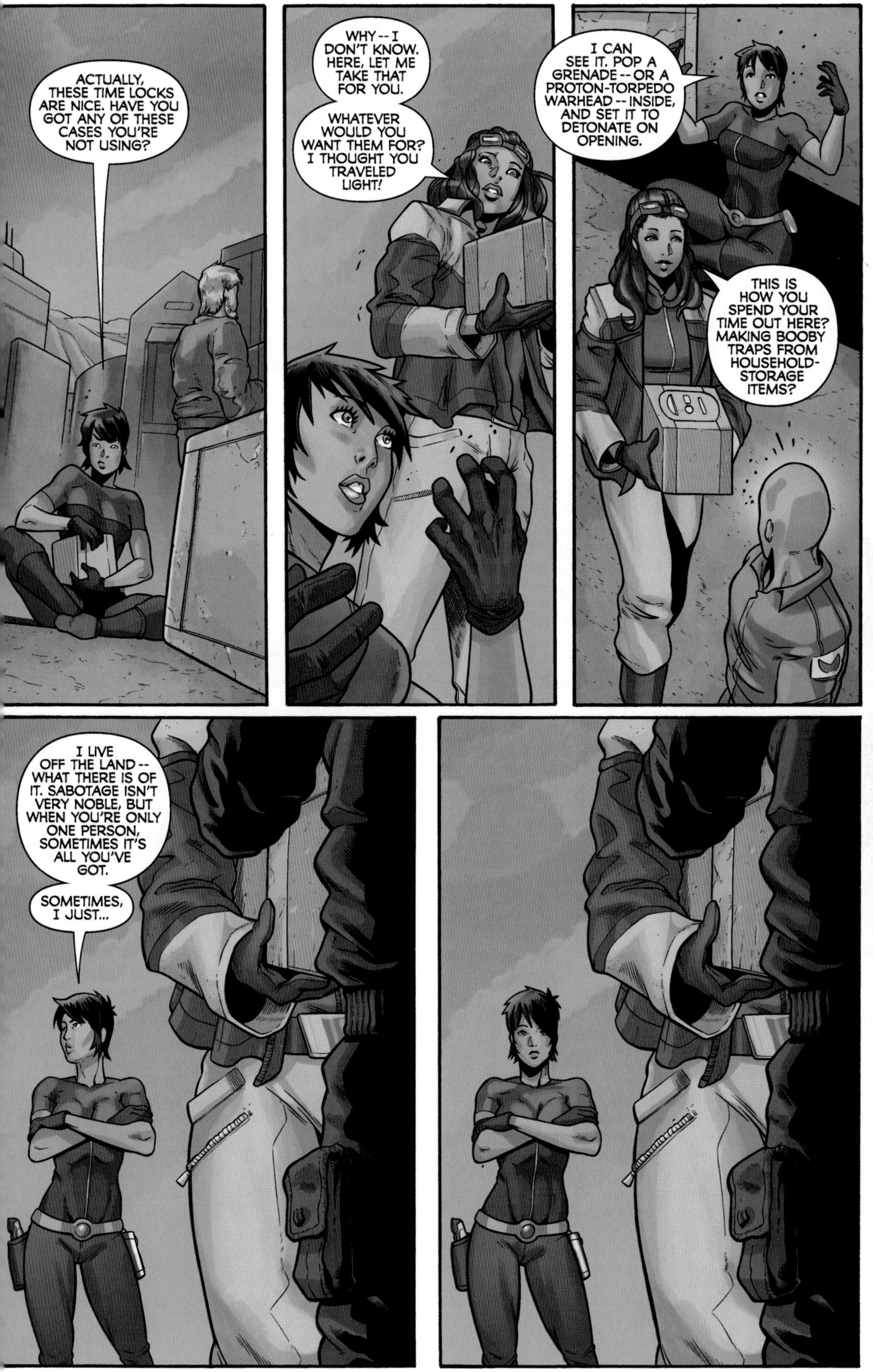
ACTUALLY, THESE TIME LOCKS ARE NICE. HAVE YOU GOT ANY OF THESE CASES YOU'RE NOT USING?
WHY -- I DON'T KNOW. HERE, LET ME TAKE THAT FOR YOU.
WHATEVER WOULD YOU WANT THEM FOR? I THOUGHT YOU TRAVELED LIGHT!
I CAN SEE IT. POP A GRENADE -- OR A PROTON-TORPEDO WARHEAD -- INSIDE, AND SET IT TO DETONATE ON OPENING.
THIS IS HOW YOU SPEND YOUR TIME OUT HERE? MAKING BOOBY TRAPS FROM HOUSEHOLD-STORAGE ITEMS?
I LIVE OFF THE LAND -- WHAT THERE IS OF IT. SABOTAGE ISN'T VERY NOBLE, BUT WHEN YOU'RE ONLY ONE PERSON, SOMETIMES IT'S ALL YOU'VE GOT.
SOMETIMES, I JUST...

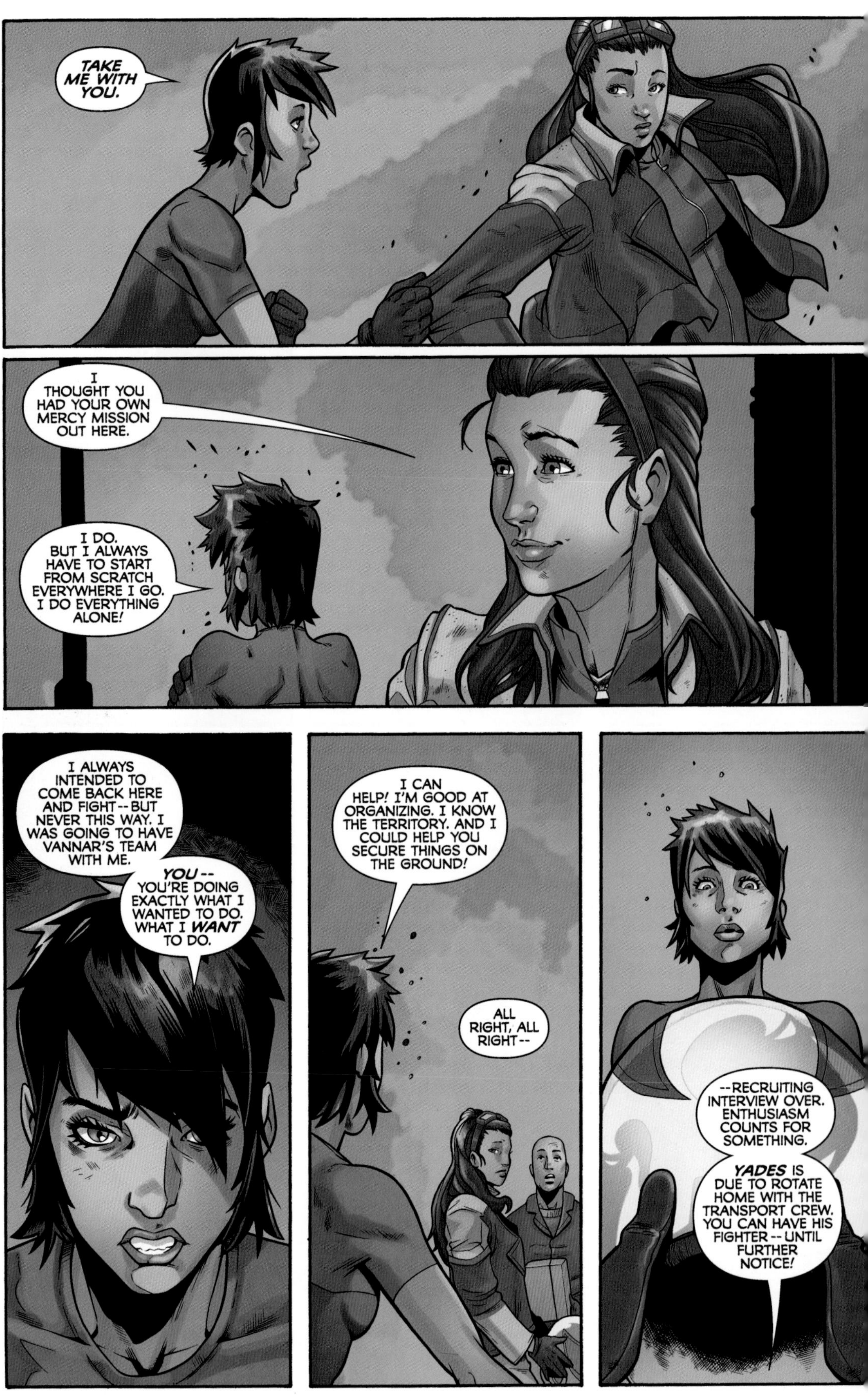

TAKE ME WITH YOU.
I THOUGHT YOU HAD YOUR OWN MERCY MISSION OUT HERE.
I DO. BUT I ALWAYS HAVE TO START FROM SCRATCH EVERYWHERE I GO. I DO EVERYTHING ALONE!
I ALWAYS INTENDED TO COME BACK HERE AND FIGHT--BUT NEVER THIS WAY. I WAS GOING TO HAVE VANNAR'S TEAM WITH ME.
YOU-- YOU'RE DOING EXACTLY WHAT I WANTED TO DO. WHAT I WANT TO DO.
I CAN HELP! I'M GOOD AT ORGANIZING. I KNOW THE TERRITORY. AND I COULD HELP YOU SECURE THINGS ON THE GROUND!
ALL RIGHT, ALL RIGHT--
--RECRUITING INTERVIEW OVER. ENTHUSIASM COUNTS FOR SOMETHING.
YADES IS DUE TO ROTATE HOME WITH THE TRANSPORT CREW. YOU CAN HAVE HIS FIGHTER--UNTIL FURTHER NOTICE!

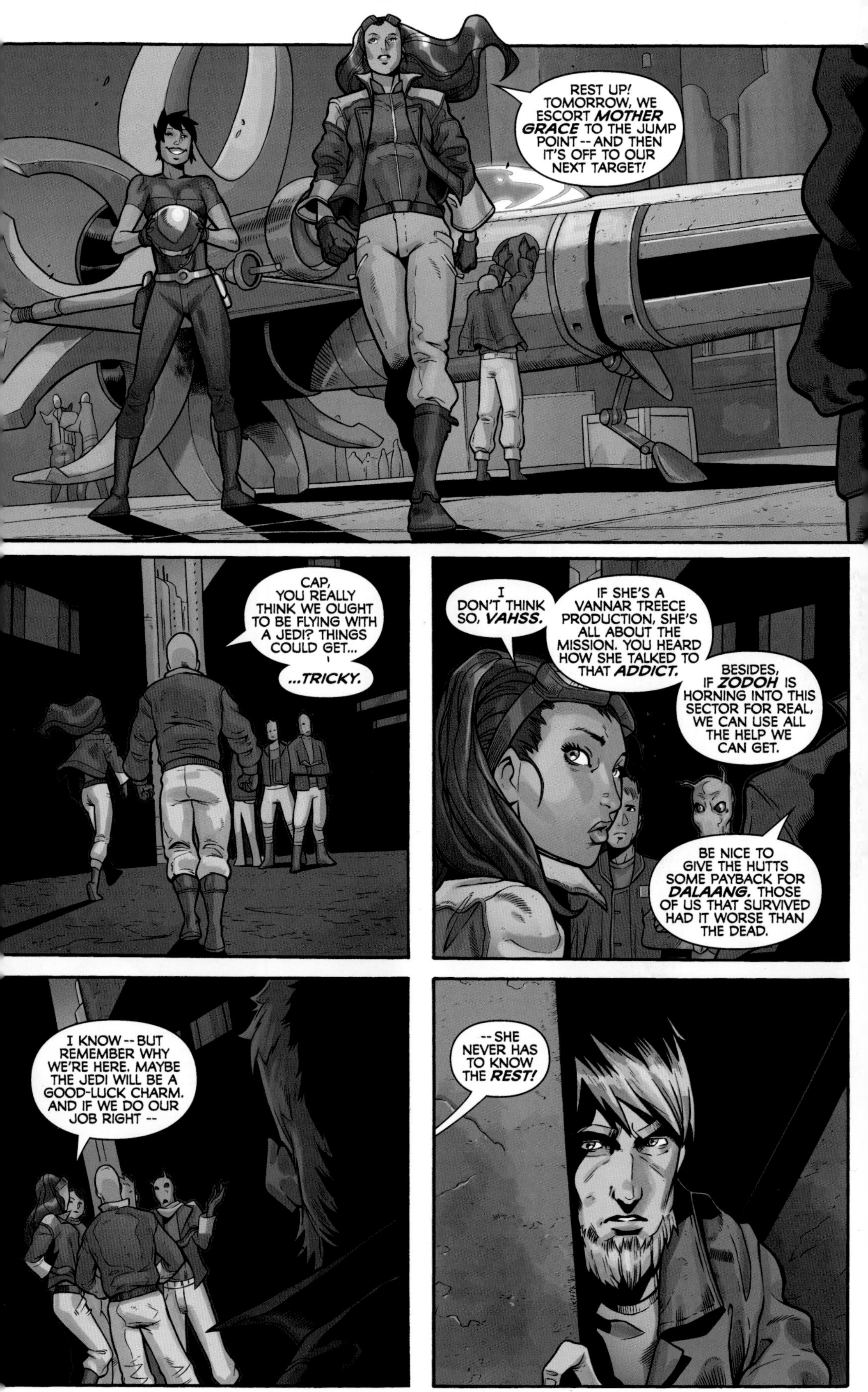
REST UP! TOMORROW, WE ESCORT MOTHER GRACE TO THE JUMP POINT -- AND THEN IT'S OFF TO OUR NEXT TARGET!
CAP, YOU REALLY THINK WE OUGHT TO BE FLYING WITH A JEDI? THINGS COULD GET...
...TRICKY.
I DON'T THINK SO, VAHSS.
IF SHE'S A VANNAR TREECE PRODUCTION, SHE'S ALL ABOUT THE MISSION. YOU HEARD HOW SHE TALKED TO THAT ADDICT.
BESIDES, IF ZODOH IS HORNING INTO THIS SECTOR FOR REAL, WE CAN USE ALL THE HELP WE CAN GET.
BE NICE TO GIVE THE HUTTS SOME PAYBACK FOR DALAANG. THOSE OF US THAT SURVIVED HAD IT WORSE THAN THE DEAD.
I KNOW -- BUT REMEMBER WHY WE'RE HERE. MAYBE THE JEDI WILL BE A GOOD-LUCK CHARM. AND IF WE DO OUR JOB RIGHT --
-- SHE NEVER HAS TO KNOW THE REST!

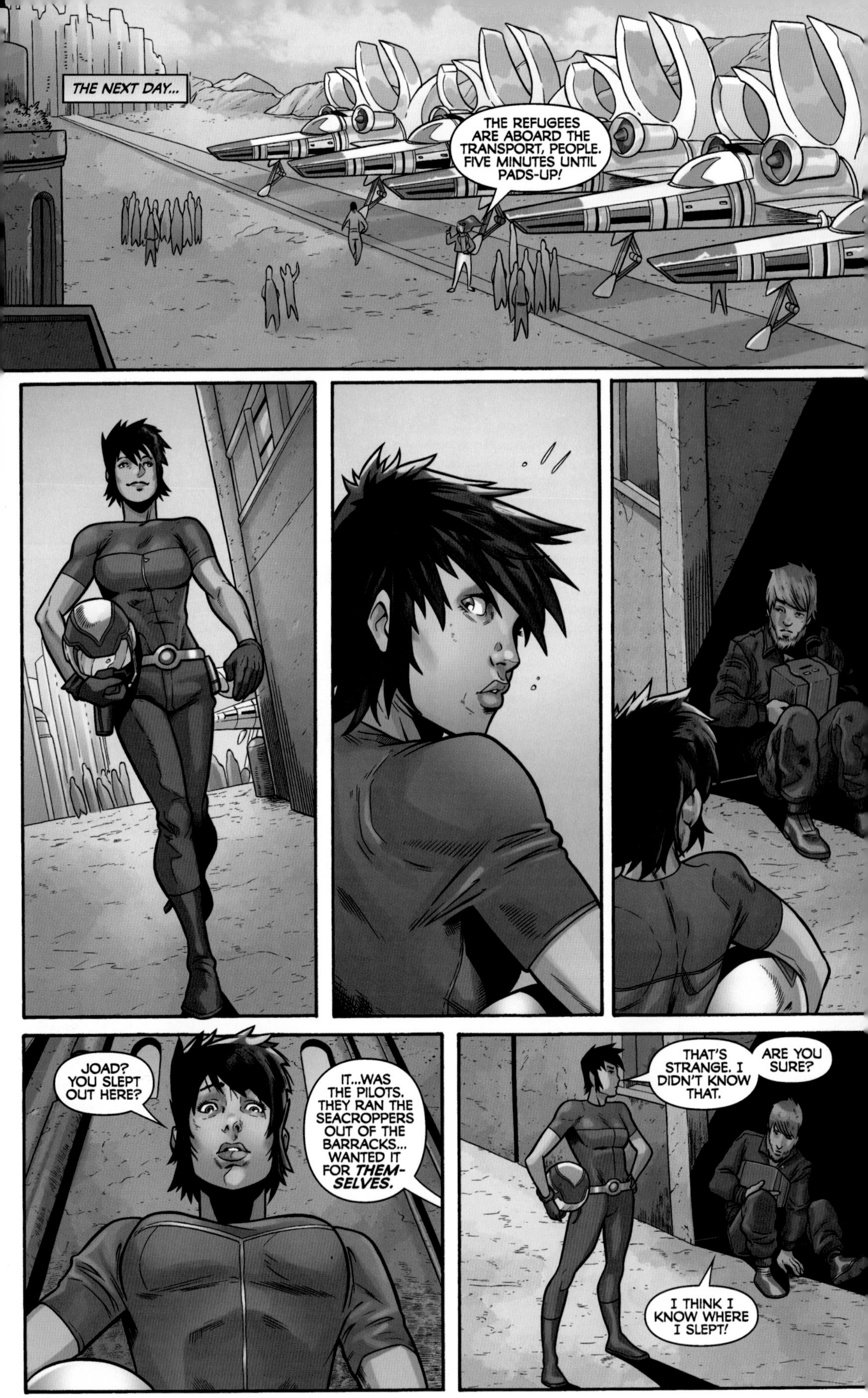
THE NEXT DAY...
THE REFUGEES ARE ABOARD THE TRANSPORT, PEOPLE. FIVE MINUTES UNTIL PADS-UP!
JOAD? YOU SLEPT OUT HERE?
IT...WAS THE PILOTS. THEY RAN THE SEACROPPERS OUT OF THE BARRACKS... WANTED IT FOR *THEMSELVES.*
THAT'S STRANGE. I DIDN'T KNOW THAT.
ARE YOU SURE?
I THINK I KNOW WHERE I SLEPT!

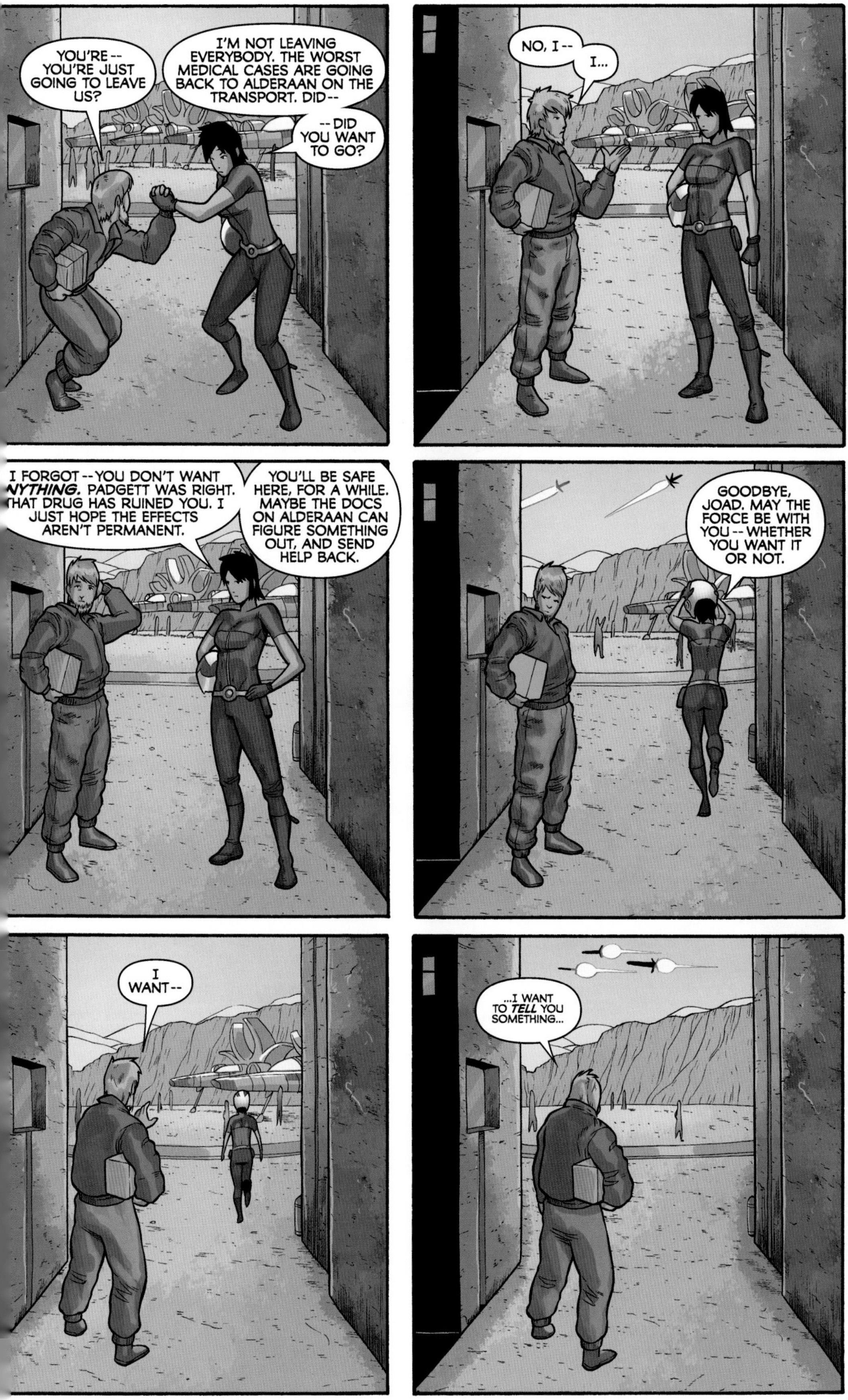
YOU'RE -- YOU'RE JUST GOING TO LEAVE US?
I'M NOT LEAVING EVERYBODY. THE WORST MEDICAL CASES ARE GOING BACK TO ALDERAAN ON THE TRANSPORT. DID--
--DID YOU WANT TO GO?
NO, I --
I...
I FORGOT --YOU DON'T WANT ANYTHING. PADGETT WAS RIGHT. THAT DRUG HAS RUINED YOU. I JUST HOPE THE EFFECTS AREN'T PERMANENT.
YOU'LL BE SAFE HERE, FOR A WHILE. MAYBE THE DOCS ON ALDERAAN CAN FIGURE SOMETHING OUT, AND SEND HELP BACK.
GOODBYE, JOAD. MAY THE FORCE BE WITH YOU -- WHETHER YOU WANT IT OR NOT.
I WANT--
...I WANT TO TELL YOU SOMETHING...

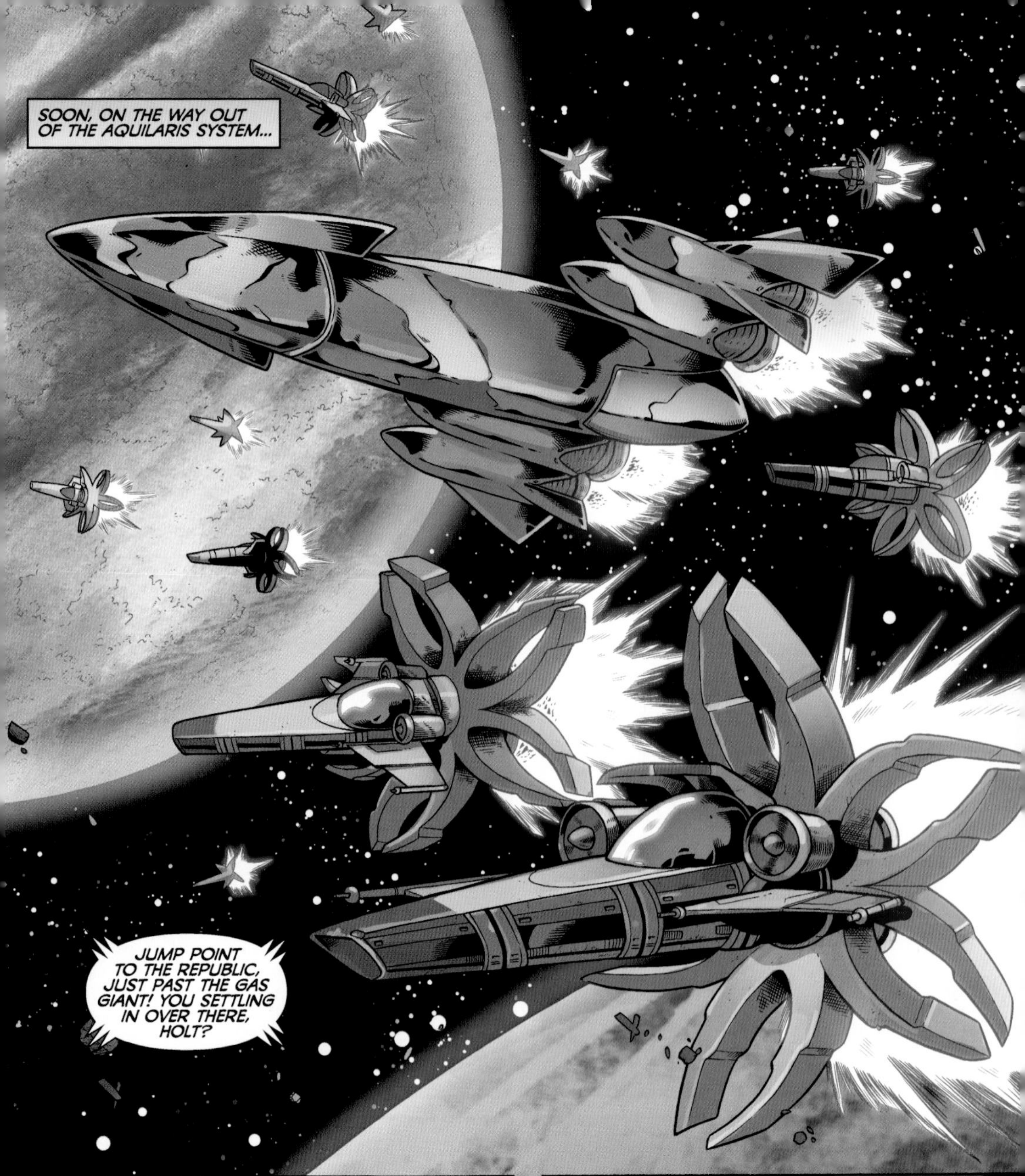

SOON, ON THE WAY OUT OF THE AQUILARIS SYSTEM...
JUMP POINT TO THE REPUBLIC, JUST PAST THE GAS GIANT! YOU SETTLING IN OVER THERE, HOLT?


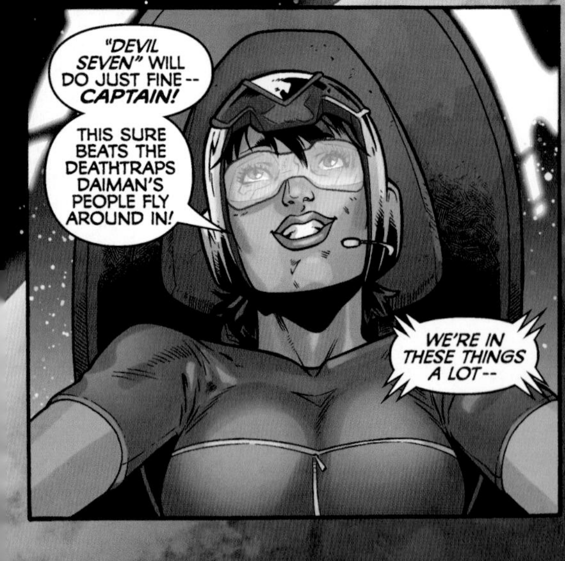

"DEVIL SEVEN" WILL DO JUST FINE-- CAPTAIN!
THIS SURE BEATS THE DEATHTRAPS DAIMAN'S PEOPLE FLY AROUND IN!
WE'RE IN THESE THINGS A LOT--


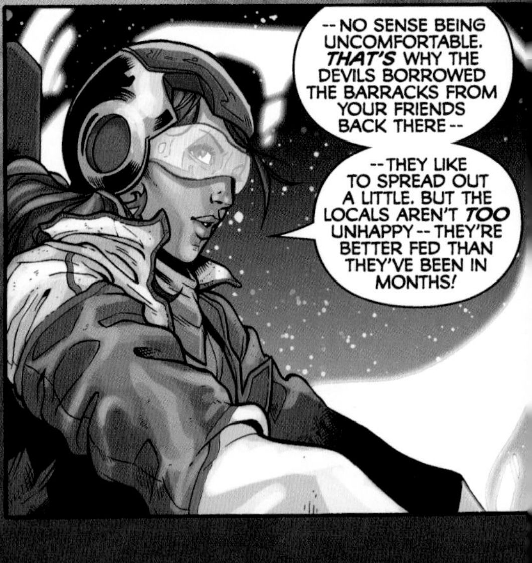

--NO SENSE BEING UNCOMFORTABLE. THAT'S WHY THE DEVILS BORROWED THE BARRACKS FROM YOUR FRIENDS BACK THERE--
--THEY LIKE TO SPREAD OUT A LITTLE. BUT THE LOCALS AREN'T TOO UNHAPPY--THEY'RE BETTER FED THAN THEY'VE BEEN IN MONTHS!

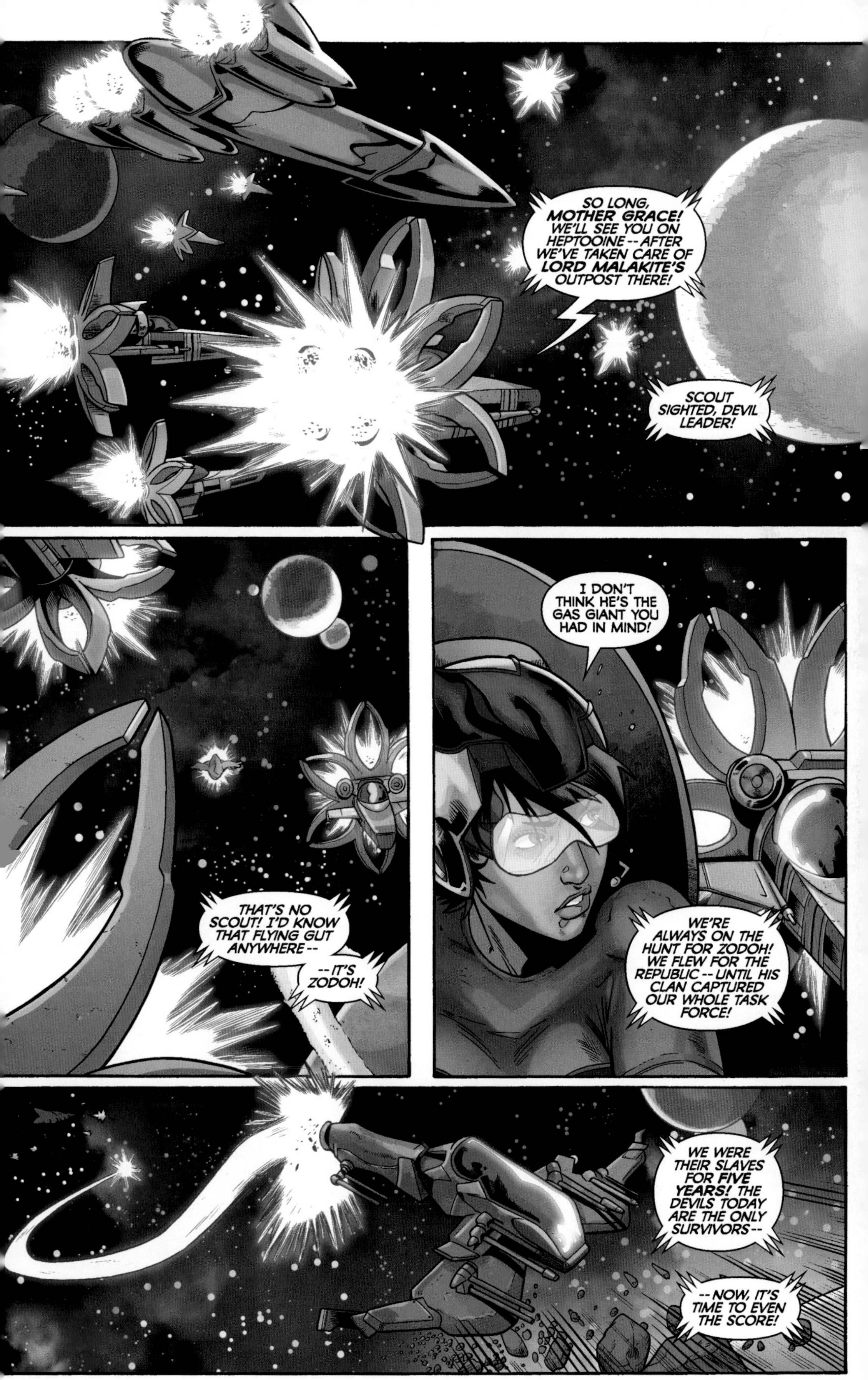
SO LONG, MOTHER GRACE! WE'LL SEE YOU ON HEPTOOINE -- AFTER WE'VE TAKEN CARE OF LORD MALAKITE'S OUTPOST THERE!
SCOUT SIGHTED, DEVIL LEADER!
THAT'S NO SCOUT! I'D KNOW THAT FLYING GUT ANYWHERE --
-- IT'S ZODOH!
I DON'T THINK HE'S THE GAS GIANT YOU HAD IN MIND!
WE'RE ALWAYS ON THE HUNT FOR ZODOH! WE FLEW FOR THE REPUBLIC -- UNTIL HIS CLAN CAPTURED OUR WHOLE TASK FORCE!
WE WERE THEIR SLAVES FOR FIVE YEARS! THE DEVILS TODAY ARE THE ONLY SURVIVORS --
-- NOW, IT'S TIME TO EVEN THE SCORE!

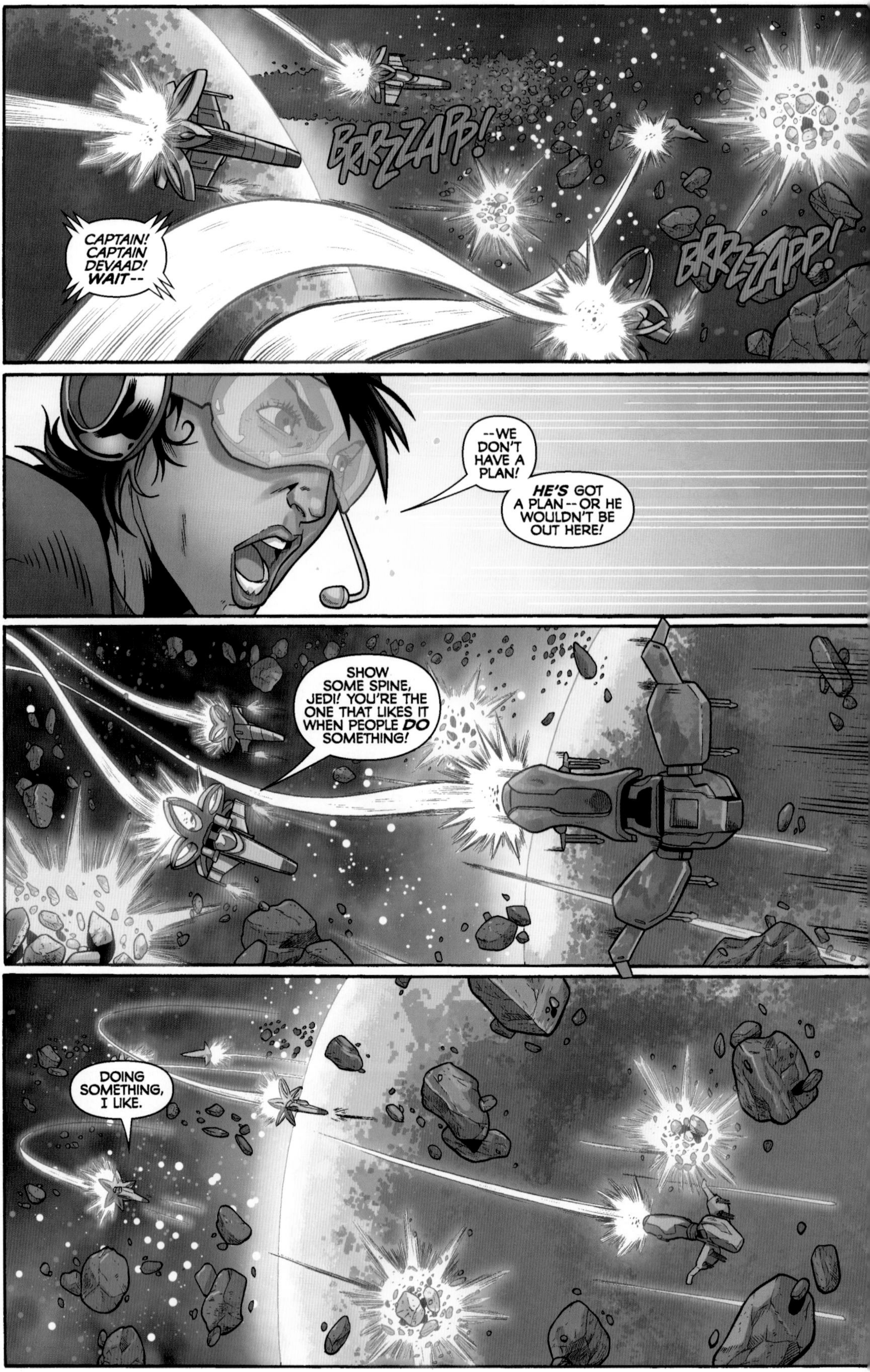
BRRZZAPP!
CAPTAIN! CAPTAIN DEVAAD! WAIT--
BRRZZAPP!
--WE DON'T HAVE A PLAN!
HE'S GOT A PLAN--OR HE WOULDN'T BE OUT HERE!
SHOW SOME SPINE, JEDI! YOU'RE THE ONE THAT LIKES IT WHEN PEOPLE DO SOMETHING!
DOING SOMETHING, I LIKE.

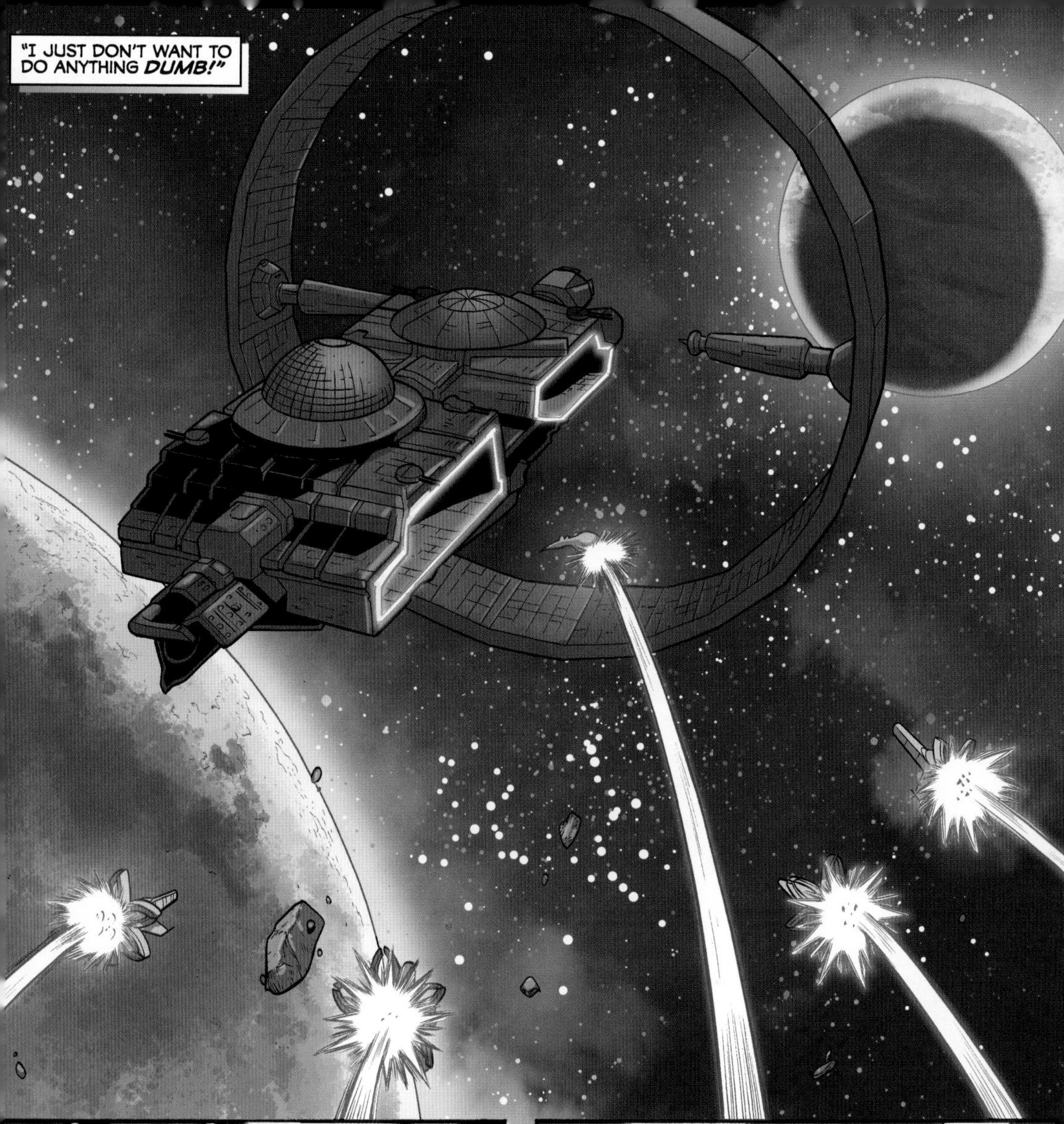
"I JUST DON'T WANT TO DO ANYTHING *DUMB!*"

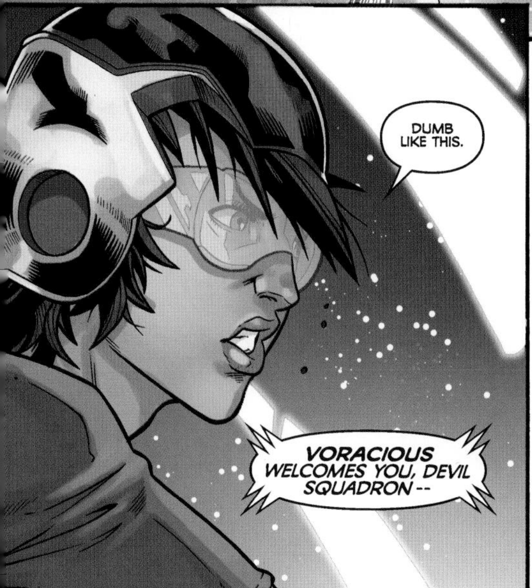
DUMB LIKE THIS.
*VORACIOUS* WELCOMES YOU, DEVIL SQUADRON --

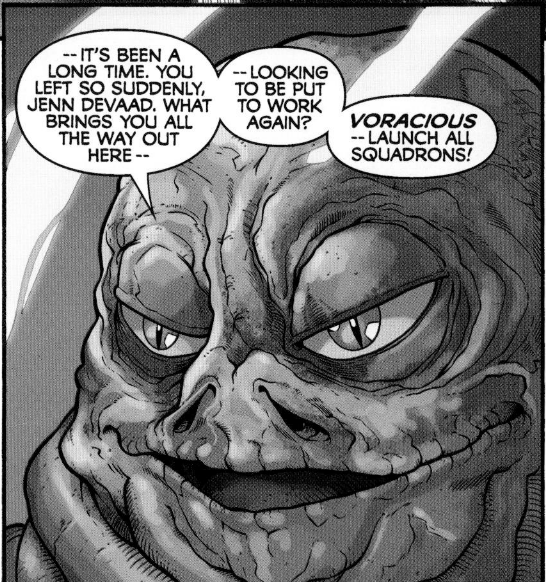
-- IT'S BEEN A LONG TIME. YOU LEFT SO SUDDENLY, JENN DEVAAD. WHAT BRINGS YOU ALL THE WAY OUT HERE --
-- LOOKING TO BE PUT TO WORK AGAIN?
*VORACIOUS* -- LAUNCH ALL SQUADRONS!

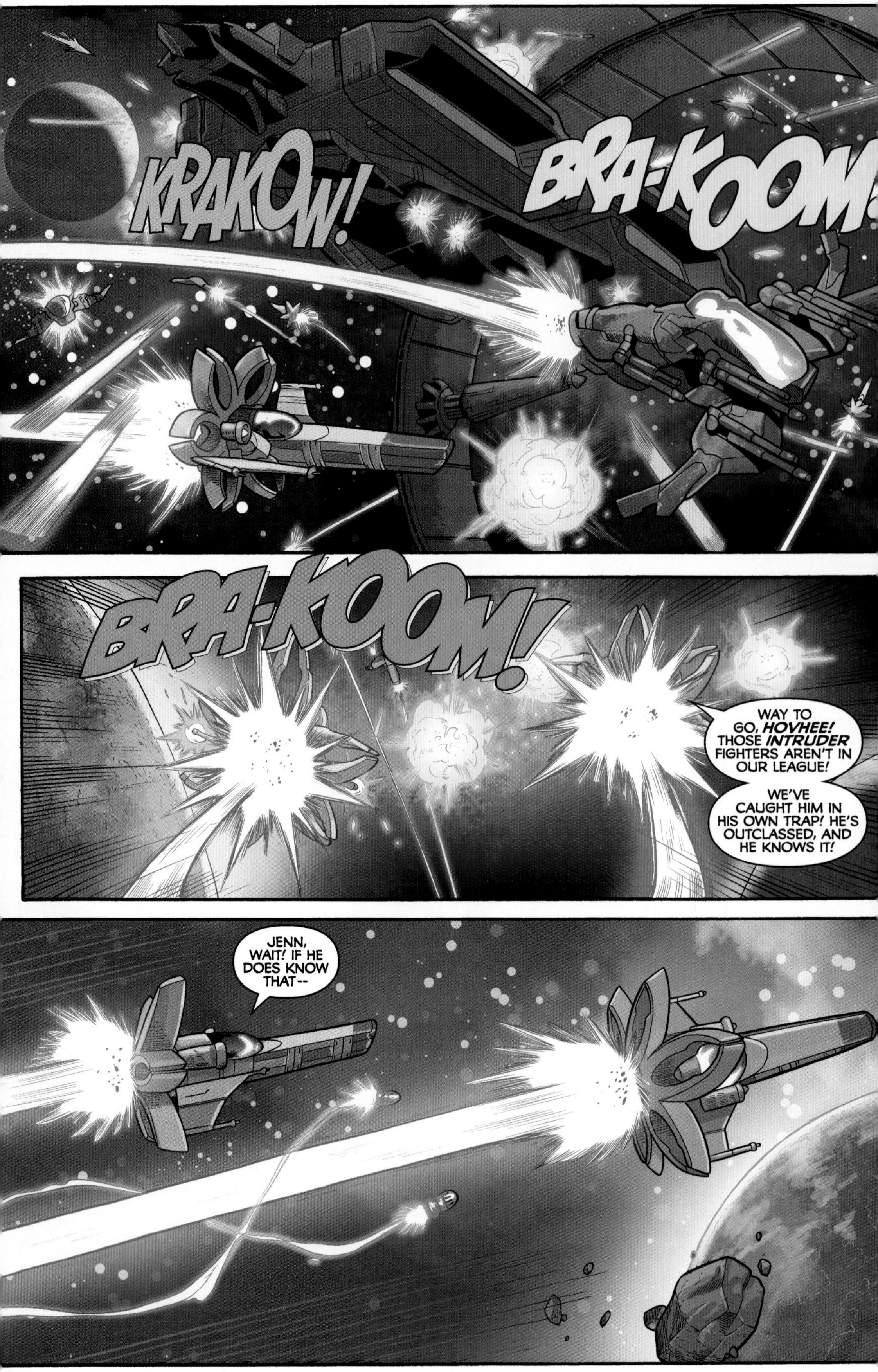
KRAKOW!
BRA-KOOM!
BRA-KOOM!
WAY TO GO, *HOVHEE!* THOSE *INTRUDER* FIGHTERS AREN'T IN OUR LEAGUE!
WE'VE CAUGHT HIM IN HIS OWN TRAP! HE'S OUTCLASSED, AND HE KNOWS IT!
JENN, WAIT! IF HE DOES KNOW THAT--

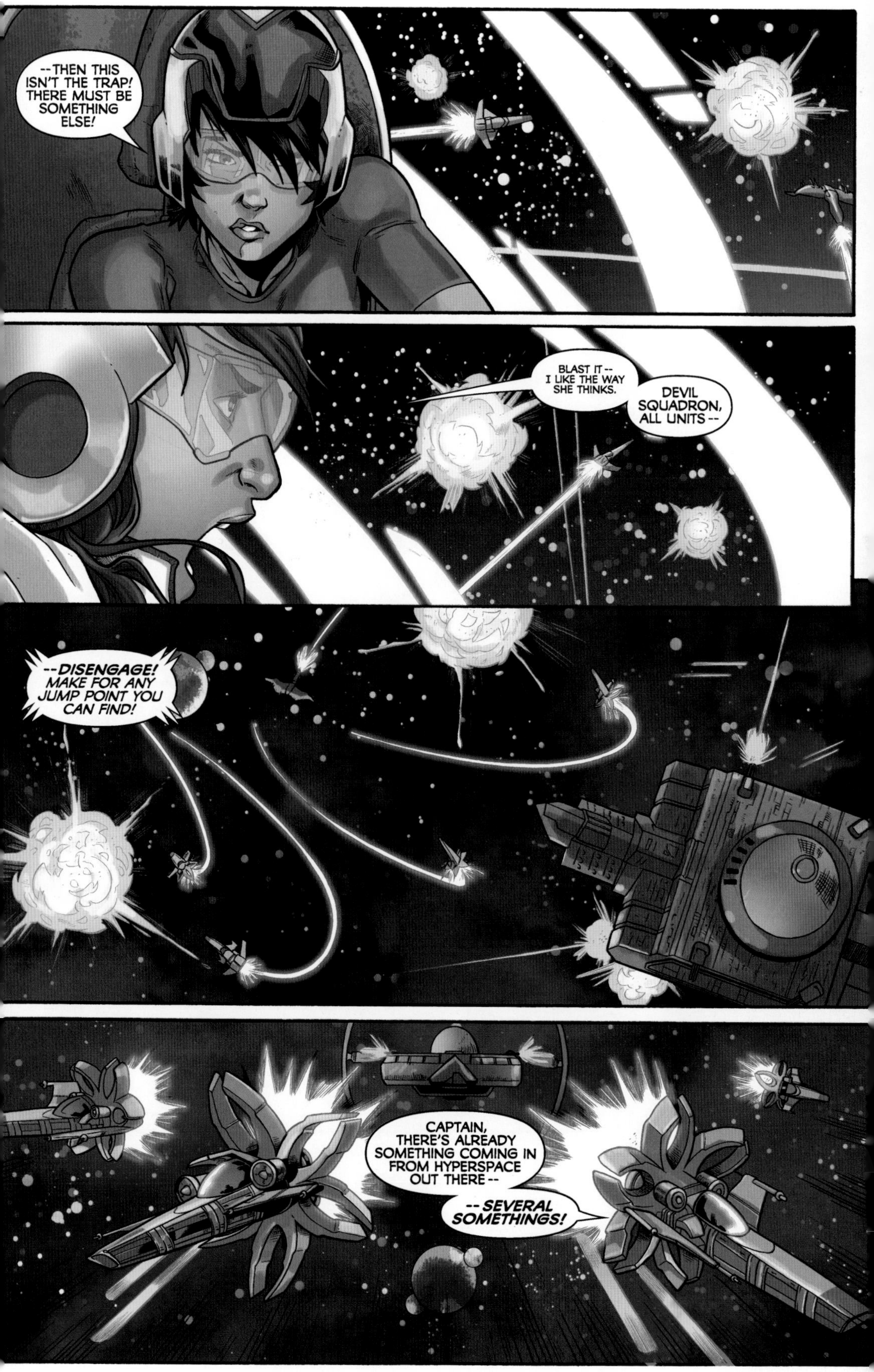
--THEN THIS ISN'T THE TRAP! THERE MUST BE SOMETHING ELSE!
BLAST IT -- I LIKE THE WAY SHE THINKS.
DEVIL SQUADRON, ALL UNITS --
--DISENGAGE! MAKE FOR ANY JUMP POINT YOU CAN FIND!
CAPTAIN, THERE'S ALREADY SOMETHING COMING IN FROM HYPERSPACE OUT THERE --
-- SEVERAL SOMETHINGS!

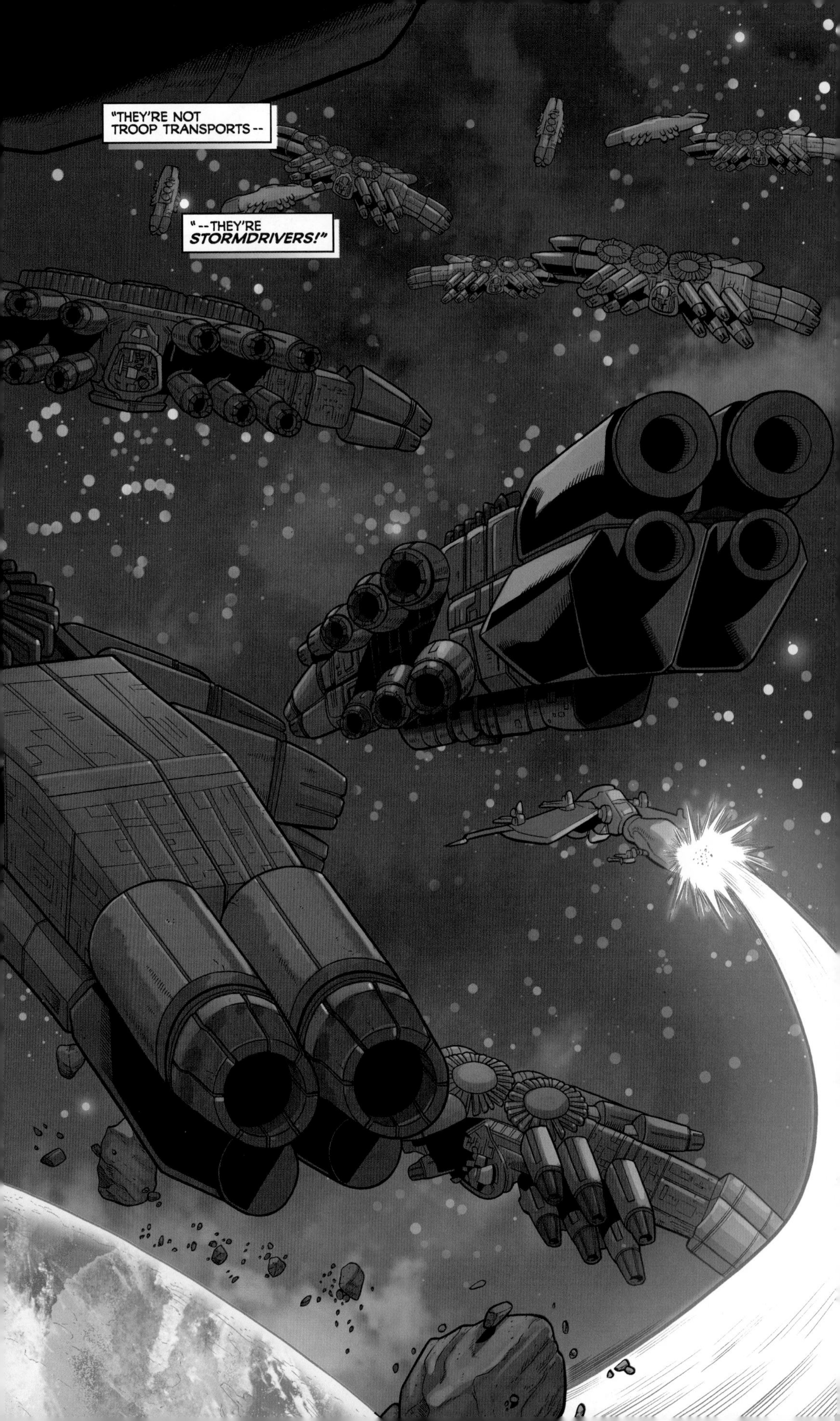
"THEY'RE NOT TROOP TRANSPORTS --
"--THEY'RE *STORMDRIVERS!*"

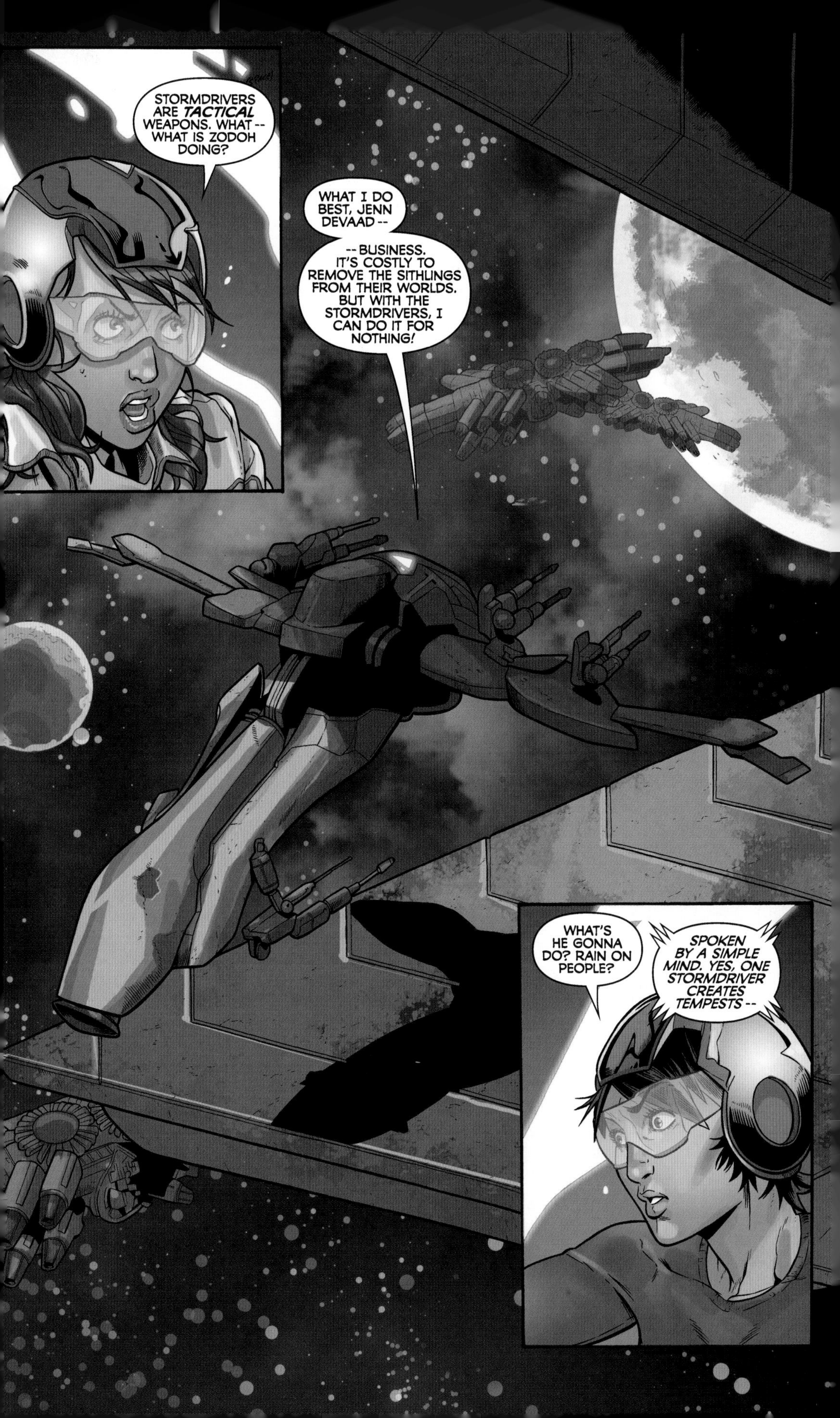
STORMDRIVERS ARE TACTICAL WEAPONS. WHAT -- WHAT IS ZODOH DOING?
WHAT I DO BEST, JENN DEVAAD --
-- BUSINESS. IT'S COSTLY TO REMOVE THE SITHLINGS FROM THEIR WORLDS. BUT WITH THE STORMDRIVERS, I CAN DO IT FOR NOTHING!
WHAT'S HE GONNA DO? RAIN ON PEOPLE?
SPOKEN BY A SIMPLE MIND. YES, ONE STORMDRIVER CREATES TEMPESTS --

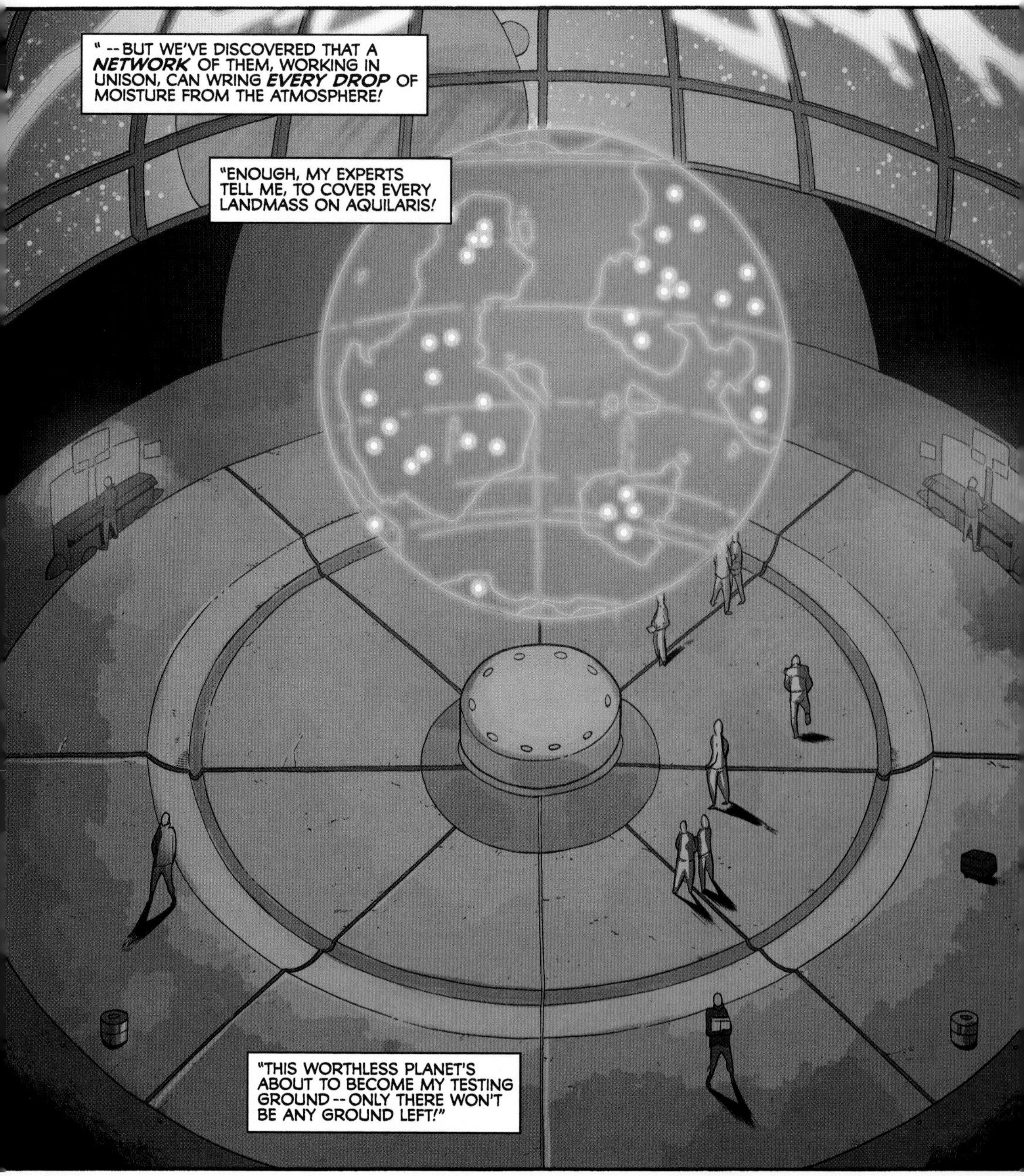
" --BUT WE'VE DISCOVERED THAT A **NETWORK** OF THEM, WORKING IN UNISON, CAN WRING **EVERY DROP** OF MOISTURE FROM THE ATMOSPHERE!
"ENOUGH, MY EXPERTS TELL ME, TO COVER EVERY LANDMASS ON AQUILARIS!
"THIS WORTHLESS PLANET'S ABOUT TO BECOME MY TESTING GROUND--ONLY THERE WON'T BE ANY GROUND LEFT!"

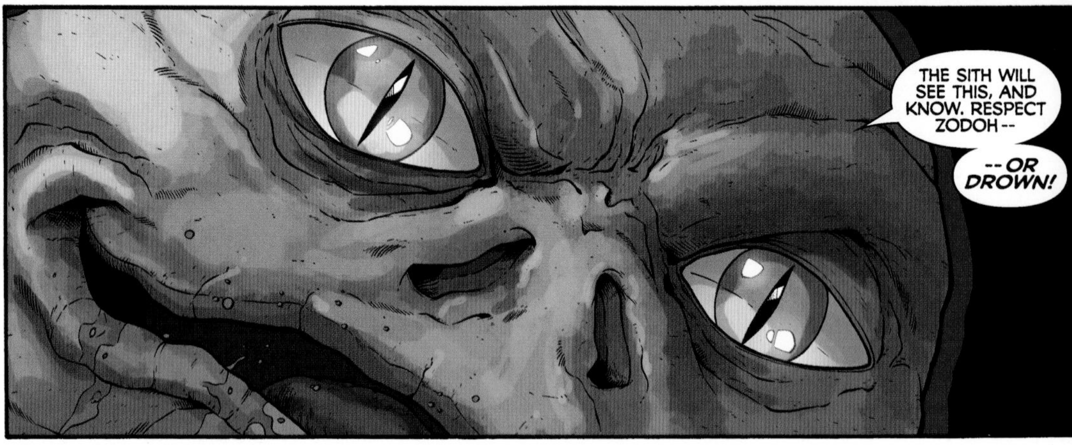
THE SITH WILL SEE THIS, AND KNOW. RESPECT ZODOH --
--**OR DROWN!**

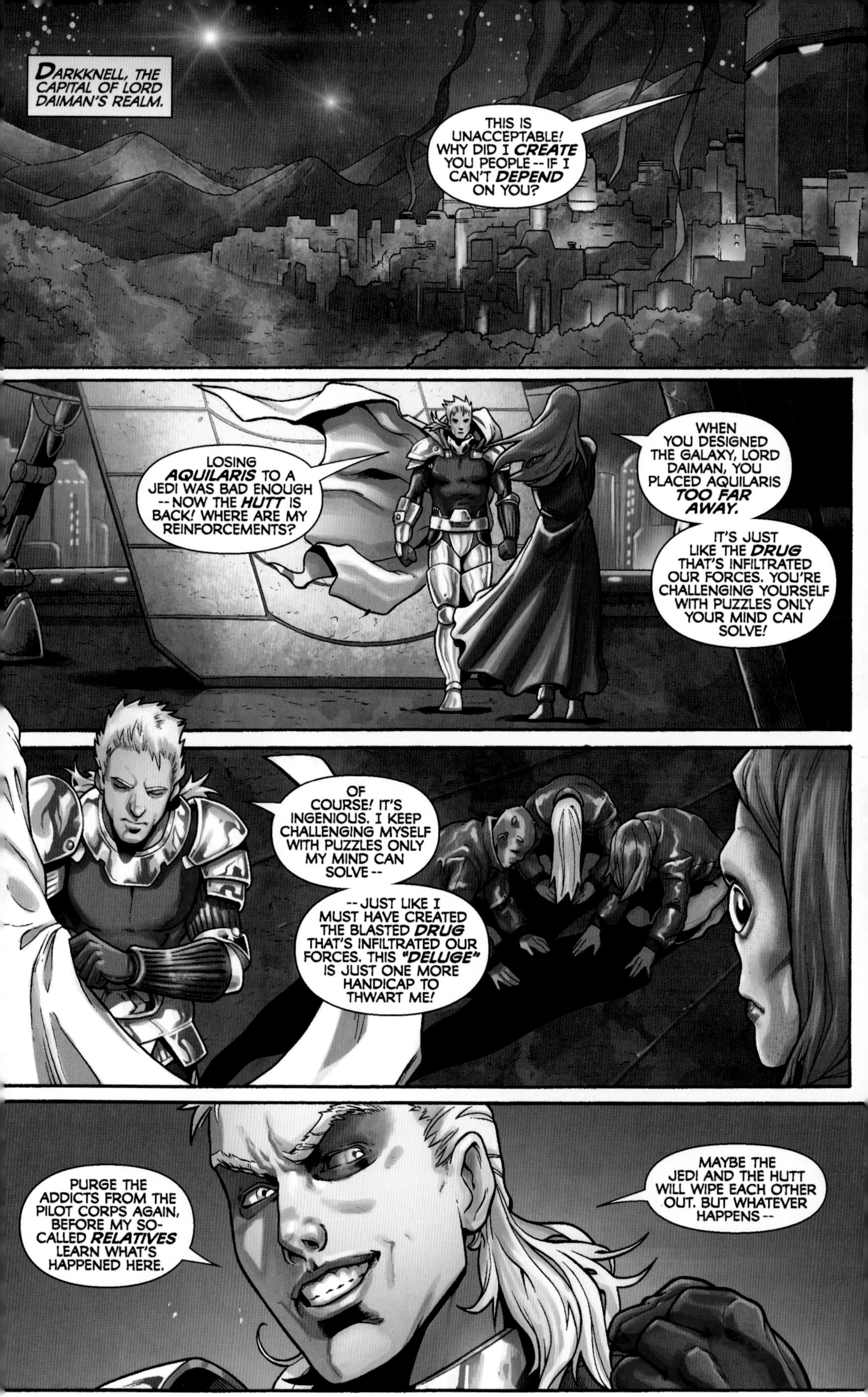
DARKKNELL, THE CAPITAL OF LORD DAIMAN'S REALM.
THIS IS UNACCEPTABLE! WHY DID I CREATE YOU PEOPLE -- IF I CAN'T DEPEND ON YOU?
LOSING AQUILARIS TO A JEDI WAS BAD ENOUGH -- NOW THE HUTT IS BACK! WHERE ARE MY REINFORCEMENTS?
WHEN YOU DESIGNED THE GALAXY, LORD DAIMAN, YOU PLACED AQUILARIS TOO FAR AWAY.
IT'S JUST LIKE THE DRUG THAT'S INFILTRATED OUR FORCES. YOU'RE CHALLENGING YOURSELF WITH PUZZLES ONLY YOUR MIND CAN SOLVE!
OF COURSE! IT'S INGENIOUS. I KEEP CHALLENGING MYSELF WITH PUZZLES ONLY MY MIND CAN SOLVE --
-- JUST LIKE I MUST HAVE CREATED THE BLASTED DRUG THAT'S INFILTRATED OUR FORCES. THIS "DELUGE" IS JUST ONE MORE HANDICAP TO THWART ME!
PURGE THE ADDICTS FROM THE PILOT CORPS AGAIN, BEFORE MY SO-CALLED RELATIVES LEARN WHAT'S HAPPENED HERE.
MAYBE THE JEDI AND THE HUTT WILL WIPE EACH OTHER OUT. BUT WHATEVER HAPPENS --

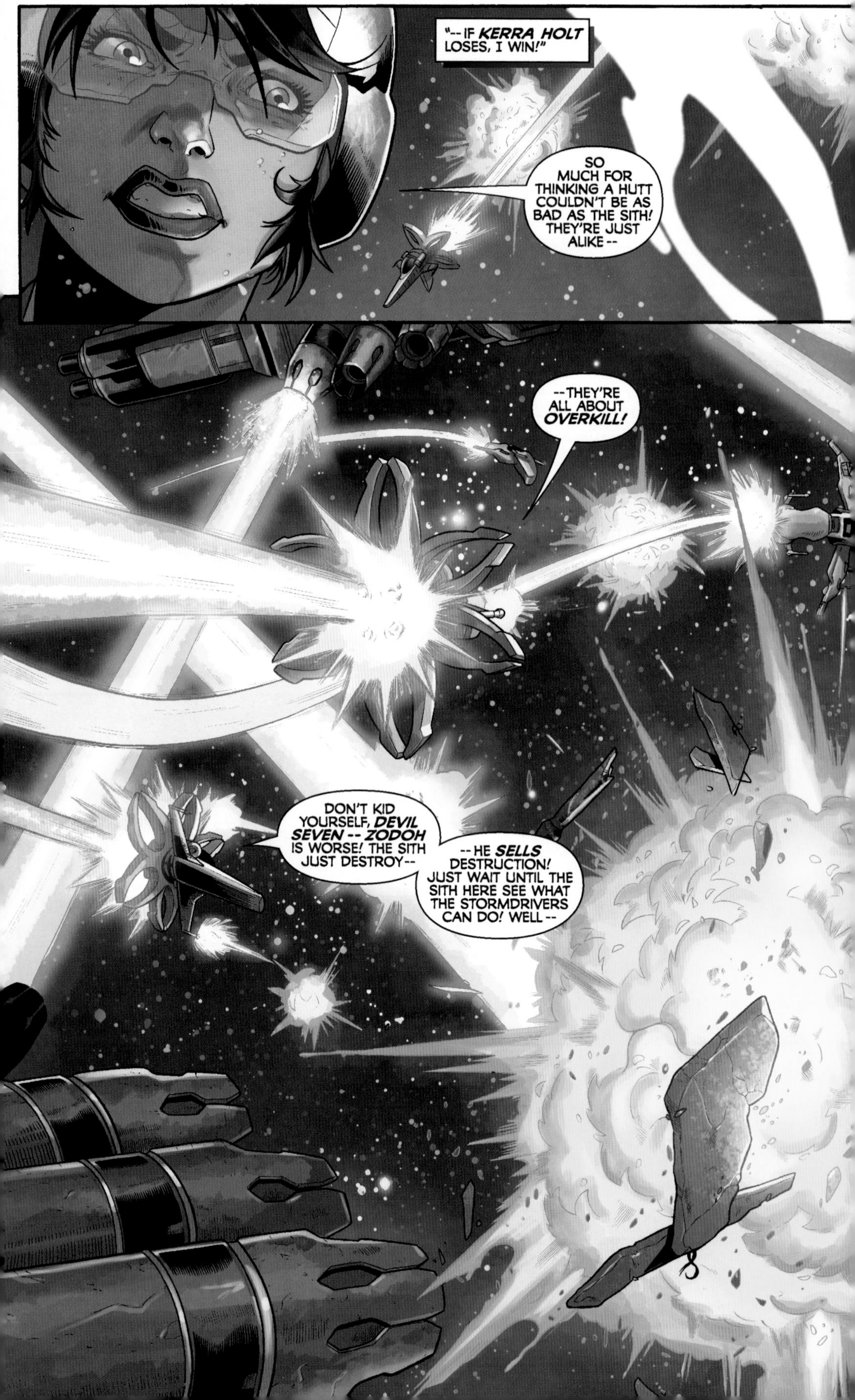
"-- IF KERRA HOLT LOSES, I WIN!"
SO MUCH FOR THINKING A HUTT COULDN'T BE AS BAD AS THE SITH! THEY'RE JUST ALIKE --
-- THEY'RE ALL ABOUT OVERKILL!
DON'T KID YOURSELF, DEVIL SEVEN -- ZODOH IS WORSE! THE SITH JUST DESTROY--
-- HE SELLS DESTRUCTION! JUST WAIT UNTIL THE SITH HERE SEE WHAT THE STORMDRIVERS CAN DO! WELL --

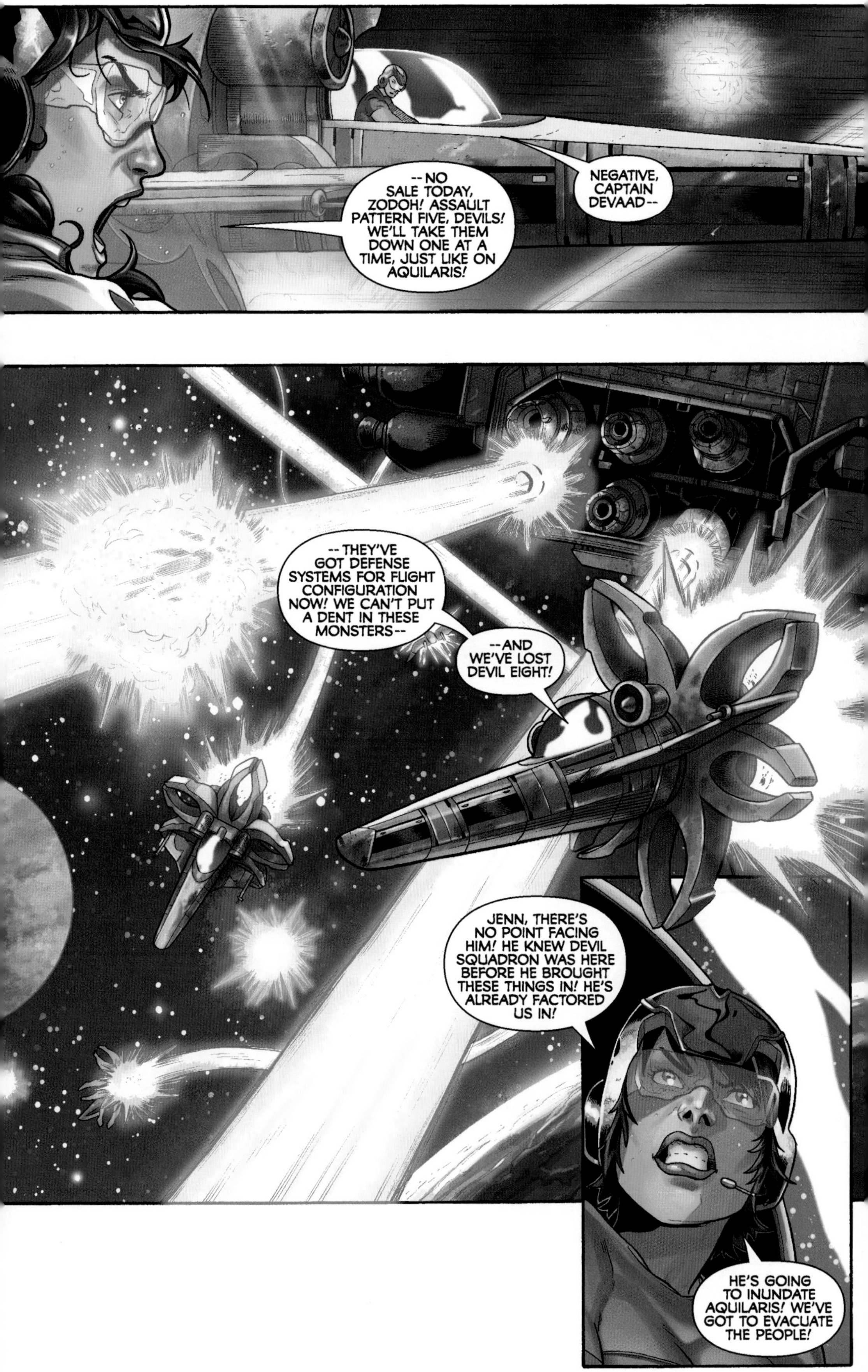
--NO SALE TODAY, ZODOH! ASSAULT PATTERN FIVE, DEVILS! WE'LL TAKE THEM DOWN ONE AT A TIME, JUST LIKE ON AQUILARIS!
NEGATIVE, CAPTAIN DEVAAD--
--THEY'VE GOT DEFENSE SYSTEMS FOR FLIGHT CONFIGURATION NOW! WE CAN'T PUT A DENT IN THESE MONSTERS--
--AND WE'VE LOST DEVIL EIGHT!
JENN, THERE'S NO POINT FACING HIM! HE KNEW DEVIL SQUADRON WAS HERE BEFORE HE BROUGHT THESE THINGS IN! HE'S ALREADY FACTORED US IN!
HE'S GOING TO INUNDATE AQUILARIS! WE'VE GOT TO EVACUATE THE PEOPLE!

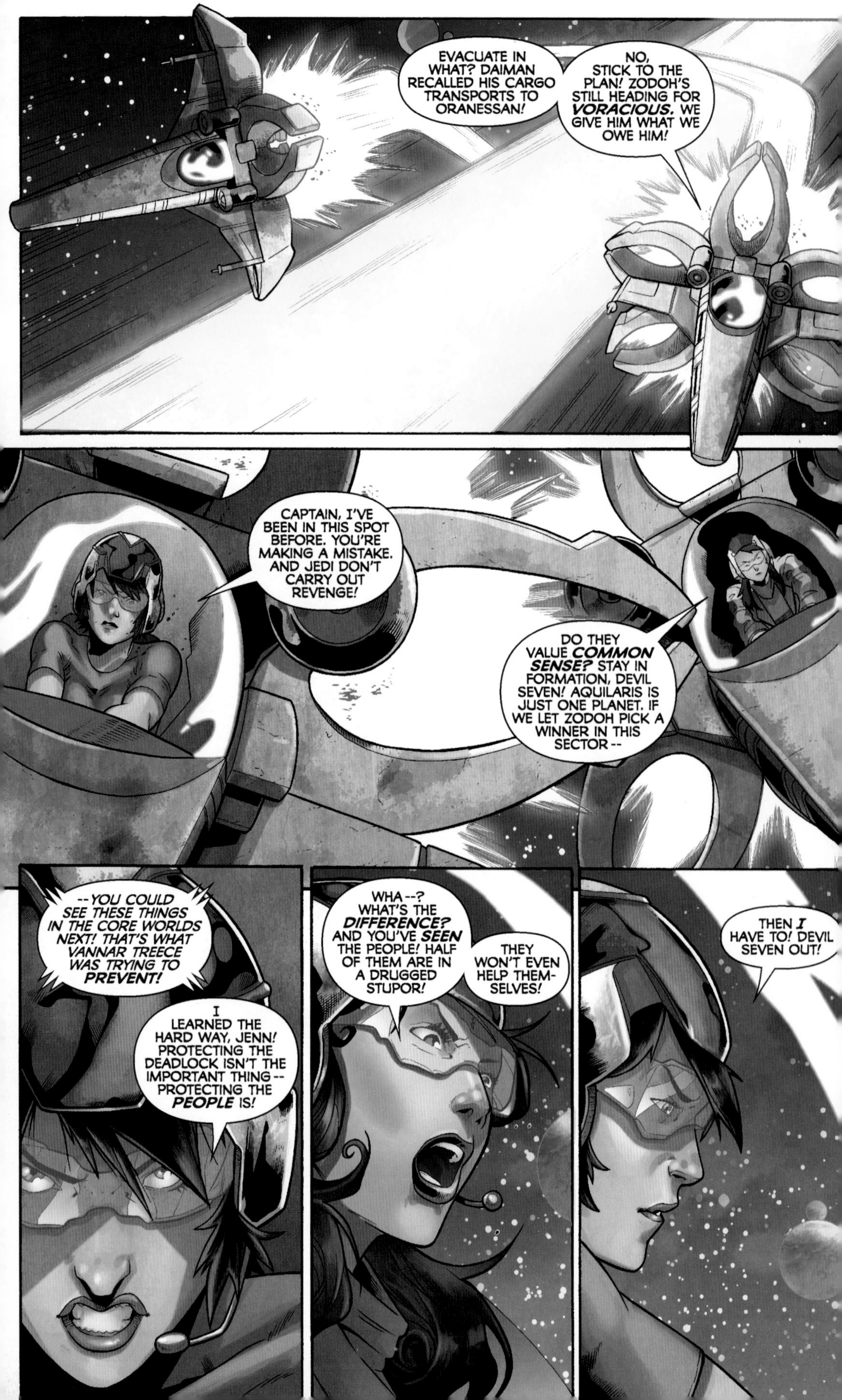
EVACUATE IN WHAT? DAIMAN RECALLED HIS CARGO TRANSPORTS TO ORANESSAN!
NO, STICK TO THE PLAN! ZODOH'S STILL HEADING FOR *VORACIOUS.* WE GIVE HIM WHAT WE OWE HIM!
CAPTAIN, I'VE BEEN IN THIS SPOT BEFORE. YOU'RE MAKING A MISTAKE. AND JEDI DON'T CARRY OUT REVENGE!
DO THEY VALUE ***COMMON SENSE?*** STAY IN FORMATION, DEVIL SEVEN! AQUILARIS IS JUST ONE PLANET. IF WE LET ZODOH PICK A WINNER IN THIS SECTOR --
*--YOU COULD SEE THESE THINGS IN THE CORE WORLDS NEXT! THAT'S WHAT VANNAR TREECE WAS TRYING TO* ***PREVENT!***
I LEARNED THE HARD WAY, JENN! PROTECTING THE DEADLOCK ISN'T THE IMPORTANT THING -- PROTECTING THE ***PEOPLE*** IS!
WHA --? WHAT'S THE ***DIFFERENCE?*** AND YOU'VE ***SEEN*** THE PEOPLE! HALF OF THEM ARE IN A DRUGGED STUPOR!
THEY WON'T EVEN HELP THEM-SELVES!
THEN ***I*** HAVE TO! DEVIL SEVEN OUT!

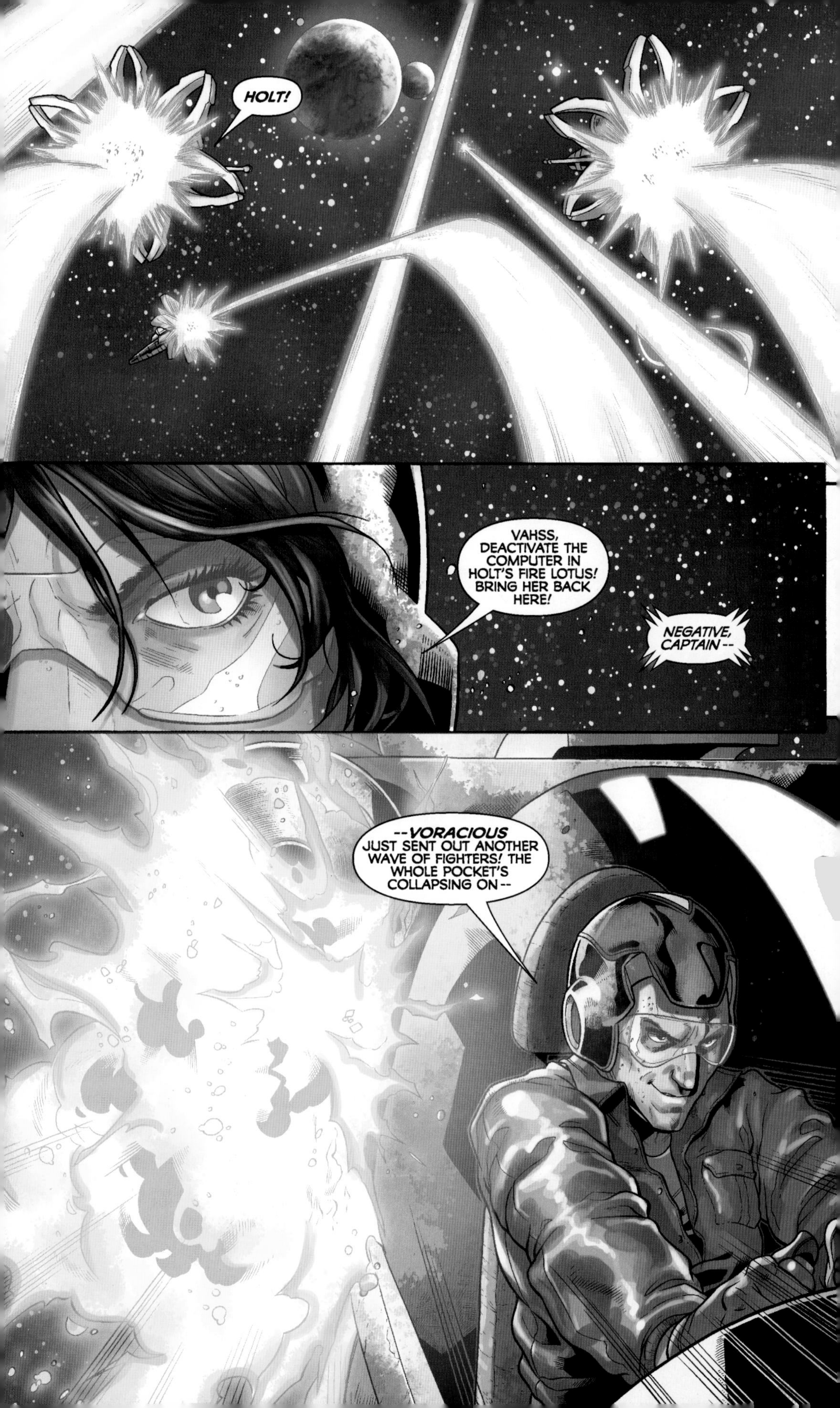
HOLT!
VAHSS, DEACTIVATE THE COMPUTER IN HOLT'S FIRE LOTUS! BRING HER BACK HERE!
NEGATIVE, CAPTAIN--
--*VORACIOUS* JUST SENT OUT ANOTHER WAVE OF FIGHTERS! THE WHOLE POCKET'S COLLAPSING ON--

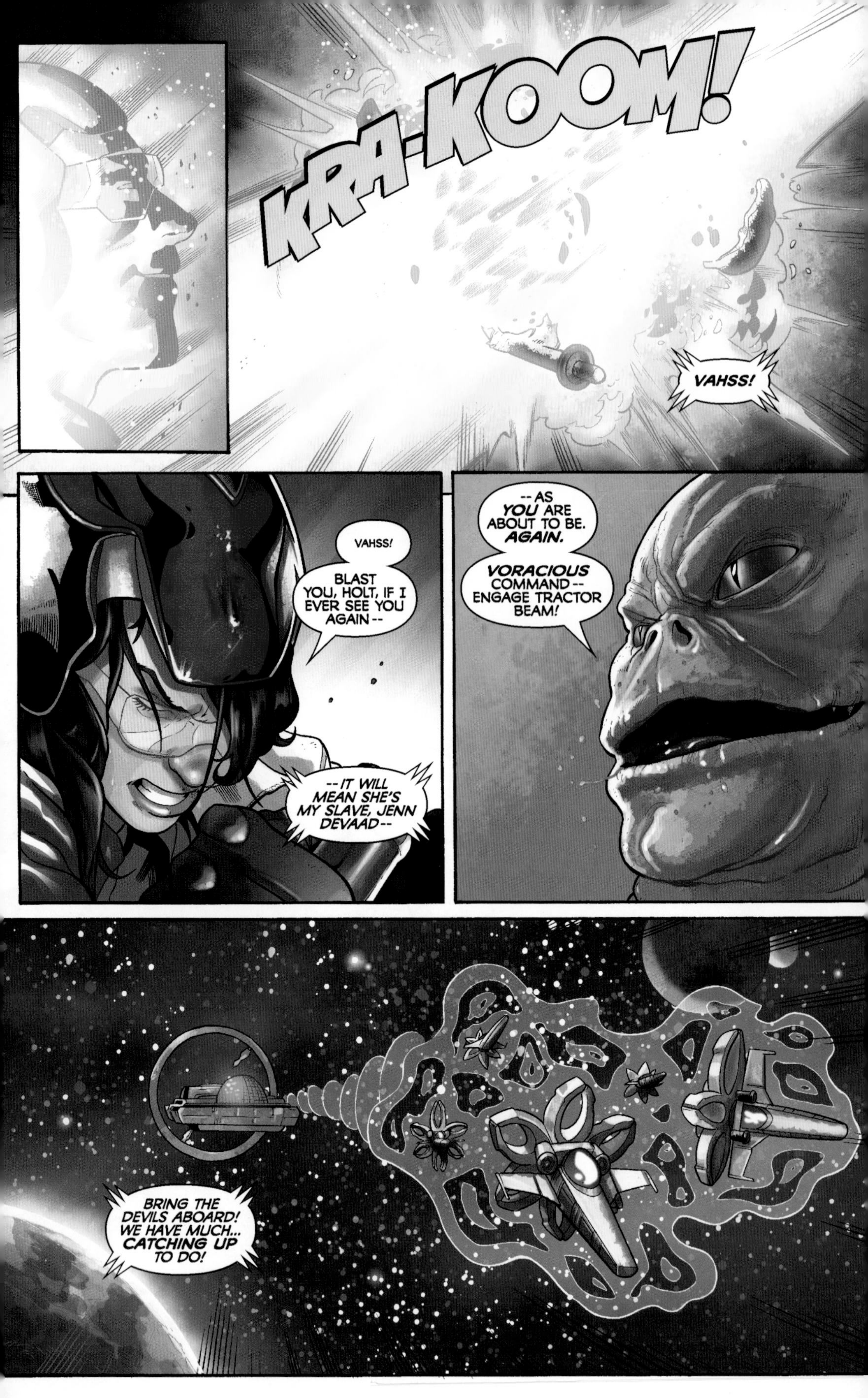
KRA-KOOM!
VAHSS!
VAHSS!
BLAST YOU, HOLT, IF I EVER SEE YOU AGAIN--
--IT WILL MEAN SHE'S MY SLAVE, JENN DEVAAD--
--AS YOU ARE ABOUT TO BE. AGAIN.
VORACIOUS COMMAND-- ENGAGE TRACTOR BEAM!
BRING THE DEVILS ABOARD! WE HAVE MUCH... CATCHING UP TO DO!

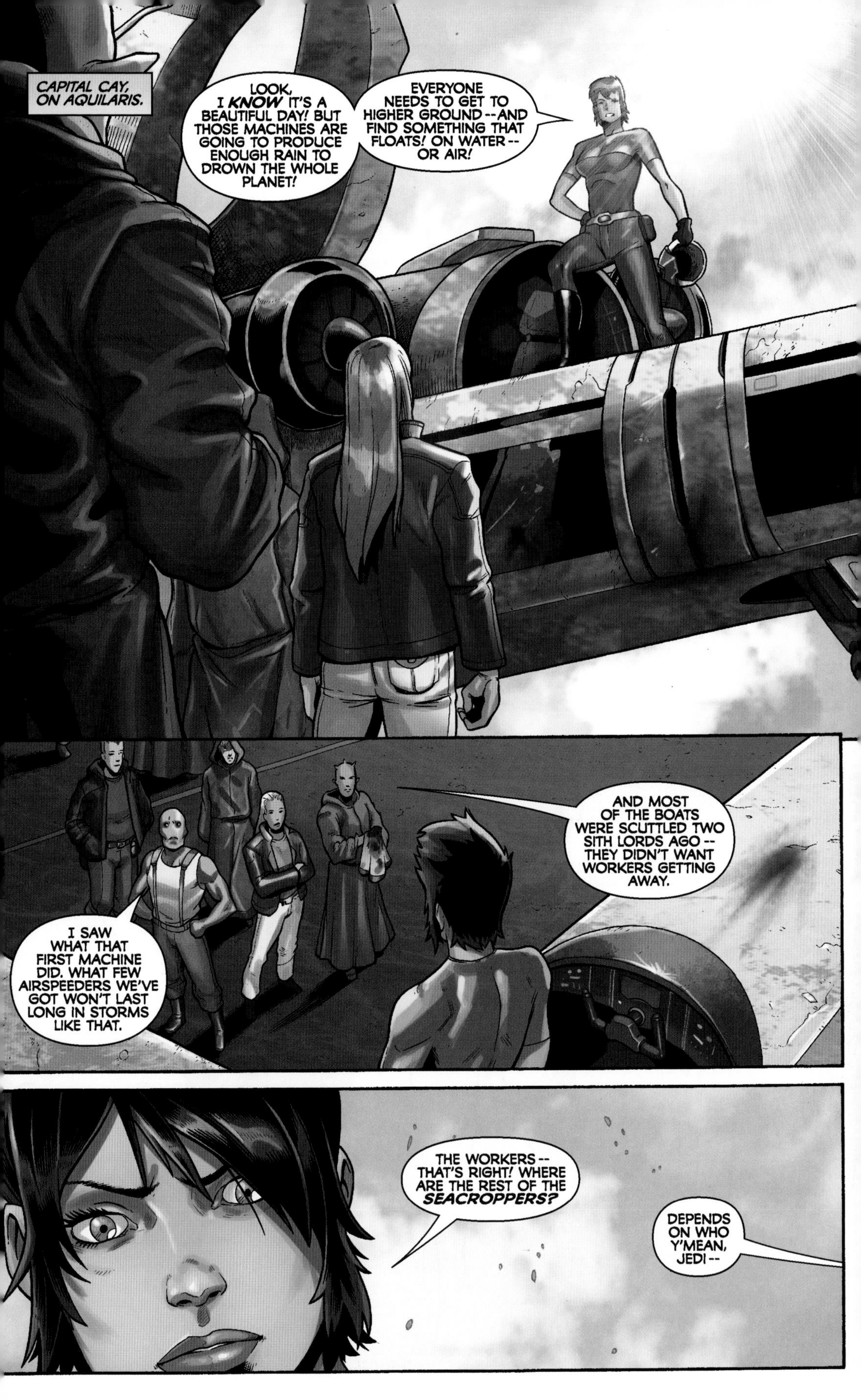
CAPITAL CAY, ON AQUILARIS.
LOOK, I KNOW IT'S A BEAUTIFUL DAY! BUT THOSE MACHINES ARE GOING TO PRODUCE ENOUGH RAIN TO DROWN THE WHOLE PLANET!
EVERYONE NEEDS TO GET TO HIGHER GROUND--AND FIND SOMETHING THAT FLOATS! ON WATER-- OR AIR!
I SAW WHAT THAT FIRST MACHINE DID. WHAT FEW AIRSPEEDERS WE'VE GOT WON'T LAST LONG IN STORMS LIKE THAT.
AND MOST OF THE BOATS WERE SCUTTLED TWO SITH LORDS AGO-- THEY DIDN'T WANT WORKERS GETTING AWAY.
THE WORKERS-- THAT'S RIGHT! WHERE ARE THE REST OF THE SEACROPPERS?
DEPENDS ON WHO Y'MEAN, JEDI--

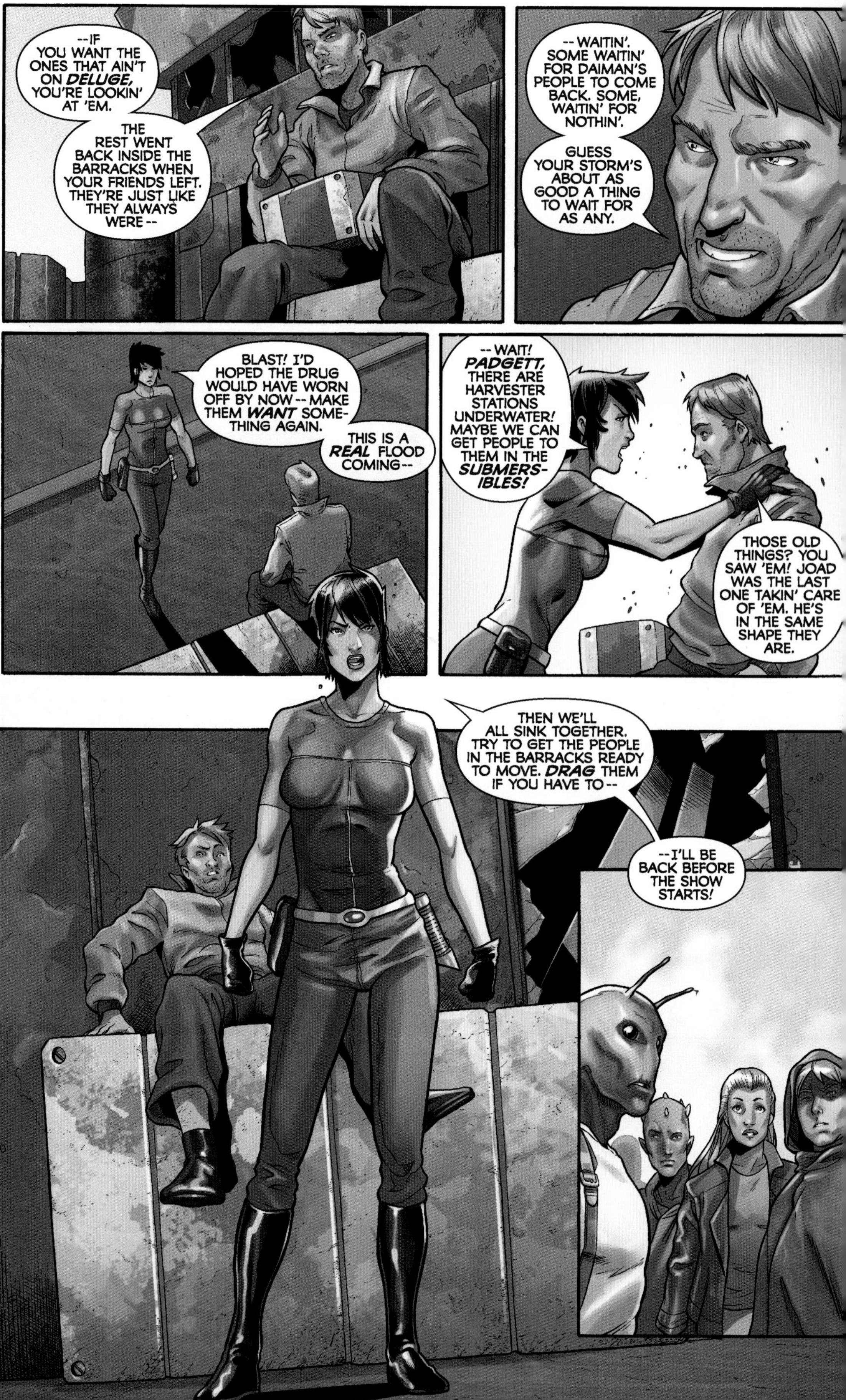
--IF YOU WANT THE ONES THAT AIN'T ON *DELUGE,* YOU'RE LOOKIN' AT 'EM.
THE REST WENT BACK INSIDE THE BARRACKS WHEN YOUR FRIENDS LEFT. THEY'RE JUST LIKE THEY ALWAYS WERE--
--WAITIN'. SOME WAITIN' FOR DAIMAN'S PEOPLE TO COME BACK. SOME, WAITIN' FOR NOTHIN'.
GUESS YOUR STORM'S ABOUT AS GOOD A THING TO WAIT FOR AS ANY.
BLAST! I'D HOPED THE DRUG WOULD HAVE WORN OFF BY NOW--MAKE THEM *WANT* SOMETHING AGAIN.
THIS IS A *REAL* FLOOD COMING--
--WAIT! *PADGETT,* THERE ARE HARVESTER STATIONS UNDERWATER! MAYBE WE CAN GET PEOPLE TO THEM IN THE *SUBMERSIBLES!*
THOSE OLD THINGS? YOU SAW 'EM! JOAD WAS THE LAST ONE TAKIN' CARE OF 'EM. HE'S IN THE SAME SHAPE THEY ARE.
THEN WE'LL ALL SINK TOGETHER. TRY TO GET THE PEOPLE IN THE BARRACKS READY TO MOVE. *DRAG* THEM IF YOU HAVE TO--
--I'LL BE BACK BEFORE THE SHOW STARTS!

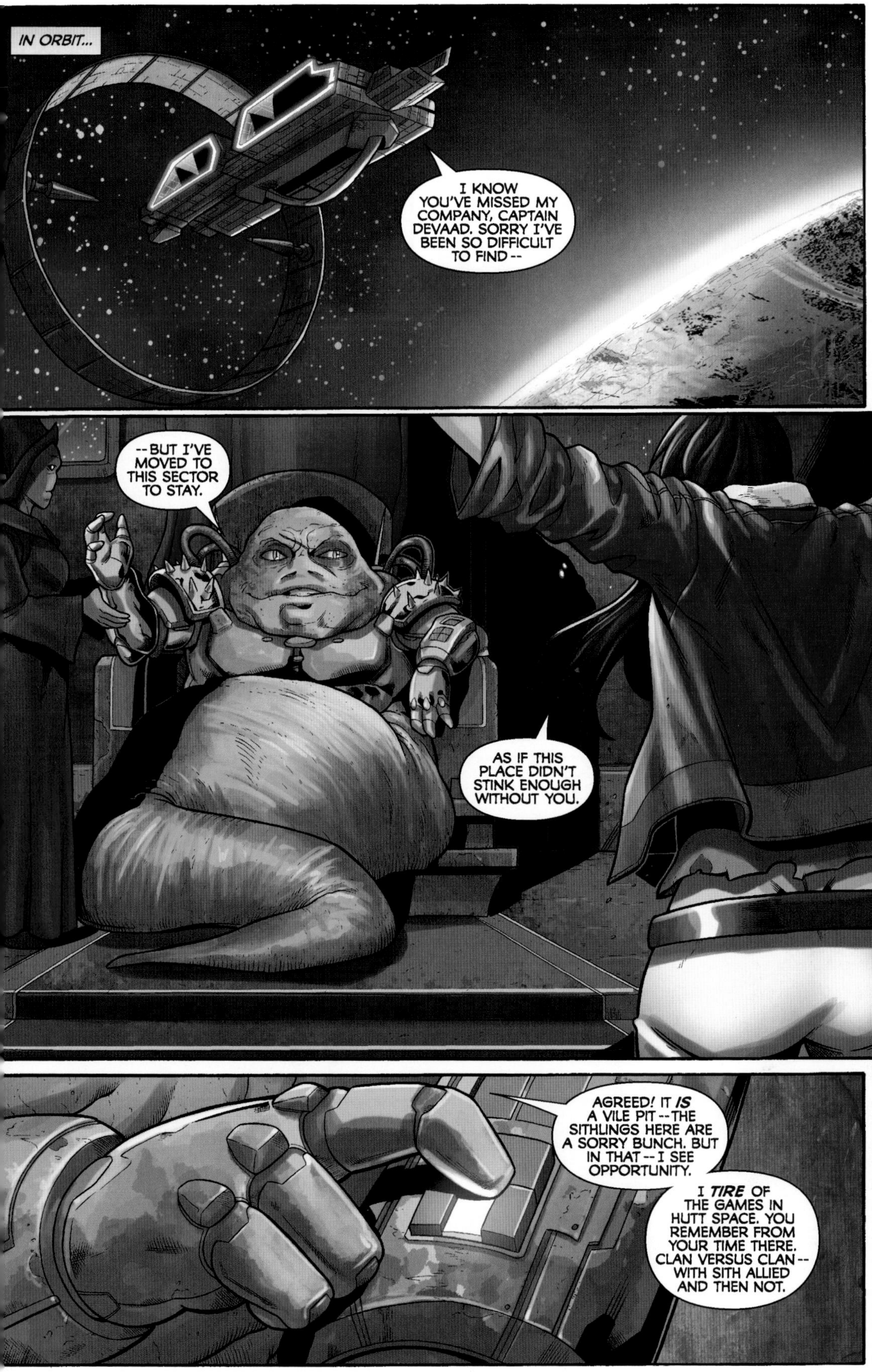
IN ORBIT...
I KNOW YOU'VE MISSED MY COMPANY, CAPTAIN DEVAAD. SORRY I'VE BEEN SO DIFFICULT TO FIND --
-- BUT I'VE MOVED TO THIS SECTOR TO STAY.
AS IF THIS PLACE DIDN'T STINK ENOUGH WITHOUT YOU.
AGREED! IT *IS* A VILE PIT -- THE SITHLINGS HERE ARE A SORRY BUNCH. BUT IN THAT -- I SEE OPPORTUNITY.
I *TIRE* OF THE GAMES IN HUTT SPACE. YOU REMEMBER FROM YOUR TIME THERE. CLAN VERSUS CLAN -- WITH SITH ALLIED AND THEN NOT.

LORDS WERE EVEN TARGETING OON GARAT, TRYING TO MAKE HER THEIR THRALL. I CAN'T TRUST ANYONE TO DO ANYTHING!

IT'S WHY I TAKE SUCH AN ACTIVE ROLE IN MY ENTERPRISES. I *HAVE* TO STAY MOBILE AND INVOLVED, OR THINGS FALL APART!

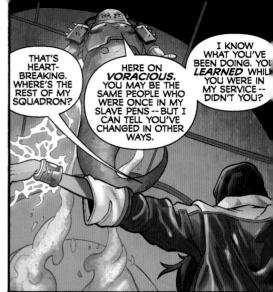

THAT'S HEART-BREAKING. WHERE'S THE REST OF MY SQUADRON?

HERE ON *VORACIOUS*. YOU MAY BE THE SAME PEOPLE WHO WERE ONCE IN MY SLAVE PENS -- BUT I CAN TELL YOU'VE CHANGED IN OTHER WAYS.

I KNOW WHAT YOU'VE BEEN DOING. YOU *LEARNED* WHILE YOU WERE IN MY SERVICE -- DIDN'T YOU?

I DON'T KNOW WHAT IN BLAZES YOU'RE TALKING ABOUT.

YES, YOU DO. I KNOW YOUR GAME, DEVAAD. I'VE BEEN DOING HIT-AND-RUN RAIDS ON THE LOCAL SITH, TOO. I KNOW THE TRAIL YOU LEAVE.

IF MY INTERROGATORS CRACK THE MINDS OF YOUR CREW, WILL THEY TELL ME? OR WILL YOU SPARE THEM THAT? THAT --

-- AND A WHOLE LOT MORE? YOU HAVE SOMETHING I WANT. IF YOU'D SAVE YOUR CREW--

--IT'S TIME TO MAKE A DEAL!

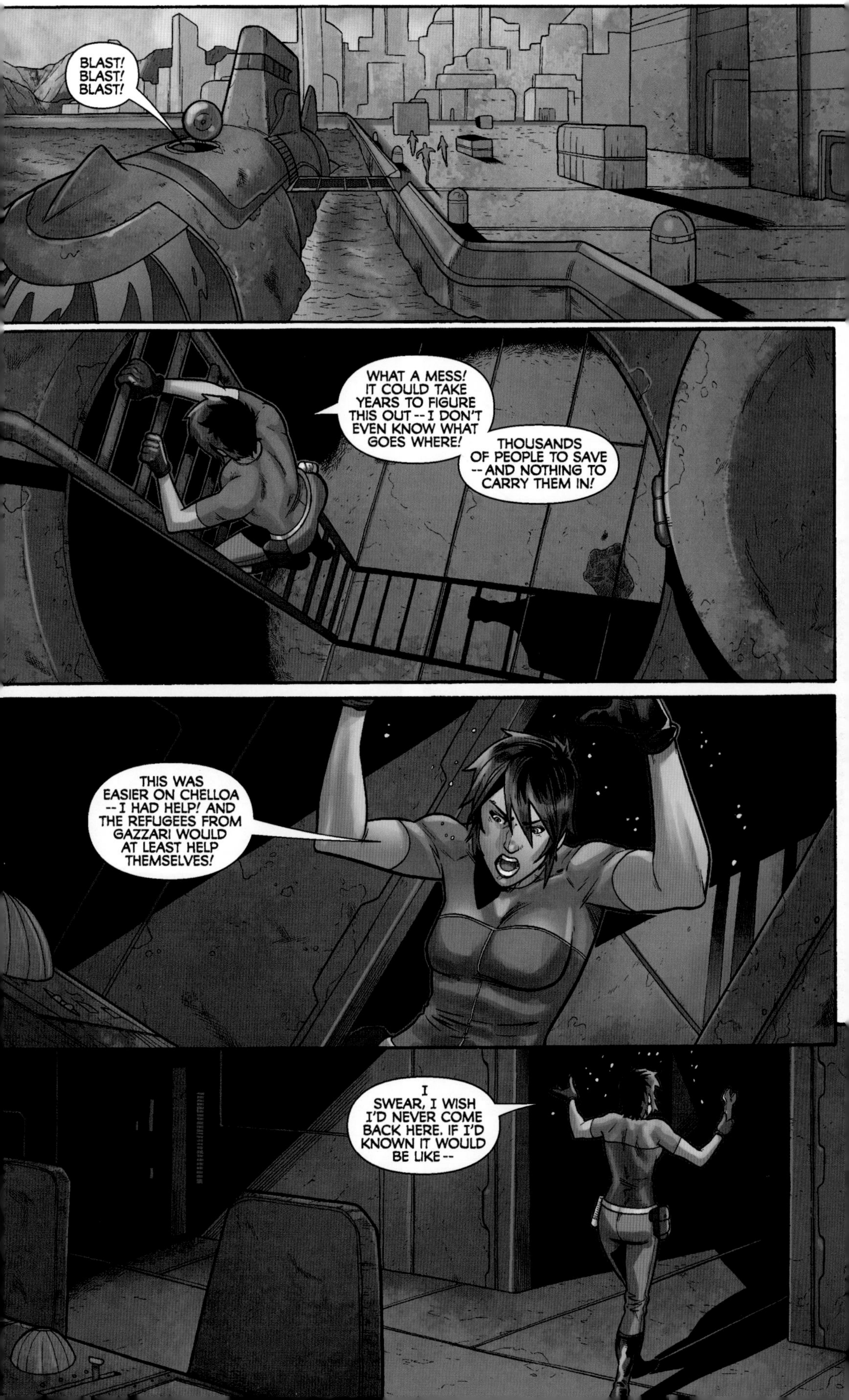
BLAST! BLAST! BLAST!
WHAT A MESS! IT COULD TAKE YEARS TO FIGURE THIS OUT--I DON'T EVEN KNOW WHAT GOES WHERE!
THOUSANDS OF PEOPLE TO SAVE--AND NOTHING TO CARRY THEM IN!
THIS WAS EASIER ON CHELLOA--I HAD HELP! AND THE REFUGEES FROM GAZZARI WOULD AT LEAST HELP THEMSELVES!
I SWEAR, I WISH I'D NEVER COME BACK HERE. IF I'D KNOWN IT WOULD BE LIKE--

LIKE WHAT?

JOAD!

THERE'S A DISASTER ON THE WAY! WHAT ARE YOU DOING *HERE*?

I WAS JUST... *REMEMBERING.* THIS PLACE -- IT'S WHERE WE *MET.*

YOUR FOLKS... WERE VISITING MY DAD. YOU WERE CURIOUS ABOUT THE SUBMERSIBLE -- SO I TOOK YOU FOR A RIDE.

WE'RE NOT IN PORT FIVE MINUTES WHEN I HEAR YOU'VE SNUCK BACK IN AND HIJACKED THE SHIP -- AT ALL OF EIGHT YEARS OLD!

I WANTED TO SEE THE HARVESTING STATIONS.

YOU RAMMED IT INTO THE HARBOR WALL!

I COME BACK HERE SOMETIMES -- TO JUST LOOK AT IT. YOU KNOW...FOR A LONG TIME, I COULDN'T REMEMBER WHY I CARED. IT'S JUST METAL.

BUT I GUESS...IT MUST HAVE *MEANT* SOMETHING.

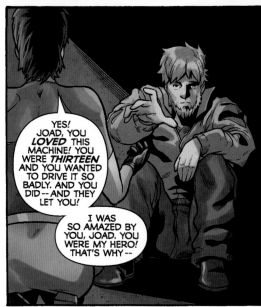

YES! JOAD, YOU *LOVED* THIS MACHINE! YOU WERE *THIRTEEN* AND YOU WANTED TO DRIVE IT SO BADLY. AND YOU DID -- AND THEY LET YOU!

I WAS SO AMAZED BY YOU, JOAD. YOU WERE MY HERO! THAT'S WHY --

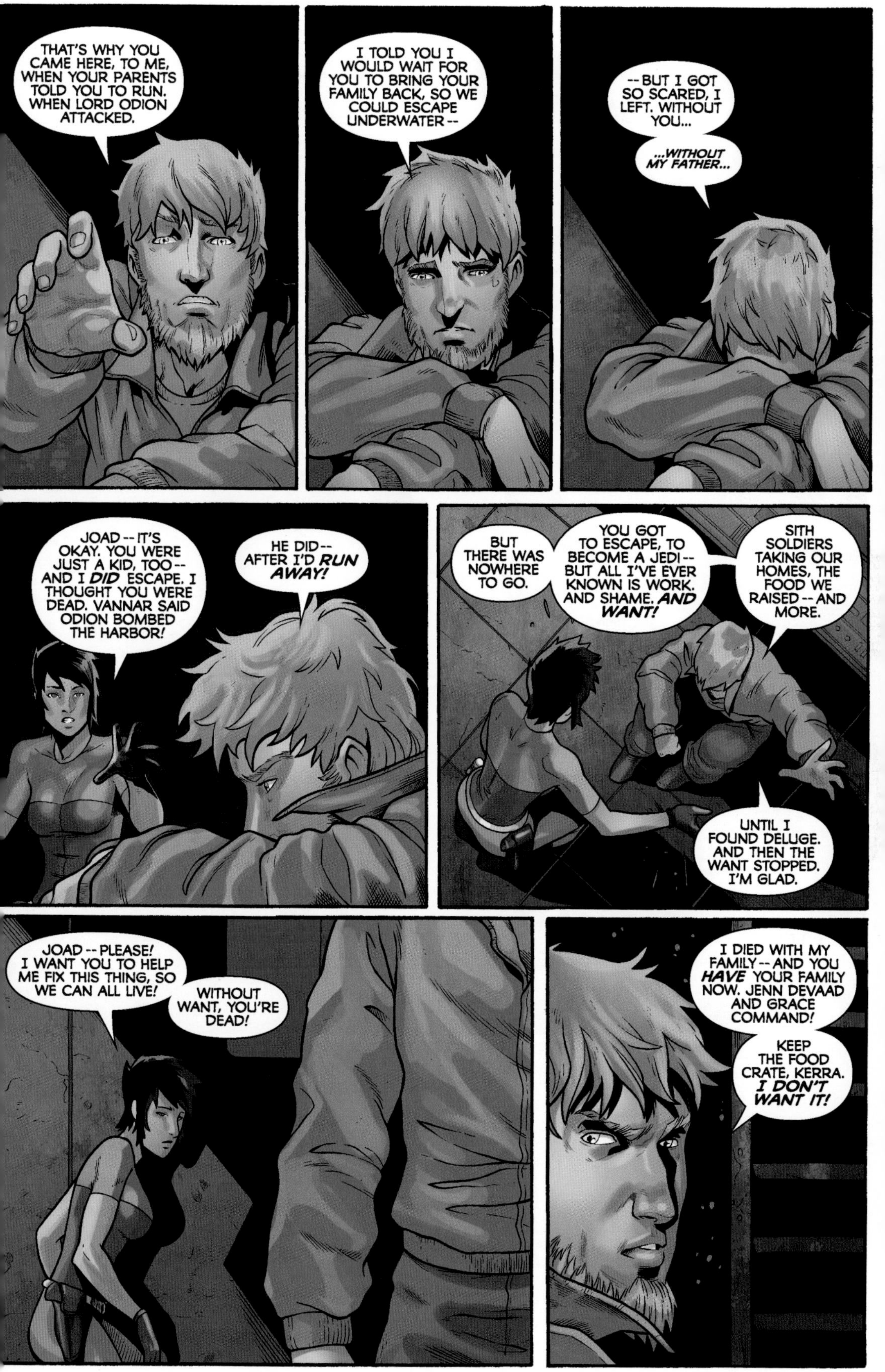
THAT'S WHY YOU CAME HERE, TO ME, WHEN YOUR PARENTS TOLD YOU TO RUN. WHEN LORD ODION ATTACKED.
I TOLD YOU I WOULD WAIT FOR YOU TO BRING YOUR FAMILY BACK, SO WE COULD ESCAPE UNDERWATER --
-- BUT I GOT SO SCARED, I LEFT. WITHOUT YOU...
...WITHOUT MY FATHER...
JOAD -- IT'S OKAY. YOU WERE JUST A KID, TOO -- AND I DID ESCAPE. I THOUGHT YOU WERE DEAD. VANNAR SAID ODION BOMBED THE HARBOR!
HE DID -- AFTER I'D RUN AWAY!
BUT THERE WAS NOWHERE TO GO.
YOU GOT TO ESCAPE, TO BECOME A JEDI -- BUT ALL I'VE EVER KNOWN IS WORK. AND SHAME. AND WANT!
SITH SOLDIERS TAKING OUR HOMES, THE FOOD WE RAISED -- AND MORE.
UNTIL I FOUND DELUGE. AND THEN THE WANT STOPPED. I'M GLAD.
JOAD -- PLEASE! I WANT YOU TO HELP ME FIX THIS THING, SO WE CAN ALL LIVE!
WITHOUT WANT, YOU'RE DEAD!
I DIED WITH MY FAMILY -- AND YOU HAVE YOUR FAMILY NOW. JENN DEVAAD AND GRACE COMMAND!
KEEP THE FOOD CRATE, KERRA. I DON'T WANT IT!

MY FAMILY?

WHAT FAMILY?

I THOUGHT JENN'S SQUADRON WAS HERE TO *HELP!* WHY AREN'T THEY *HERE?*

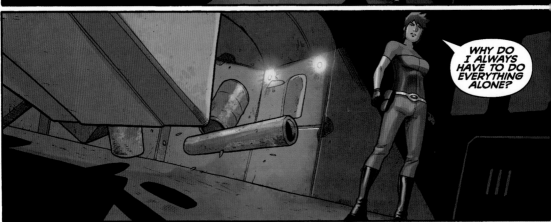

WHY DO I ALWAYS HAVE TO DO EVERYTHING ALONE?

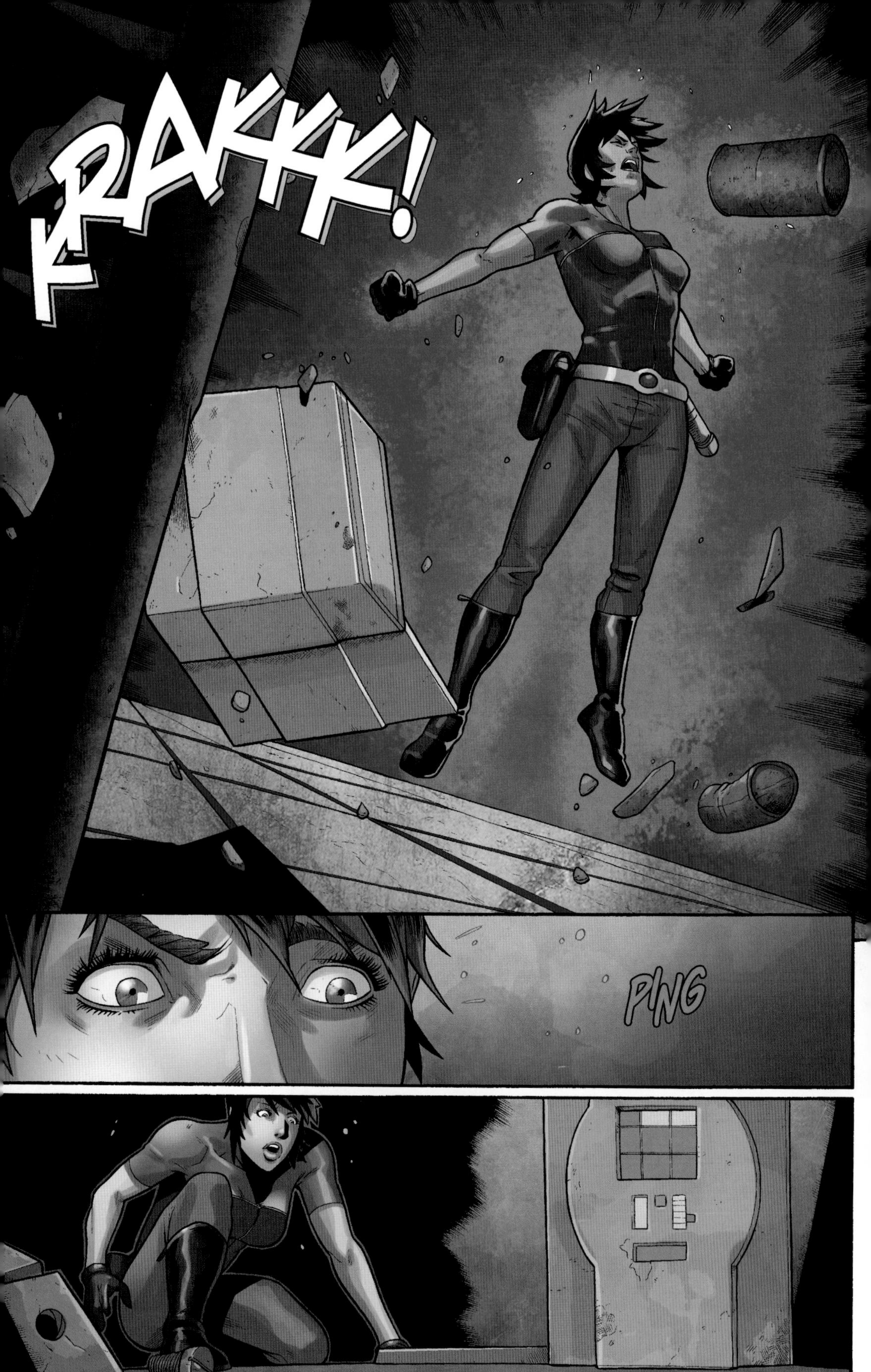
KRAKK!
PING

SOON.

YOU'RE CLEARED TO PASS, SHUTTLE. WE'VE GOT A SCHEDULE TO KEEP. DO YOUR JOB AND GET OUT-- OR GET SOAKED!

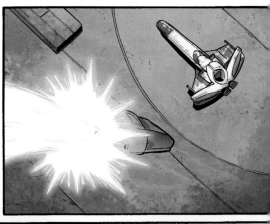

--THAT JEDI LADY'S CRAZIER THAN I AM. I DON'T KNOW WHERE YOU EXPECT TO GO--

--THERE AIN'T A HILL ON THIS PLANET THAT'S MORE THAN A PIMPLE.

SHUT UP AND HELP, PADGETT. SHE'S RIGHT. *SOMETHING'S* ABOUT TO--

*YOU!* YOU CAME BACK FOR US!

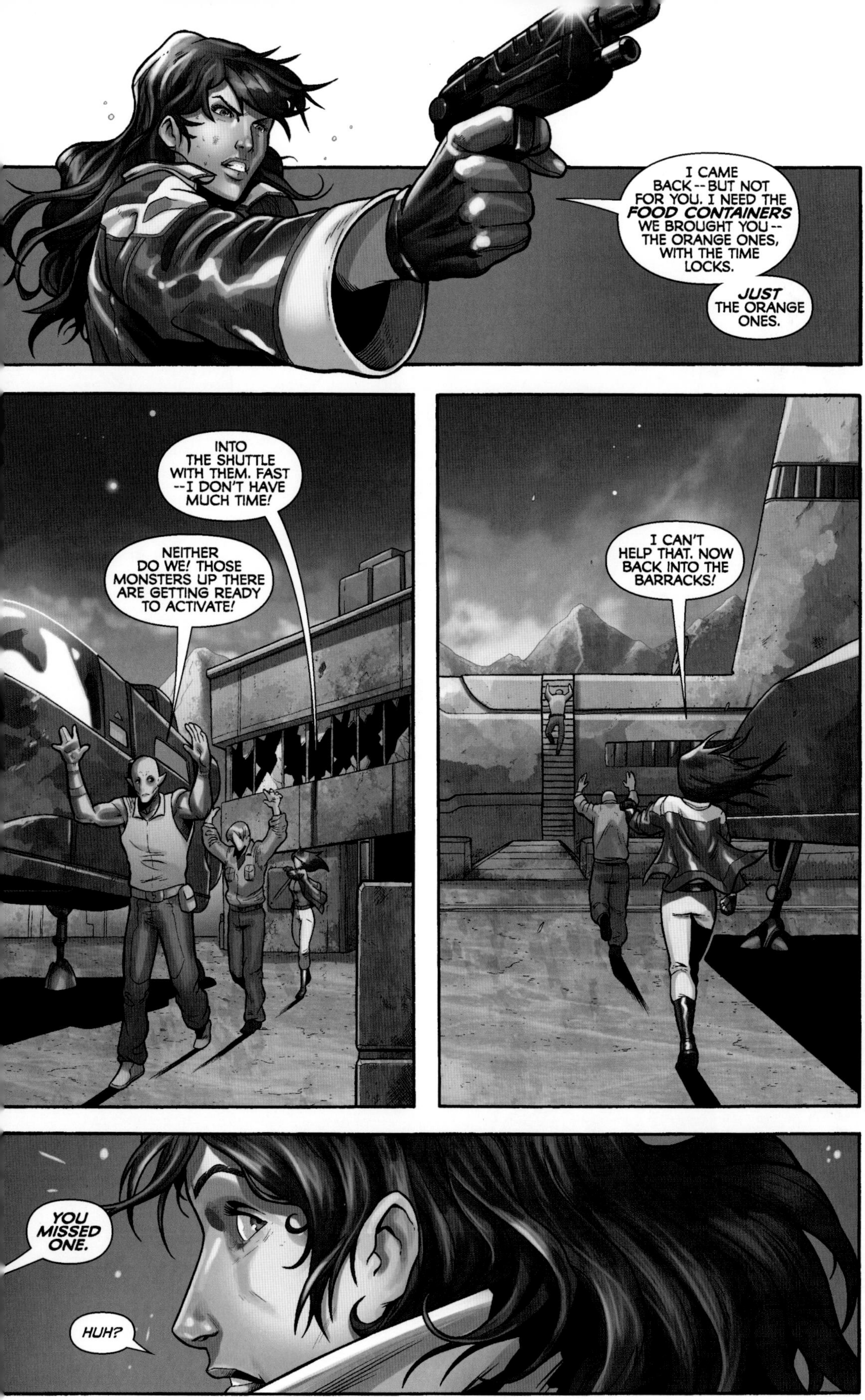
I CAME BACK--BUT NOT FOR YOU. I NEED THE FOOD CONTAINERS WE BROUGHT YOU--THE ORANGE ONES, WITH THE TIME LOCKS.
JUST THE ORANGE ONES.
INTO THE SHUTTLE WITH THEM. FAST--I DON'T HAVE MUCH TIME!
NEITHER DO WE! THOSE MONSTERS UP THERE ARE GETTING READY TO ACTIVATE!
I CAN'T HELP THAT. NOW BACK INTO THE BARRACKS!
YOU MISSED ONE.
HUH?

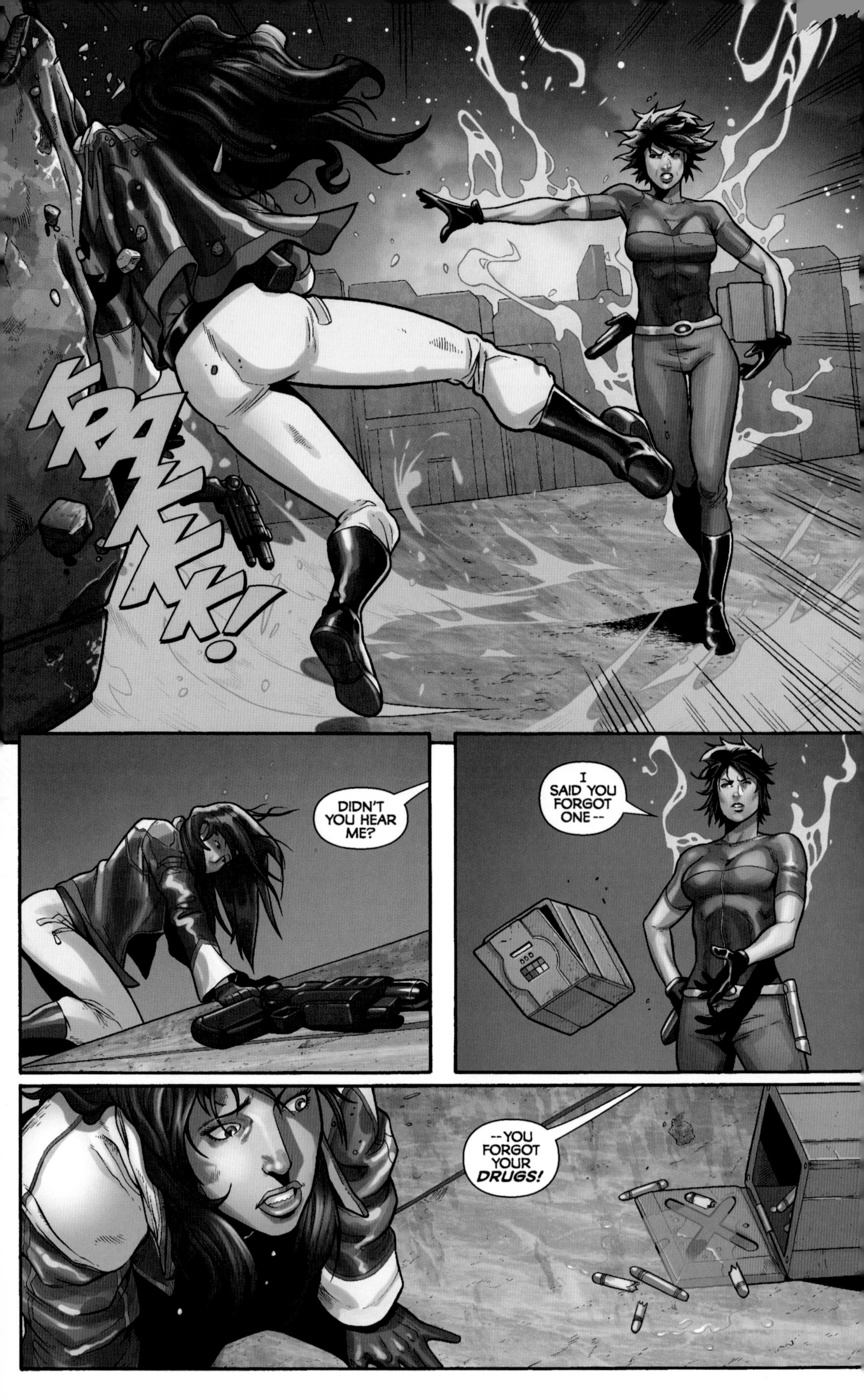

KRAAKKK!
DIDN'T YOU HEAR ME?
I SAID YOU FORGOT ONE--
--YOU FORGOT YOUR DRUGS!

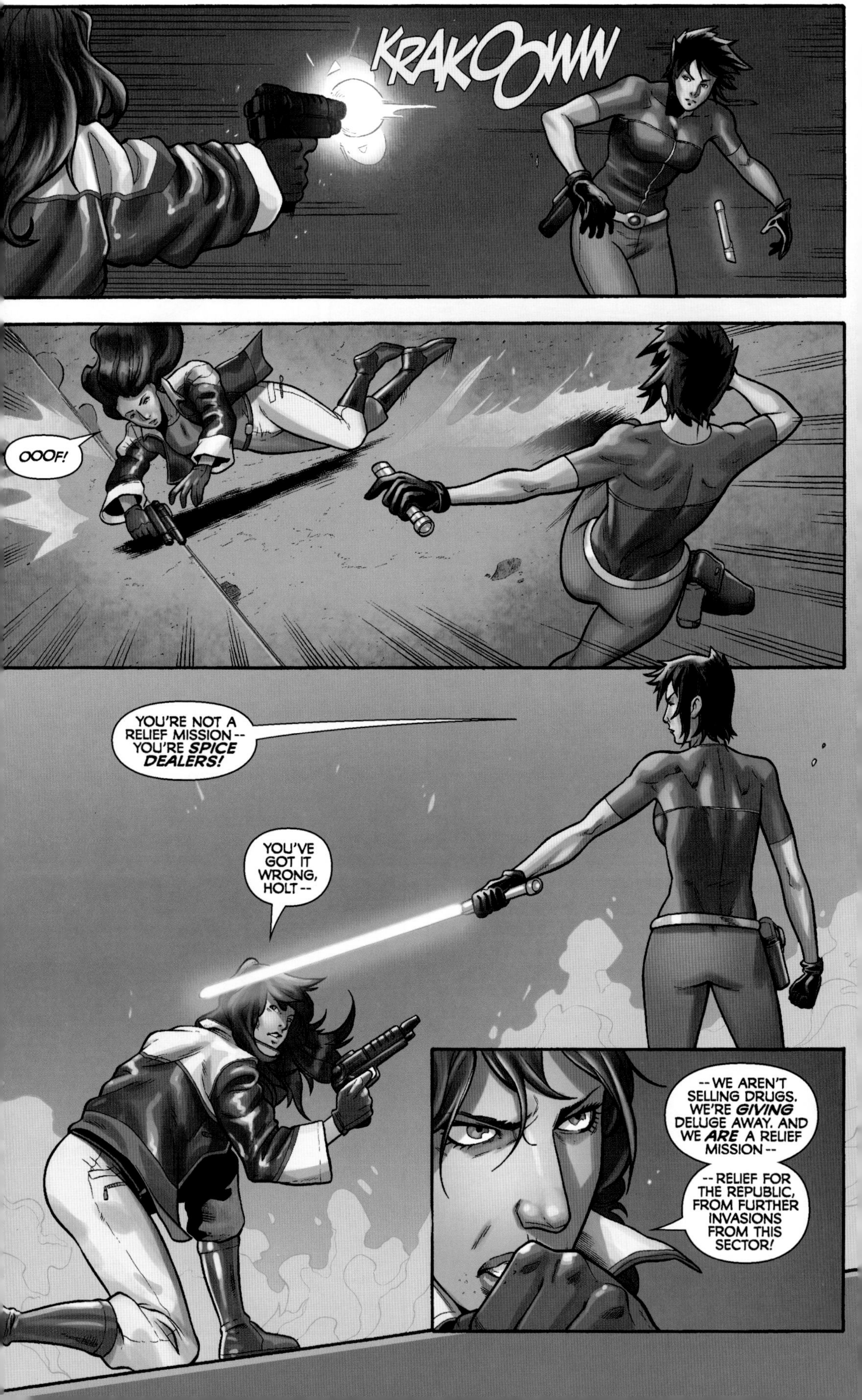
KRAKOOWW
OOOF!
YOU'RE NOT A RELIEF MISSION -- YOU'RE *SPICE DEALERS!*
YOU'VE GOT IT WRONG, HOLT --
-- WE AREN'T SELLING DRUGS. WE'RE *GIVING* DELUGE AWAY. AND WE *ARE* A RELIEF MISSION --
-- RELIEF FOR THE REPUBLIC, FROM FURTHER INVASIONS FROM THIS SECTOR!

TREECE WASN'T THE ONLY ONE WORKING OUT HERE. BARON LEMAYNE CREATED GRACE COMMAND AS A FRONT FOR HIS OWN INTEL OPS--

--INCLUDING *OPERATION DELUGE.* WE LEAVE THE DRUGS WITH THE SLAVES WE FREE. BY THE TIME THE CASES OPEN, THE SITH ARE BACK--

--AND THE DRUG'S INTO THE MILITARY. EVEN ONE DOSE IS ENOUGH TO NEUTRALIZE A WARRIOR FOR THE SITH--

--AND EVERY CASE HOLDS TWO THOUSAND!

THE SLAVES ARE GETTING INTO IT, TOO-- OR HAVEN'T YOU *LOOKED AROUND?*

HOLT, *GROW UP!* THEY'RE JUST ANOTHER ASSET FOR THE SITH -- AND THEY'RE NOT ON OUR SIDE. DON'T YOU KNOW WHO WE *ARE?*

I TOLD YOU DEVIL SQUADRON IS ALL THAT'S LEFT OF THE REPUBLIC TASK FORCE THAT WENT TO DALAANG. WE WERE GROUNDED, NEEDING SHELTER --

--BUT YOUR PRECIOUS *PEOPLE* WERE TOO AFRAID TO HIDE US! THEY *BETRAYED* US -- FIVE YEARS IN ZODOH'S LABOR CAMPS!

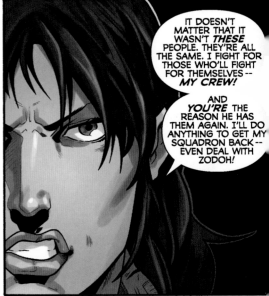

IT DOESN'T MATTER THAT IT WASN'T *THESE* PEOPLE. THEY'RE ALL THE SAME. I FIGHT FOR THOSE WHO'LL FIGHT FOR THEMSELVES -- *MY CREW!*

AND *YOU'RE* THE REASON HE HAS THEM AGAIN. I'LL DO ANYTHING TO GET MY SQUADRON BACK -- EVEN DEAL WITH ZODOH!

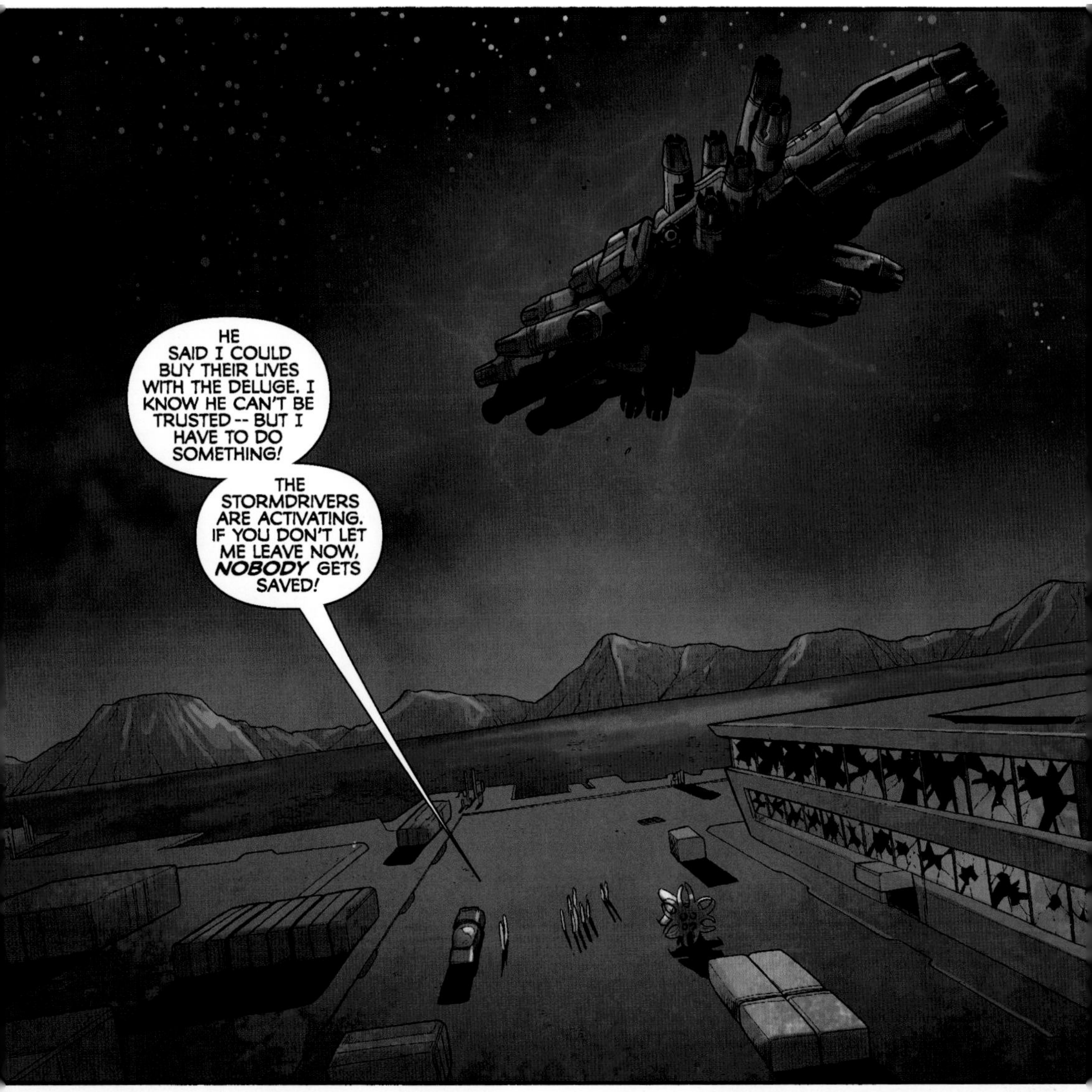
HE SAID I COULD BUY THEIR LIVES WITH THE DELUGE. I KNOW HE CAN'T BE TRUSTED -- BUT I HAVE TO DO SOMETHING!
THE STORMDRIVERS ARE ACTIVATING. IF YOU DON'T LET ME LEAVE NOW, NOBODY GETS SAVED!

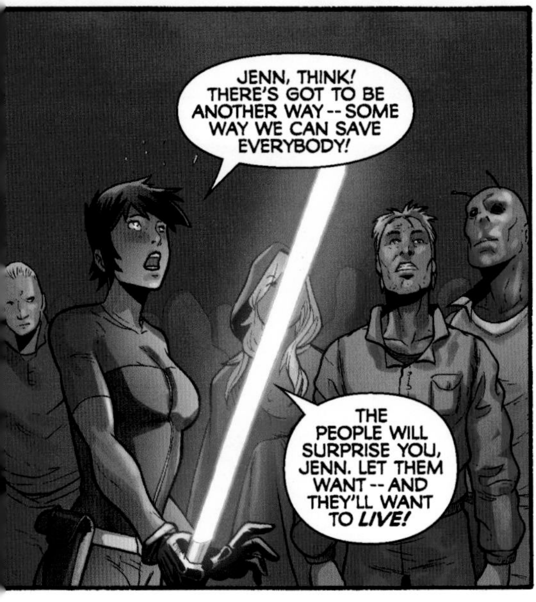
JENN, THINK! THERE'S GOT TO BE ANOTHER WAY -- SOME WAY WE CAN SAVE EVERYBODY!
THE PEOPLE WILL SURPRISE YOU, JENN. LET THEM WANT -- AND THEY'LL WANT TO LIVE!

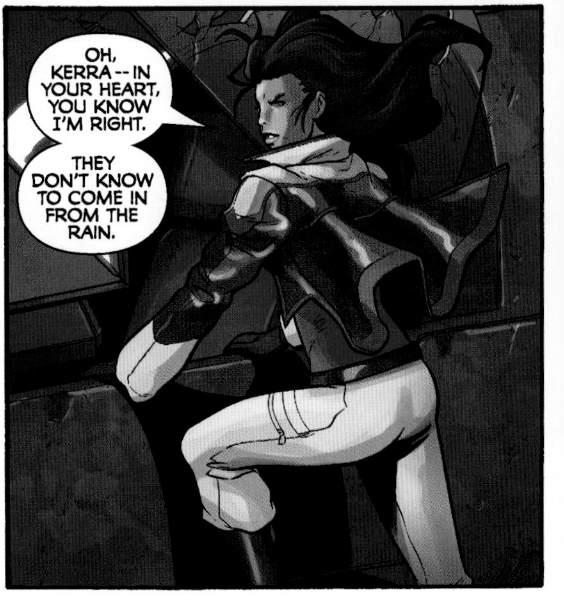
OH, KERRA -- IN YOUR HEART, YOU KNOW I'M RIGHT.
THEY DON'T KNOW TO COME IN FROM THE RAIN.

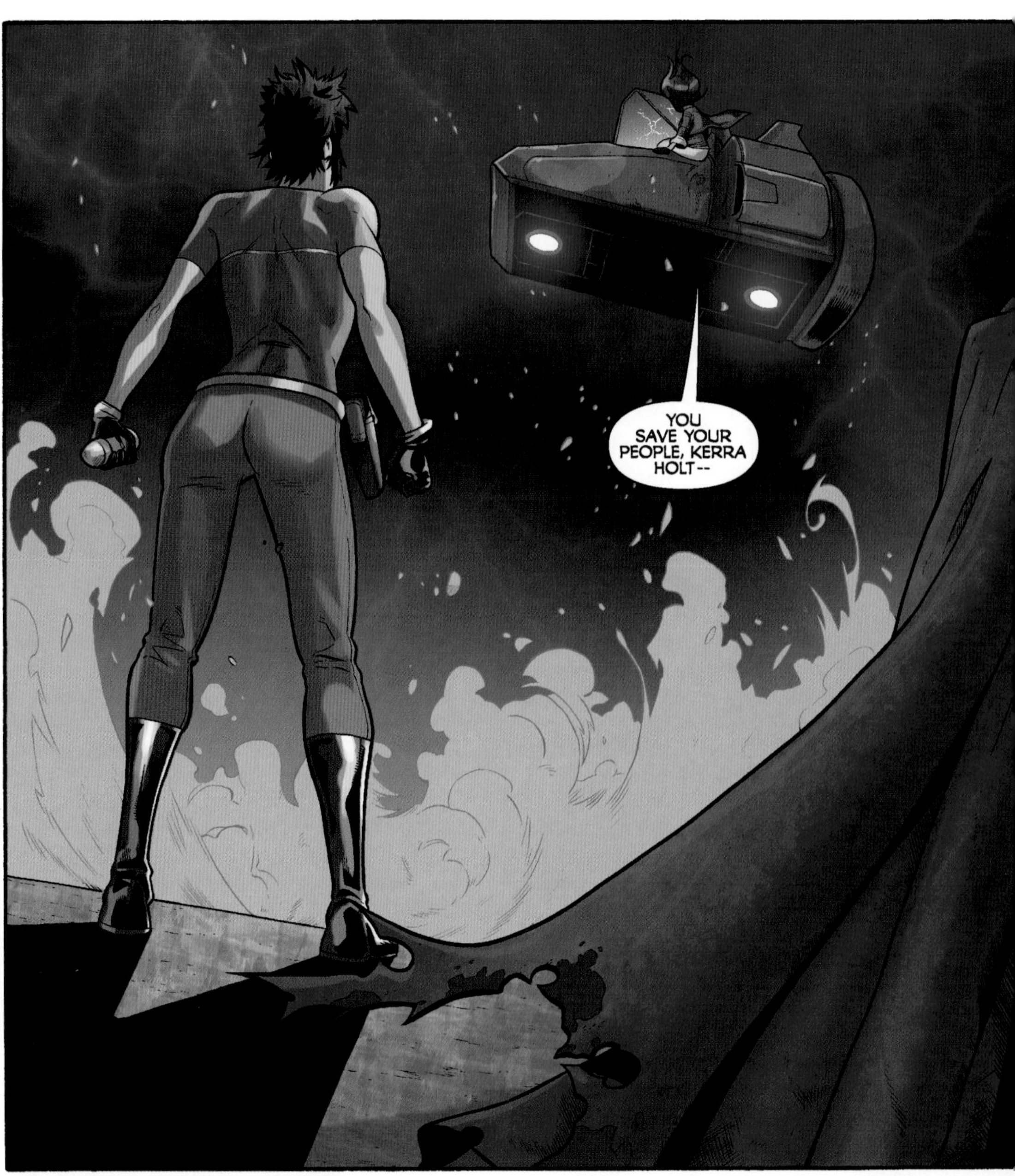
YOU SAVE YOUR PEOPLE, KERRA HOLT--

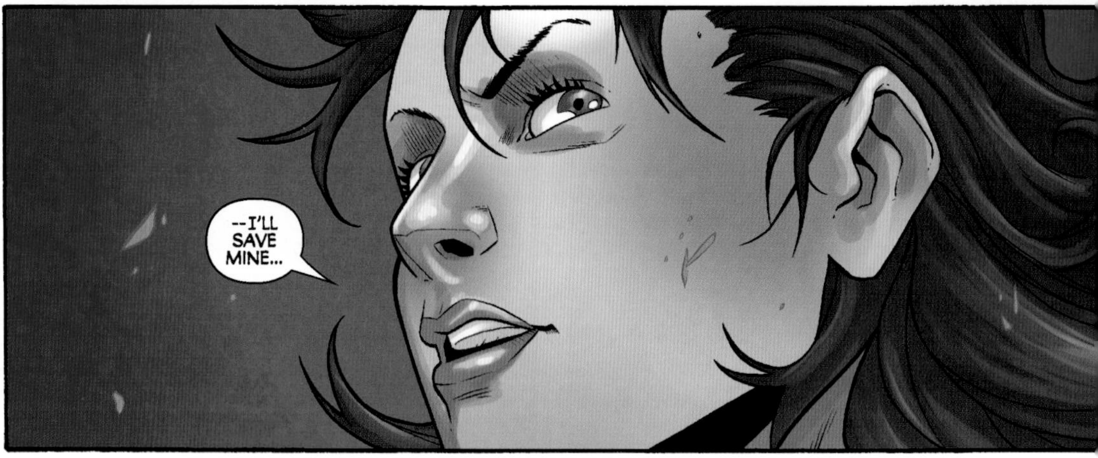
--I'LL SAVE MINE...

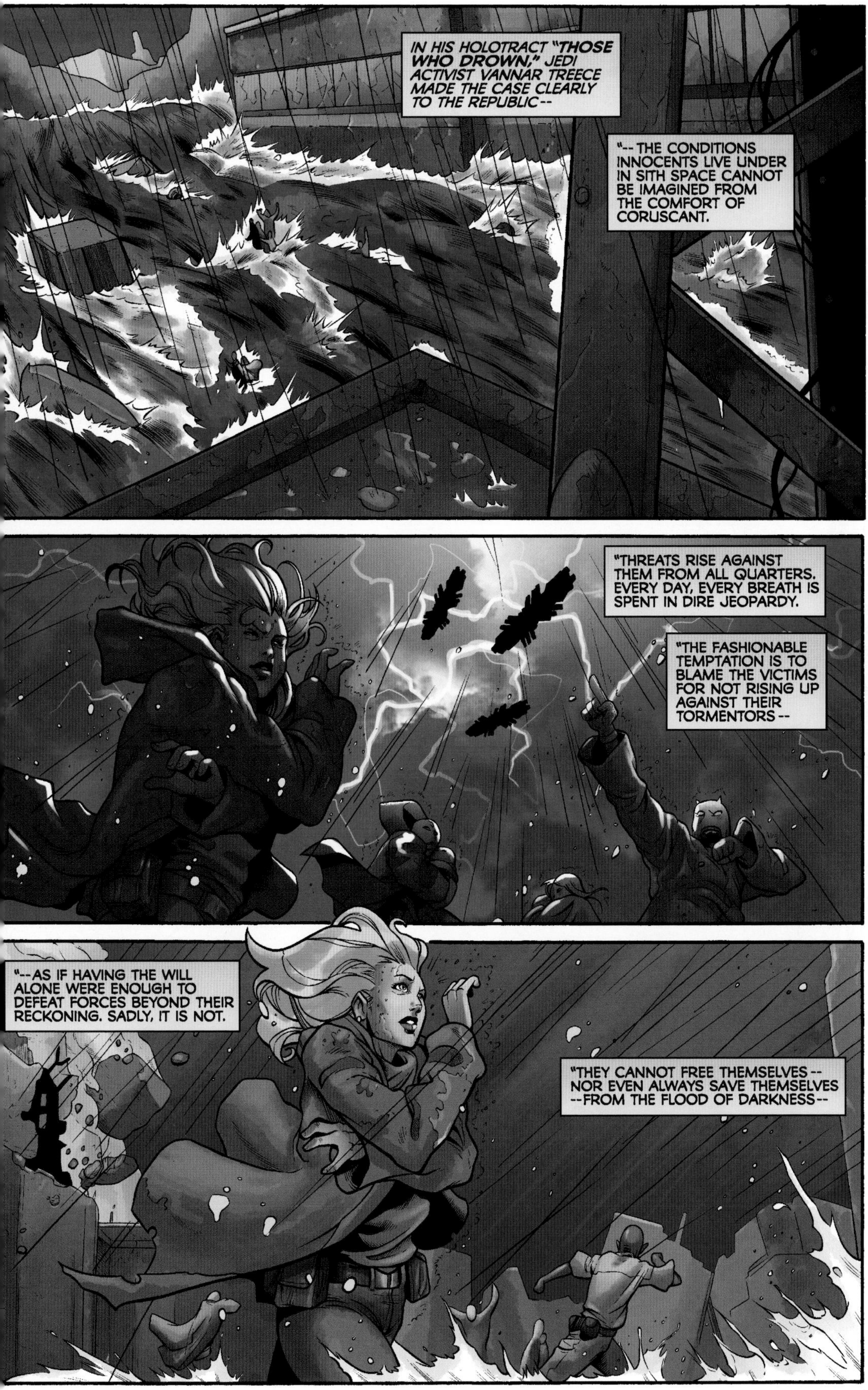
IN HIS HOLOTRACT "THOSE WHO DROWN," JEDI ACTIVIST VANNAR TREECE MADE THE CASE CLEARLY TO THE REPUBLIC--
"--THE CONDITIONS INNOCENTS LIVE UNDER IN SITH SPACE CANNOT BE IMAGINED FROM THE COMFORT OF CORUSCANT.
"THREATS RISE AGAINST THEM FROM ALL QUARTERS. EVERY DAY, EVERY BREATH IS SPENT IN DIRE JEOPARDY.
"THE FASHIONABLE TEMPTATION IS TO BLAME THE VICTIMS FOR NOT RISING UP AGAINST THEIR TORMENTORS--
"--AS IF HAVING THE WILL ALONE WERE ENOUGH TO DEFEAT FORCES BEYOND THEIR RECKONING. SADLY, IT IS NOT.
"THEY CANNOT FREE THEMSELVES--NOR EVEN ALWAYS SAVE THEMSELVES--FROM THE FLOOD OF DARKNESS--

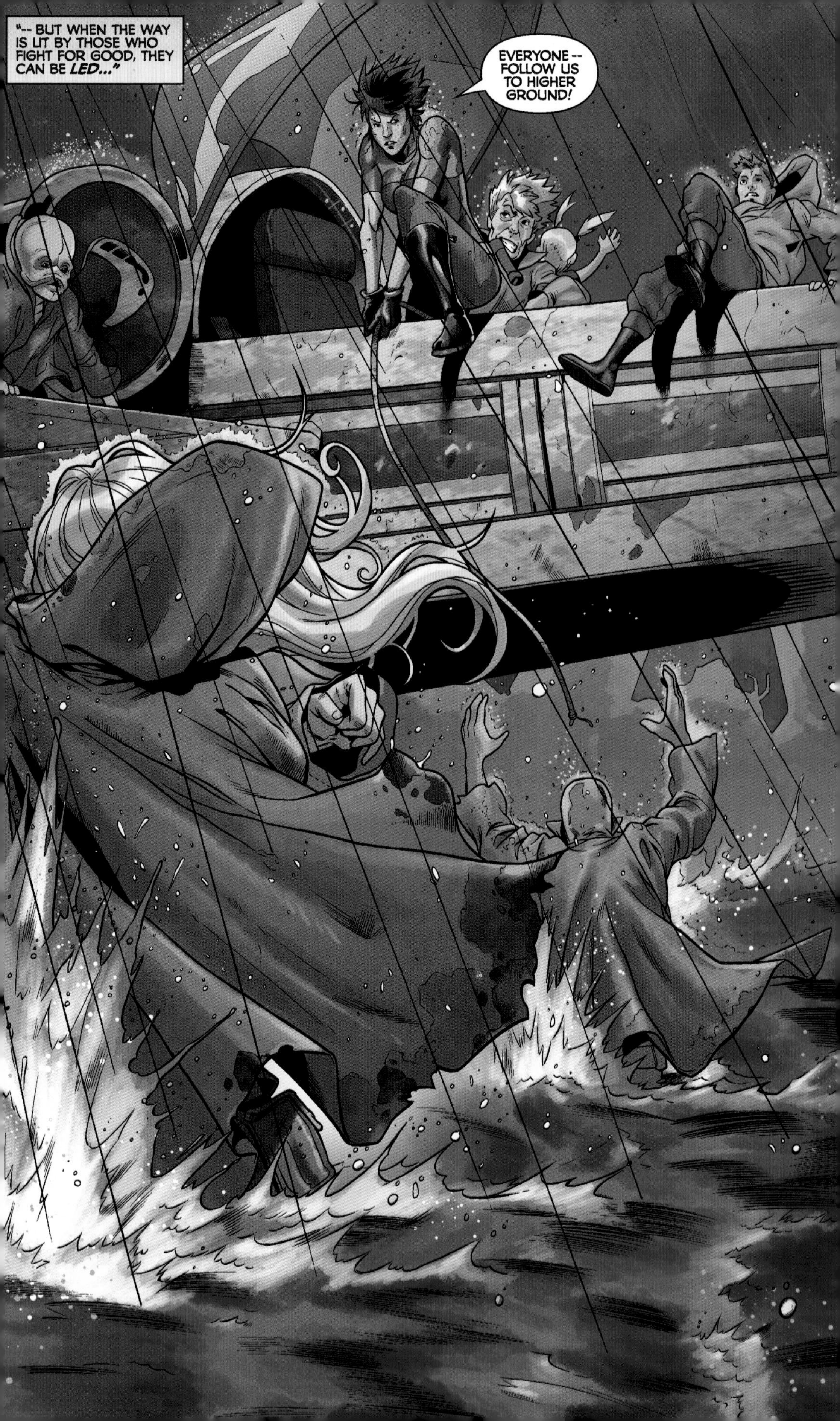
"-- BUT WHEN THE WAY IS LIT BY THOSE WHO FIGHT FOR GOOD, THEY CAN BE *LED*..."
EVERYONE -- FOLLOW US TO HIGHER GROUND!

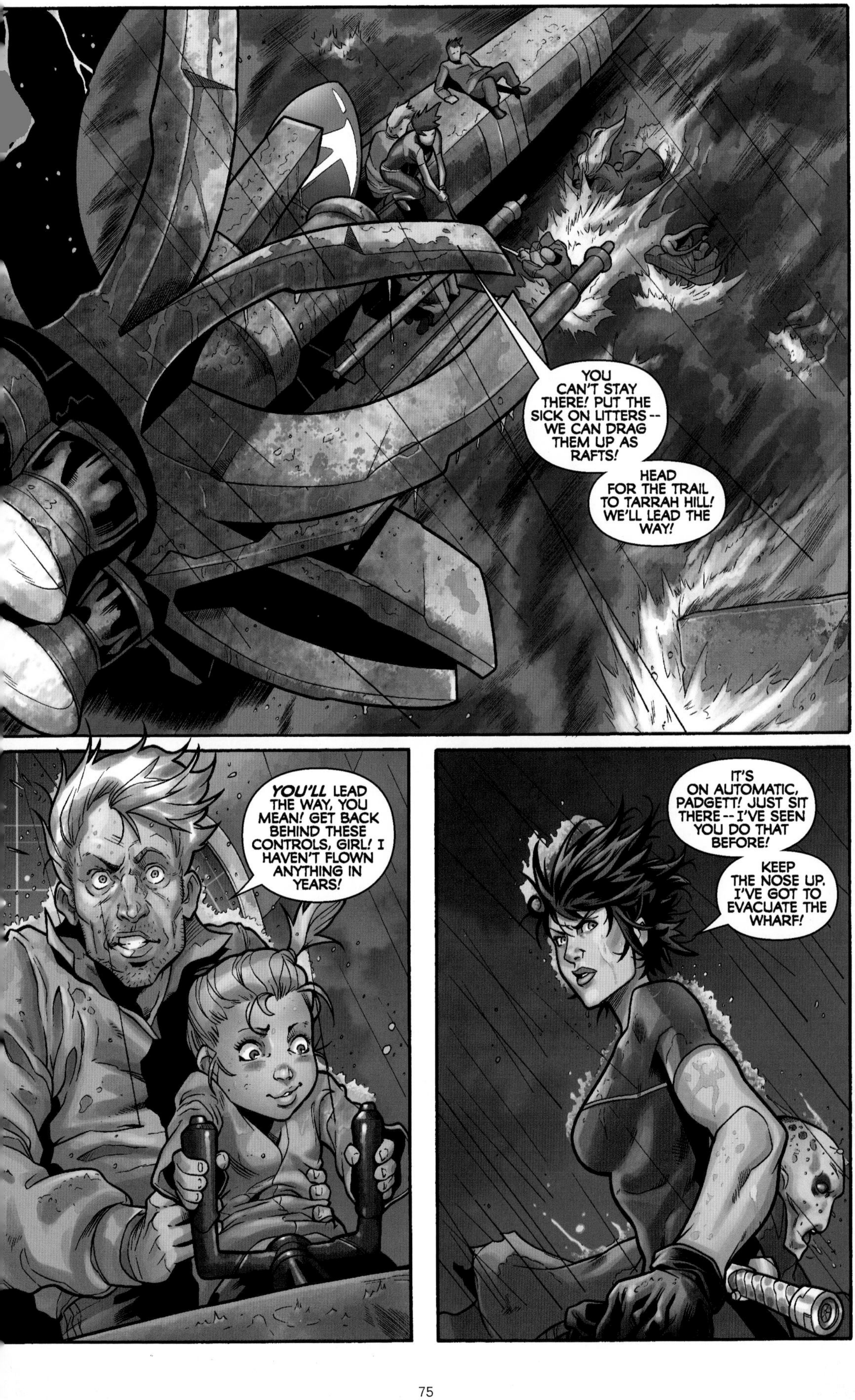
YOU CAN'T STAY THERE! PUT THE SICK ON LITTERS -- WE CAN DRAG THEM UP AS RAFTS!
HEAD FOR THE TRAIL TO TARRAH HILL! WE'LL LEAD THE WAY!
*YOU'LL* LEAD THE WAY, YOU MEAN! GET BACK BEHIND THESE CONTROLS, GIRL! I HAVEN'T FLOWN ANYTHING IN YEARS!
IT'S ON AUTOMATIC, PADGETT! JUST SIT THERE -- I'VE SEEN YOU DO THAT BEFORE!
KEEP THE NOSE UP. I'VE GOT TO EVACUATE THE WHARF!

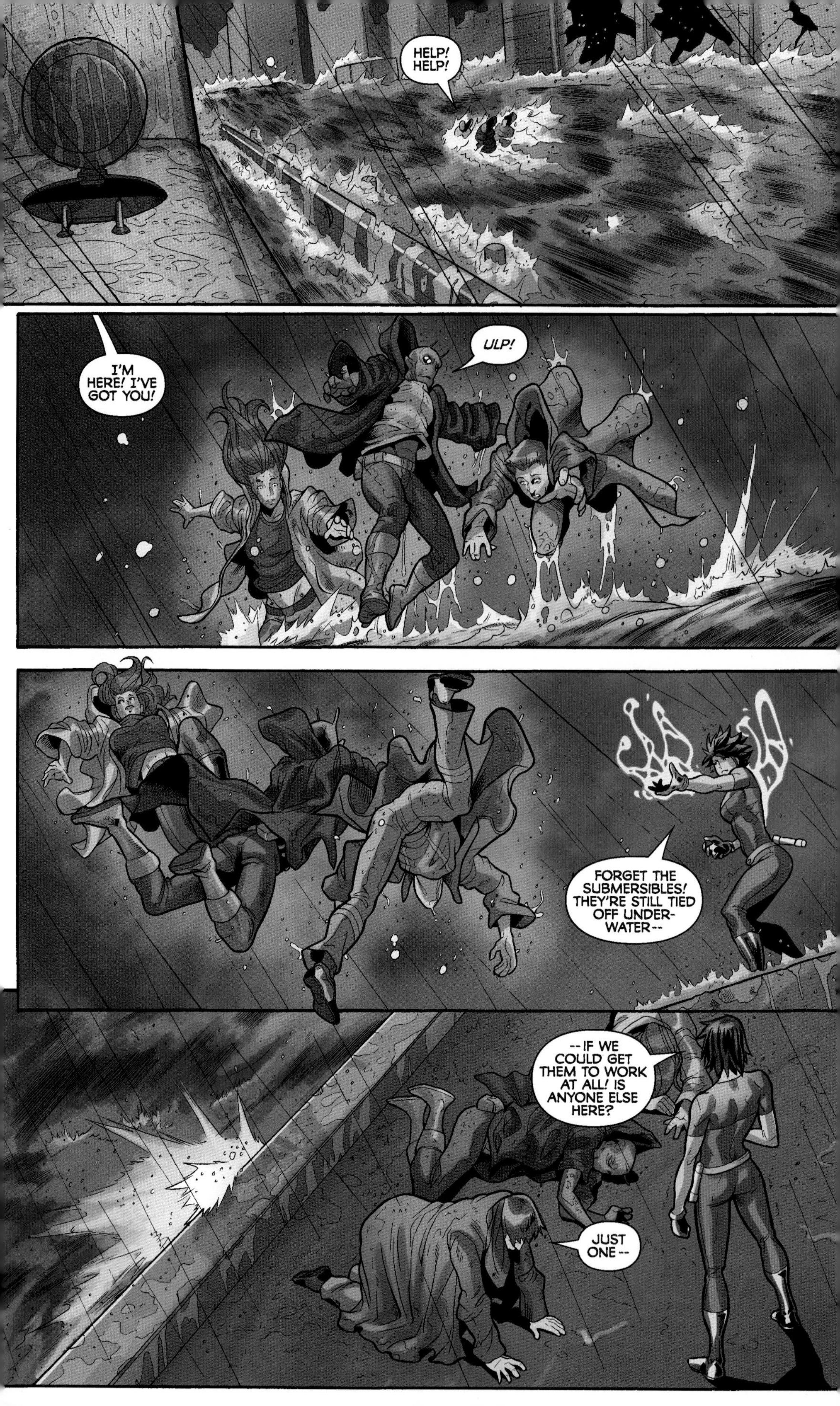
HELP! HELP!
I'M HERE! I'VE GOT YOU!
ULP!
FORGET THE SUBMERSIBLES! THEY'RE STILL TIED OFF UNDER-WATER--
--IF WE COULD GET THEM TO WORK AT ALL! IS ANYONE ELSE HERE?
JUST ONE--

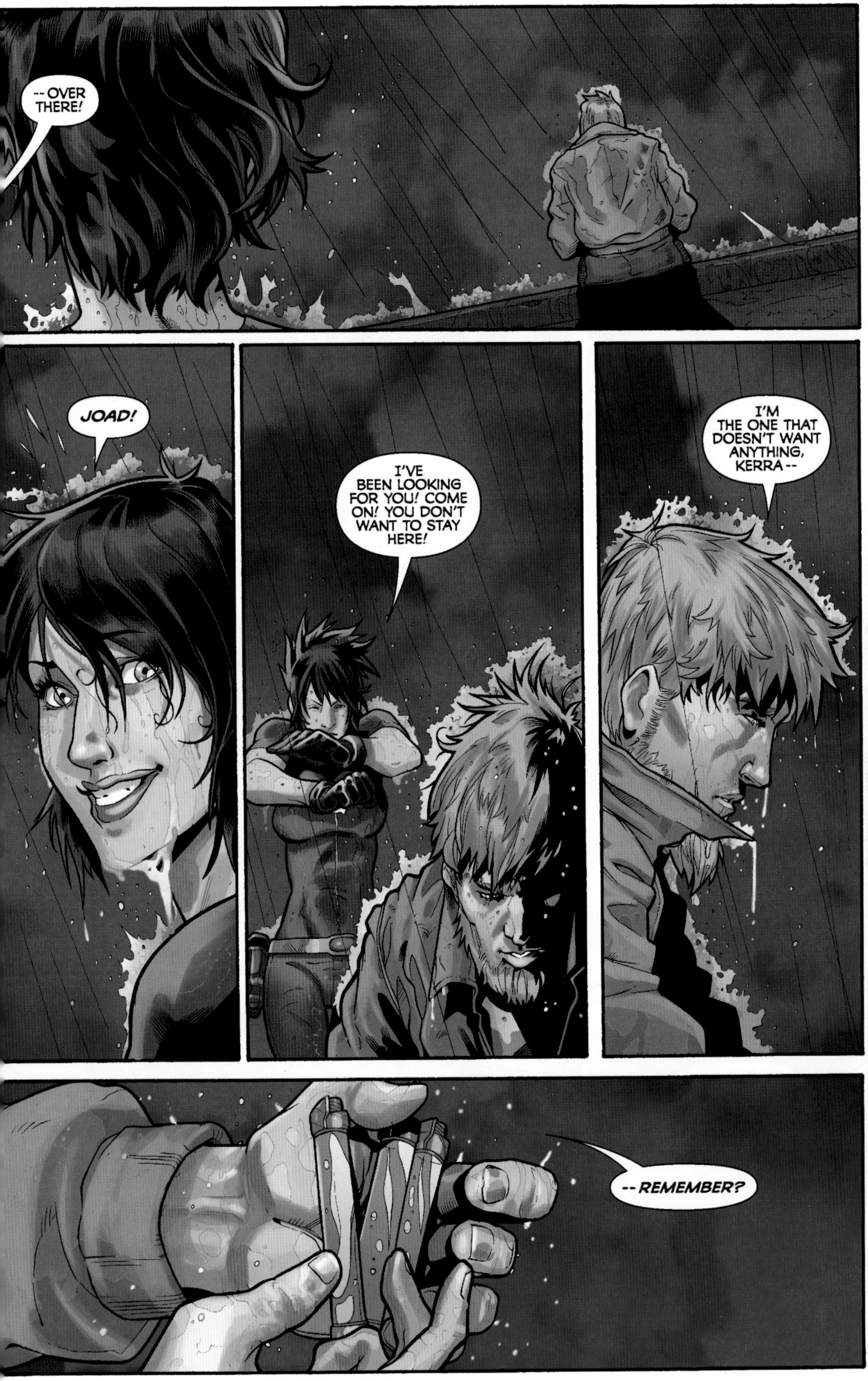
-- OVER THERE!
JOAD!
I'VE BEEN LOOKING FOR YOU! COME ON! YOU DON'T WANT TO STAY HERE!
I'M THE ONE THAT DOESN'T WANT ANYTHING, KERRA --
-- REMEMBER?

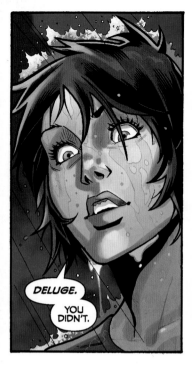

DELUGE. YOU DIDN'T.

NO, I DIDN'T. YOUR F-FRIEND DEVAAD M-MISSED A FEW IN THE STREET. WHEN YOU WERE GONE, I P-PICKED THEM UP.

I W-WANTED TO PICK THEM UP.

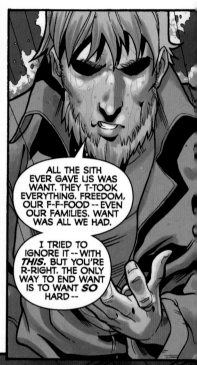

ALL THE SITH EVER GAVE US WAS WANT. THEY T-TOOK EVERYTHING. FREEDOM, OUR F-F-FOOD -- EVEN OUR FAMILIES. WANT WAS ALL WE HAD.

I TRIED TO IGNORE IT -- WITH *THIS.* BUT YOU'RE R-RIGHT. THE ONLY WAY TO END WANT IS TO WANT *SO* HARD --

-- THAT YOU *DO* SOMETHING ABOUT IT!

YES, JOAD! YOUR FRIENDS -- THEY'RE COMING OUT OF IT, TOO. FOCUSED ON THEIR SURVIVAL!

FOCUSED BY YOU, YOU MEAN. FOR A LITTLE SNEAK -- YOU'VE COME A LONG WAY!

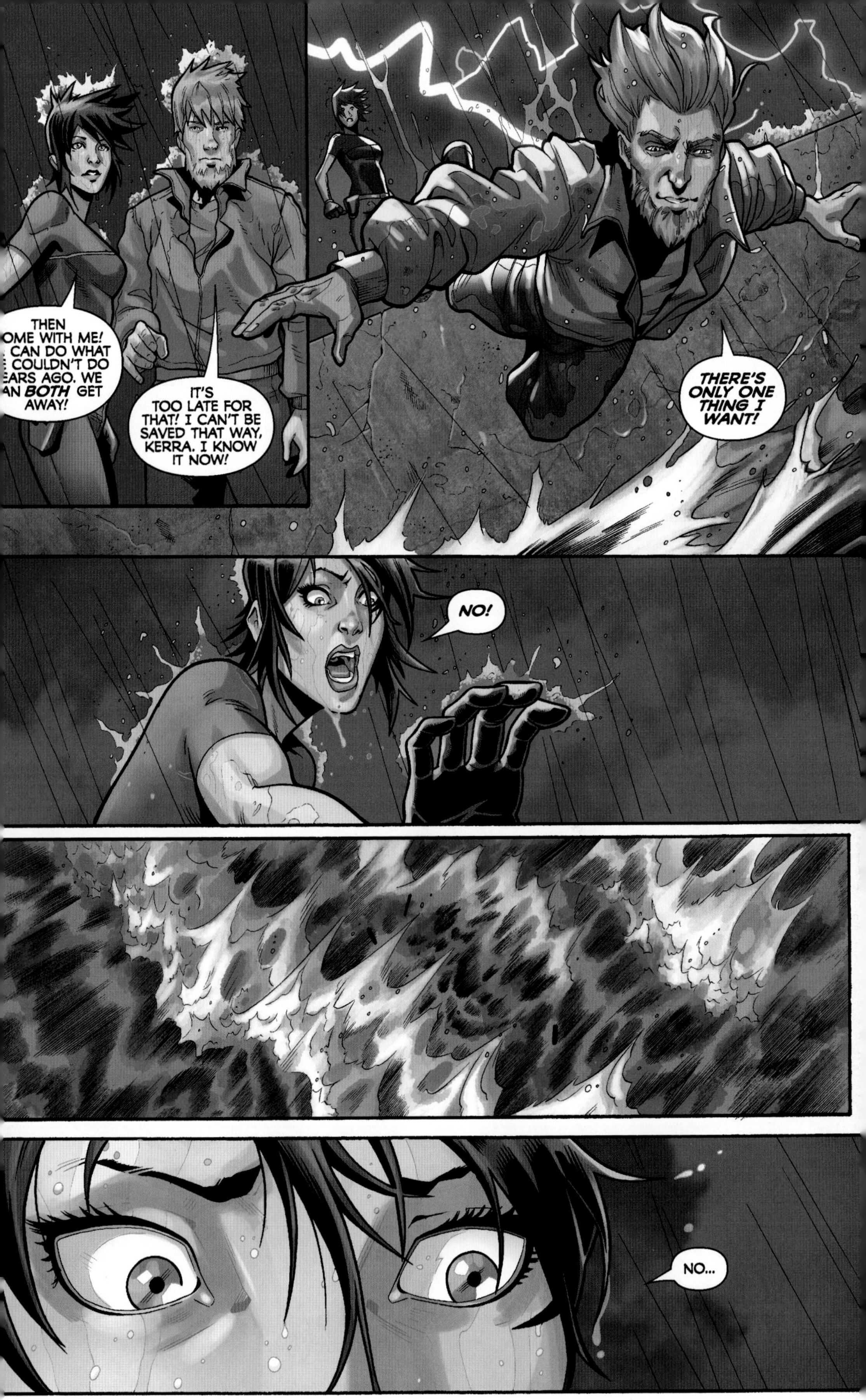
THEN OME WITH ME! CAN DO WHAT COULDN'T DO EARS AGO. WE AN *BOTH* GET AWAY!
IT'S TOO LATE FOR THAT! I CAN'T BE SAVED THAT WAY, KERRA. I KNOW IT NOW!
*THERE'S ONLY ONE THING I WANT!*
*NO!*
NO...

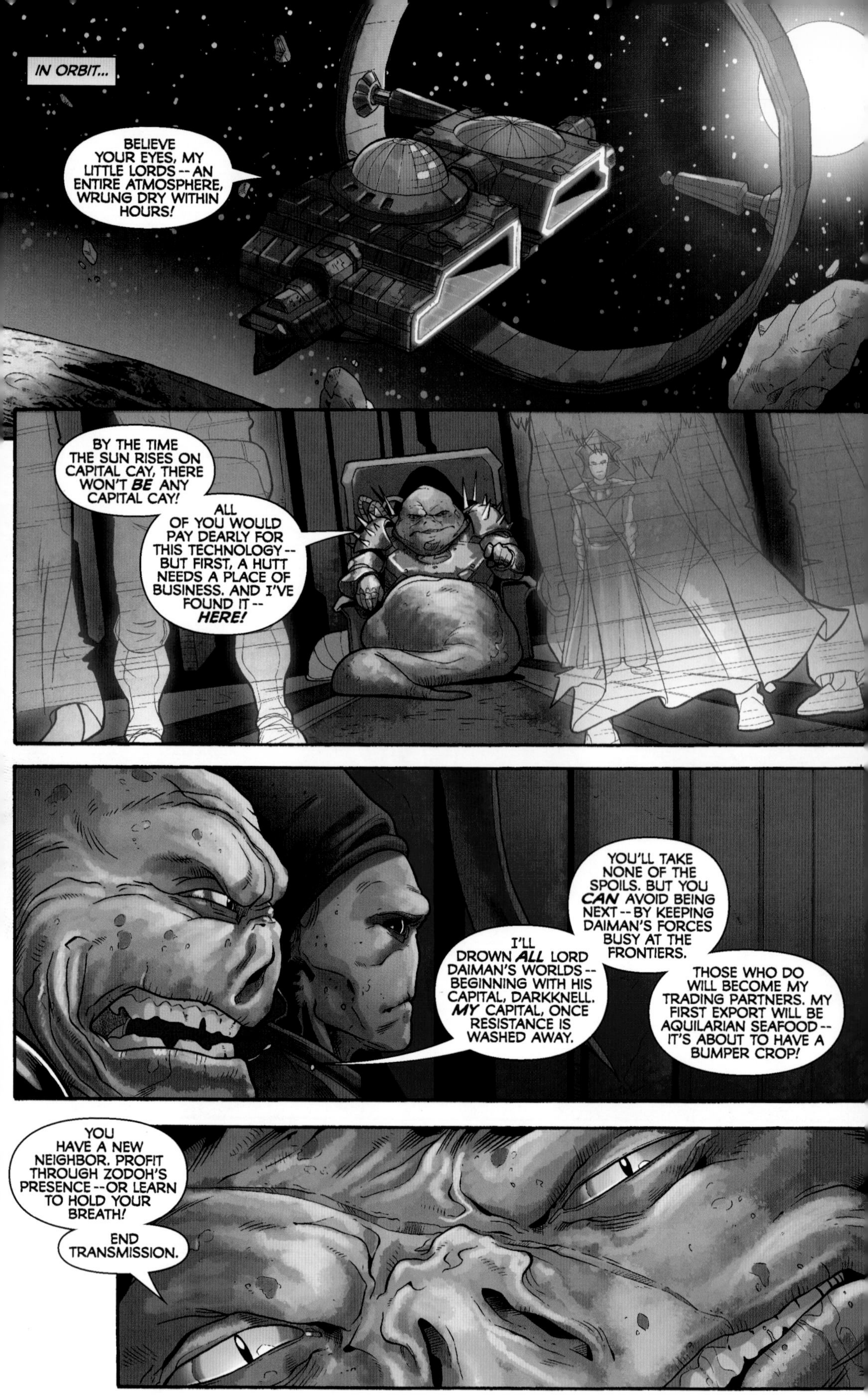
IN ORBIT...
BELIEVE YOUR EYES, MY LITTLE LORDS -- AN ENTIRE ATMOSPHERE, WRUNG DRY WITHIN HOURS!
BY THE TIME THE SUN RISES ON CAPITAL CAY, THERE WON'T BE ANY CAPITAL CAY!
ALL OF YOU WOULD PAY DEARLY FOR THIS TECHNOLOGY -- BUT FIRST, A HUTT NEEDS A PLACE OF BUSINESS. AND I'VE FOUND IT -- HERE!
I'LL DROWN ALL LORD DAIMAN'S WORLDS -- BEGINNING WITH HIS CAPITAL, DARKKNELL. MY CAPITAL, ONCE RESISTANCE IS WASHED AWAY.
YOU'LL TAKE NONE OF THE SPOILS. BUT YOU CAN AVOID BEING NEXT -- BY KEEPING DAIMAN'S FORCES BUSY AT THE FRONTIERS.
THOSE WHO DO WILL BECOME MY TRADING PARTNERS. MY FIRST EXPORT WILL BE AQUILARIAN SEAFOOD -- IT'S ABOUT TO HAVE A BUMPER CROP!
YOU HAVE A NEW NEIGHBOR. PROFIT THROUGH ZODOH'S PRESENCE -- OR LEARN TO HOLD YOUR BREATH!
END TRANSMISSION.

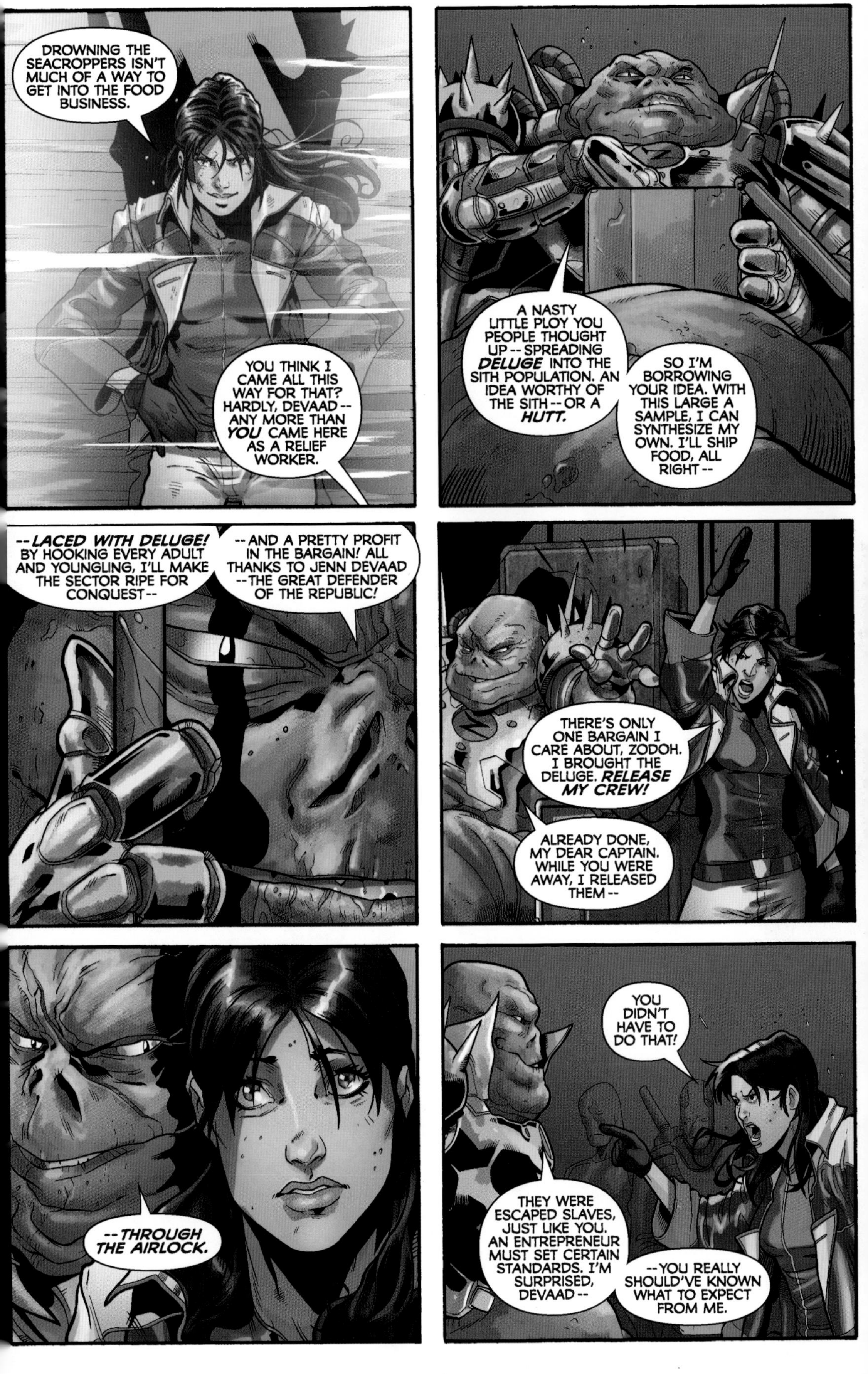

DROWNING THE SEACROPPERS ISN'T MUCH OF A WAY TO GET INTO THE FOOD BUSINESS.
YOU THINK I CAME ALL THIS WAY FOR THAT? HARDLY, DEVAAD -- ANY MORE THAN YOU CAME HERE AS A RELIEF WORKER.
A NASTY LITTLE PLOY YOU PEOPLE THOUGHT UP -- SPREADING DELUGE INTO THE SITH POPULATION. AN IDEA WORTHY OF THE SITH -- OR A HUTT.
SO I'M BORROWING YOUR IDEA. WITH THIS LARGE A SAMPLE, I CAN SYNTHESIZE MY OWN. I'LL SHIP FOOD, ALL RIGHT --
-- LACED WITH DELUGE! BY HOOKING EVERY ADULT AND YOUNGLING, I'LL MAKE THE SECTOR RIPE FOR CONQUEST --
-- AND A PRETTY PROFIT IN THE BARGAIN! ALL THANKS TO JENN DEVAAD -- THE GREAT DEFENDER OF THE REPUBLIC!
THERE'S ONLY ONE BARGAIN I CARE ABOUT, ZODOH. I BROUGHT THE DELUGE. RELEASE MY CREW!
ALREADY DONE, MY DEAR CAPTAIN. WHILE YOU WERE AWAY, I RELEASED THEM --
-- THROUGH THE AIRLOCK.
YOU DIDN'T HAVE TO DO THAT!
THEY WERE ESCAPED SLAVES, JUST LIKE YOU. AN ENTREPRENEUR MUST SET CERTAIN STANDARDS. I'M SURPRISED, DEVAAD --
-- YOU REALLY SHOULD'VE KNOWN WHAT TO EXPECT FROM ME.

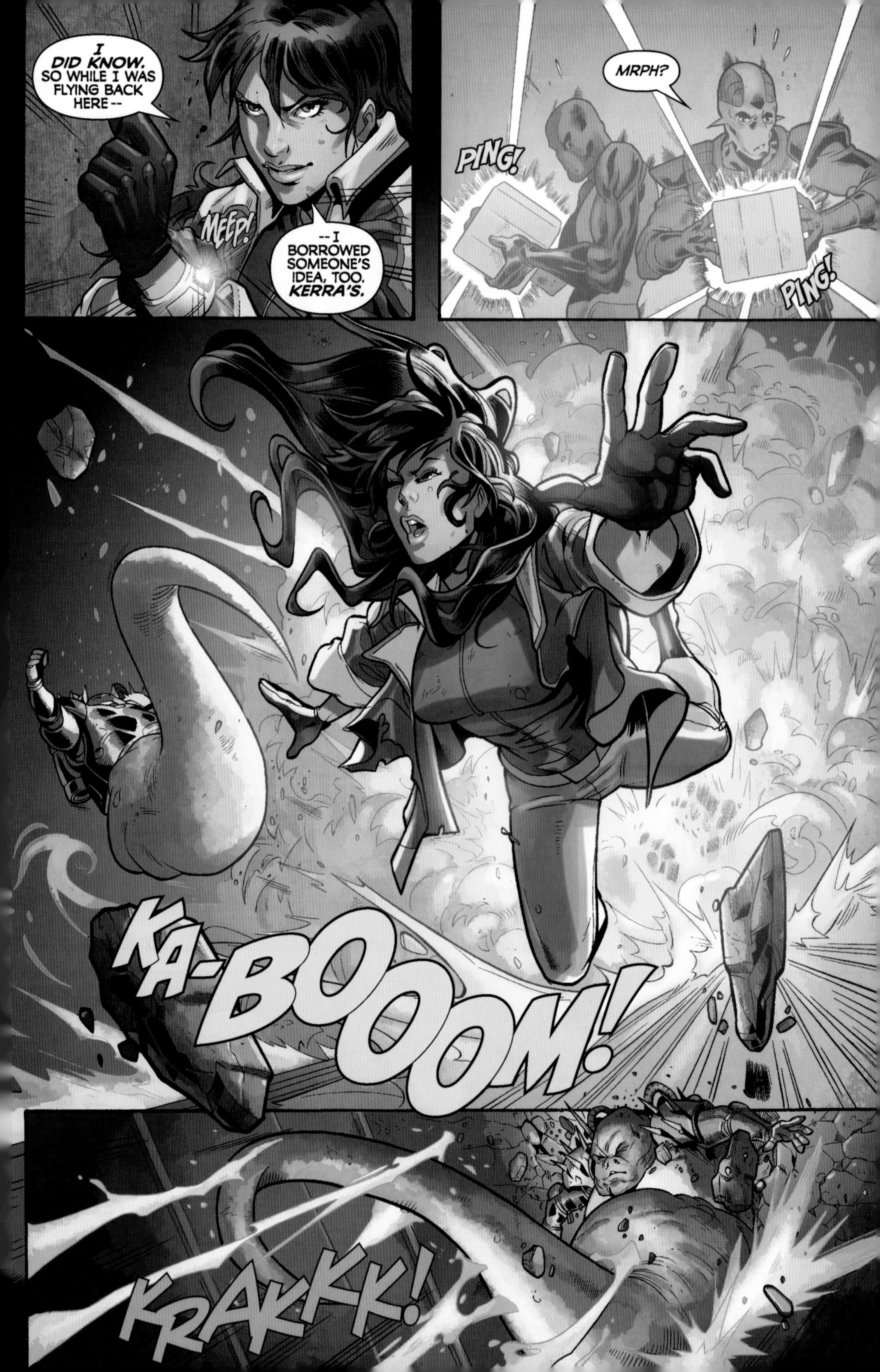
I DID KNOW. SO WHILE I WAS FLYING BACK HERE --
MEEP!
-- I BORROWED SOMEONE'S IDEA, TOO. KERRA'S.
MRPH?
PING!
PING!
KA-BOOOOM!
KRAKKK!

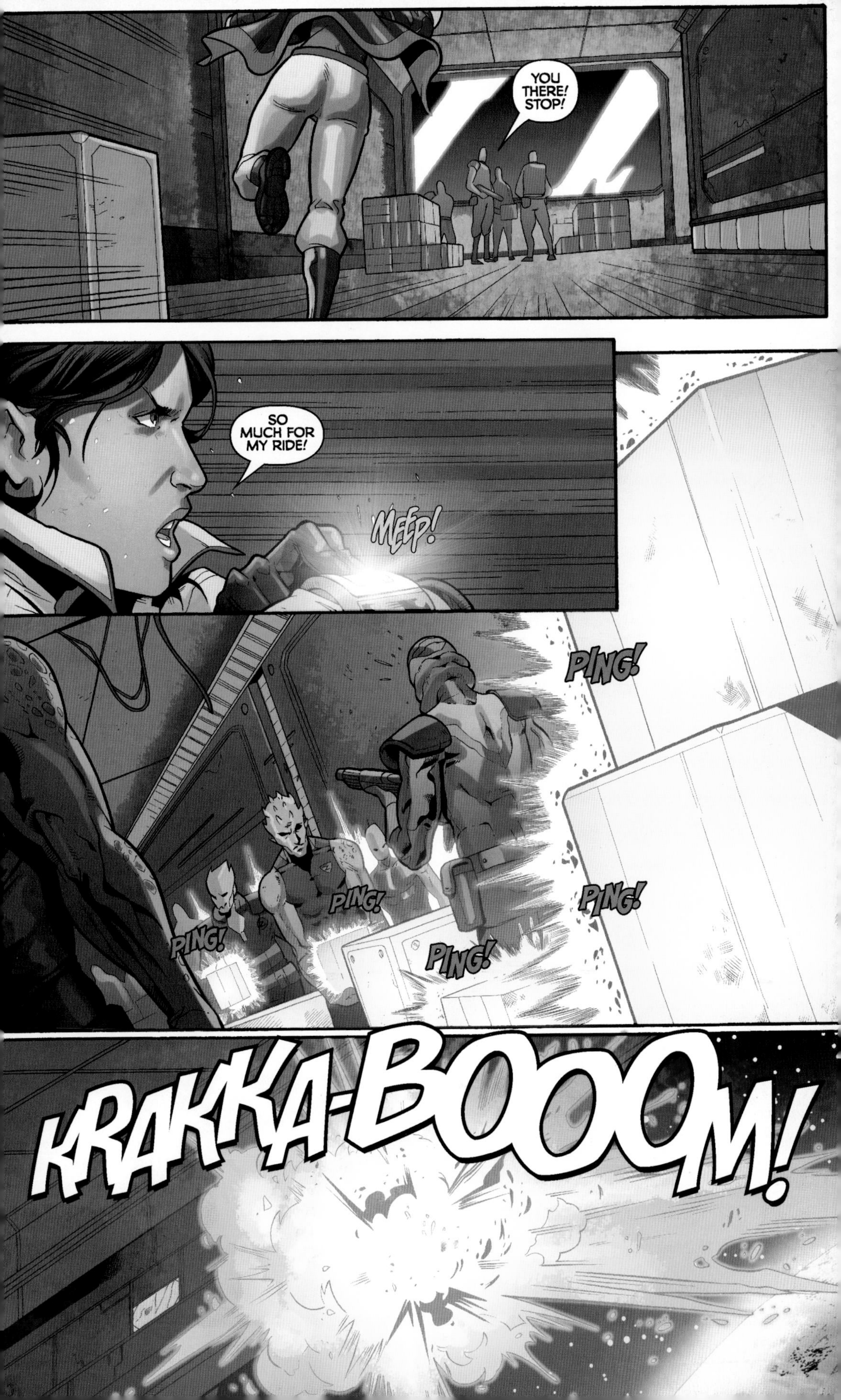

YOU THERE! STOP!
SO MUCH FOR MY RIDE!
MEEP!
PING!
PING!
PING!
PING!
PING!
KRAKKA-BOOOM!

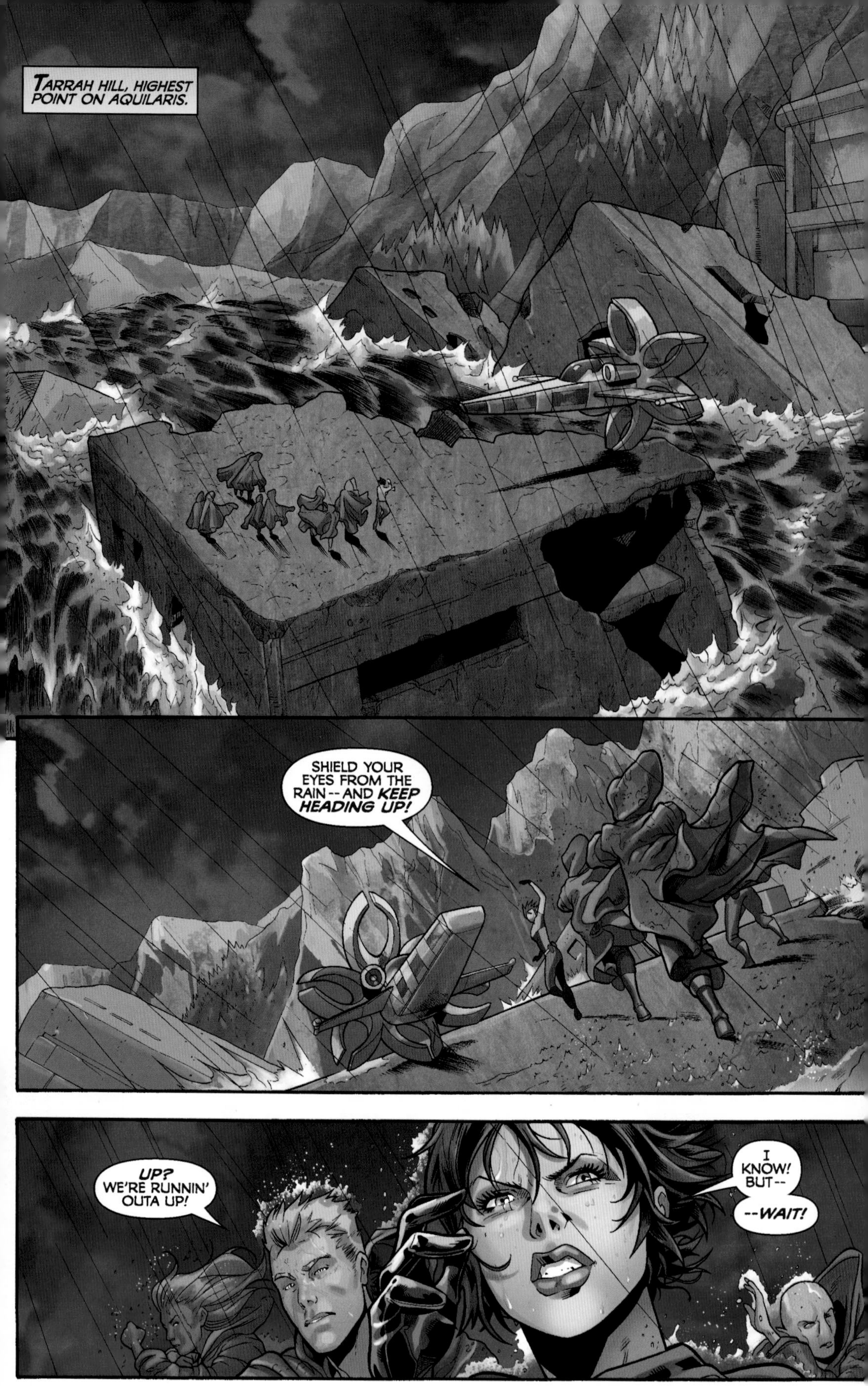
TARRAH HILL, HIGHEST POINT ON AQUILARIS.
SHIELD YOUR EYES FROM THE RAIN -- AND KEEP HEADING UP!
UP? WE'RE RUNNIN' OUTA UP!
I KNOW! BUT--
--WAIT!

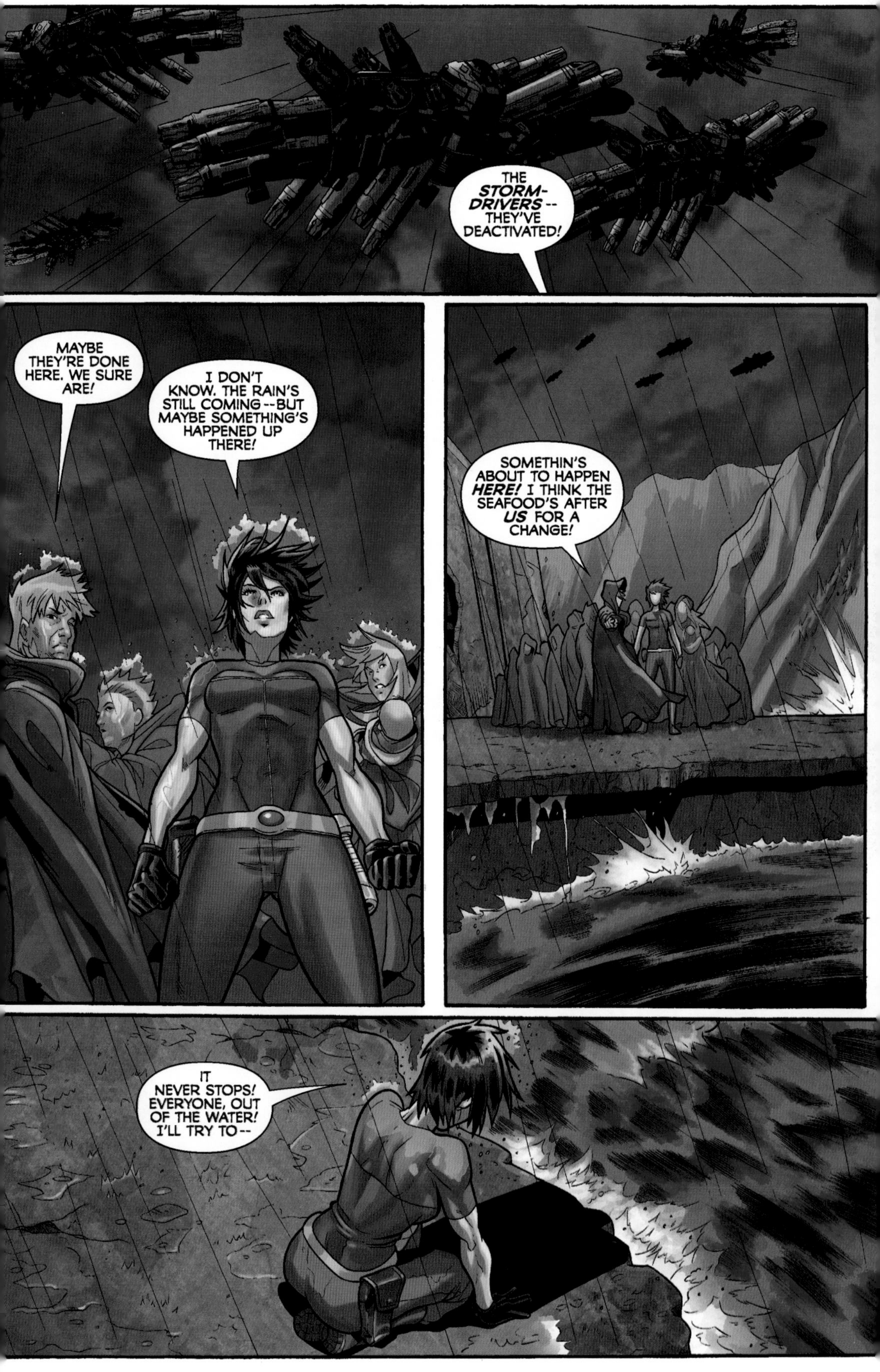
THE STORM-DRIVERS -- THEY'VE DEACTIVATED!
MAYBE THEY'RE DONE HERE. WE SURE ARE!
I DON'T KNOW. THE RAIN'S STILL COMING --BUT MAYBE SOMETHING'S HAPPENED UP THERE!
SOMETHIN'S ABOUT TO HAPPEN HERE! I THINK THE SEAFOOD'S AFTER US FOR A CHANGE!
IT NEVER STOPS! EVERYONE, OUT OF THE WATER! I'LL TRY TO--

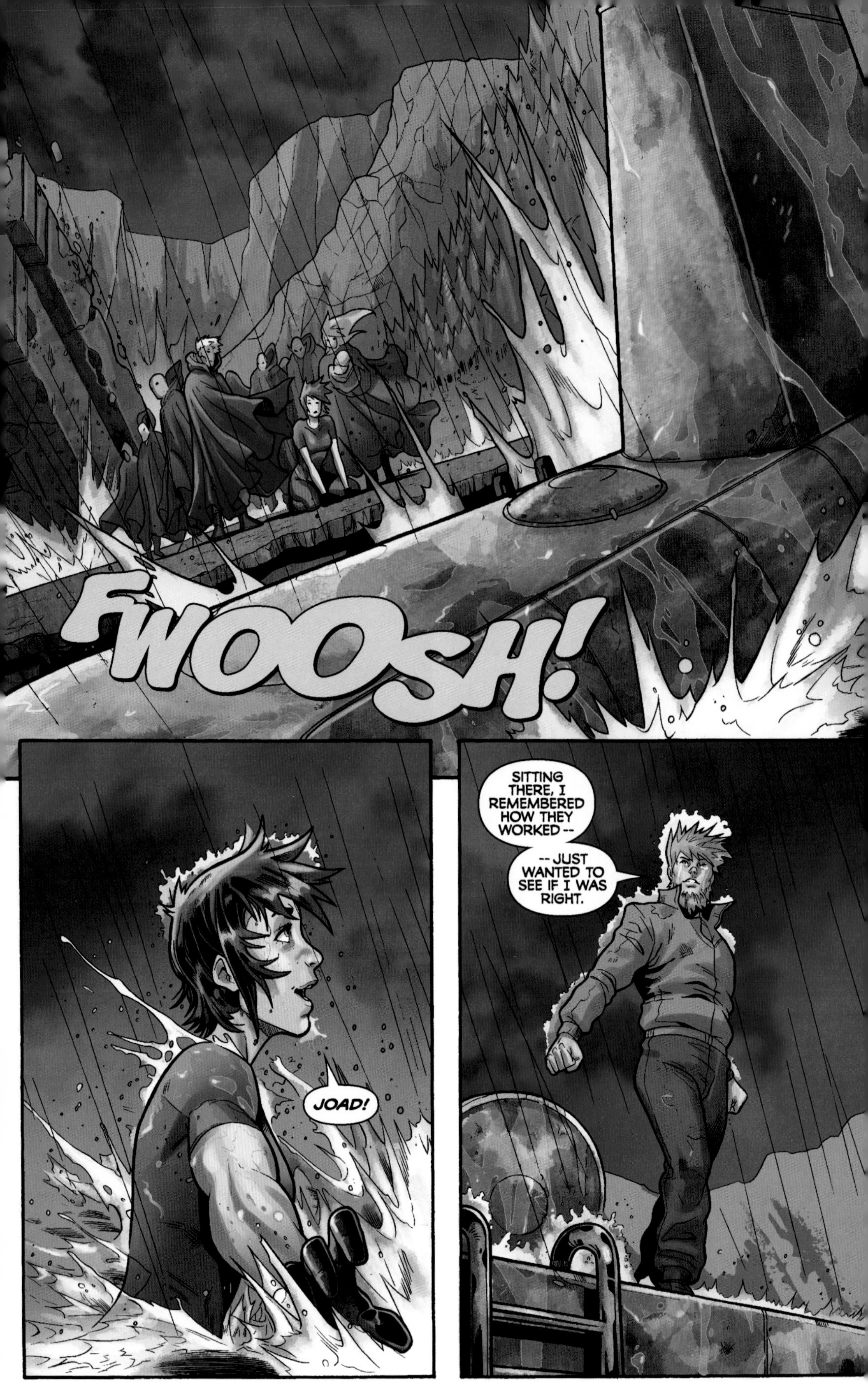
FWOOSH!
JOAD!
SITTING THERE, I REMEMBERED HOW THEY WORKED --
-- JUST WANTED TO SEE IF I WAS RIGHT.

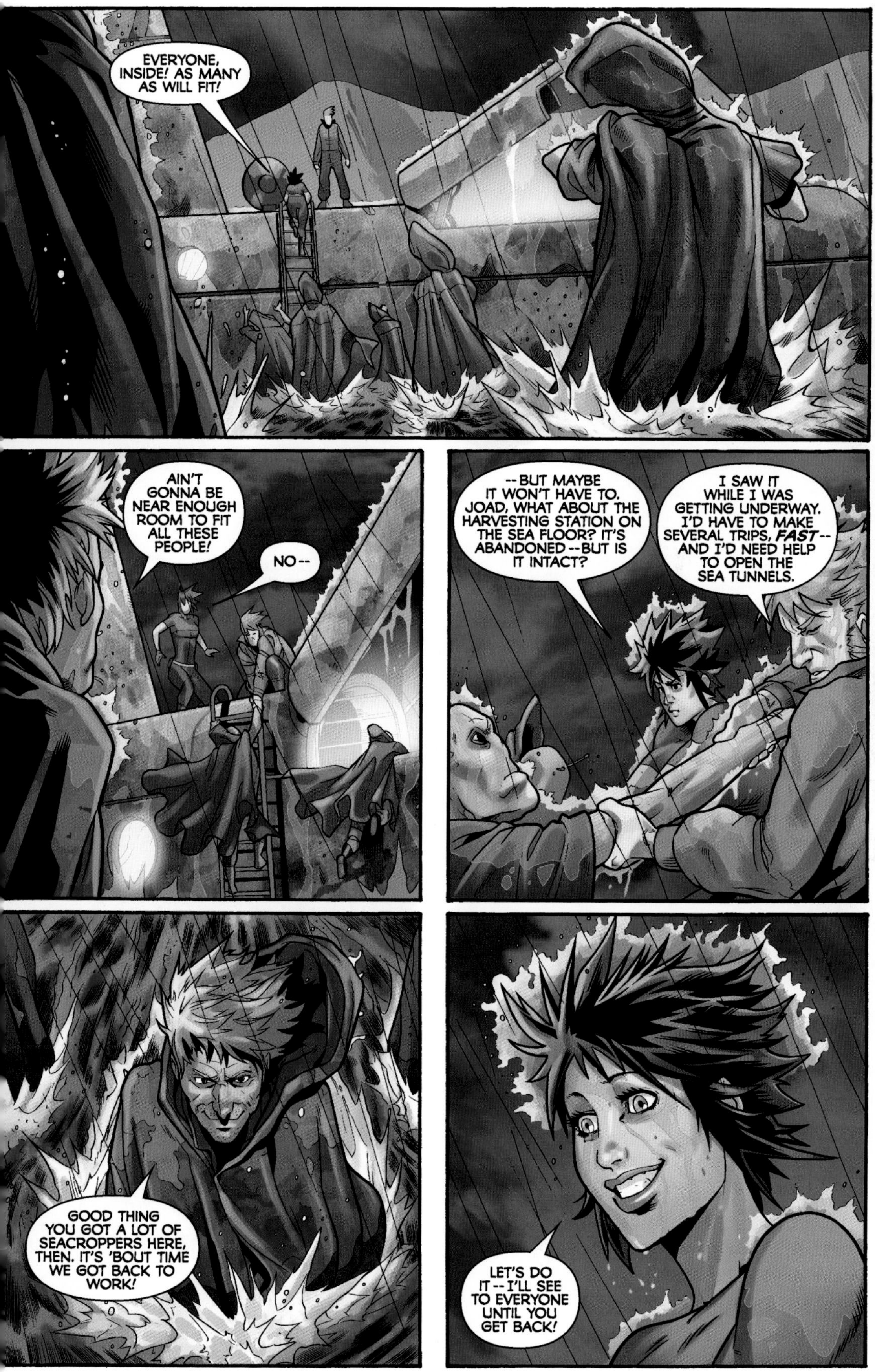
EVERYONE, INSIDE! AS MANY AS WILL FIT!
AIN'T GONNA BE NEAR ENOUGH ROOM TO FIT ALL THESE PEOPLE!
NO--
--BUT MAYBE IT WON'T HAVE TO. JOAD, WHAT ABOUT THE HARVESTING STATION ON THE SEA FLOOR? IT'S ABANDONED--BUT IS IT INTACT?
I SAW IT WHILE I WAS GETTING UNDERWAY. I'D HAVE TO MAKE SEVERAL TRIPS, FAST-- AND I'D NEED HELP TO OPEN THE SEA TUNNELS.
GOOD THING YOU GOT A LOT OF SEACROPPERS HERE, THEN. IT'S 'BOUT TIME WE GOT BACK TO WORK!
LET'S DO IT--I'LL SEE TO EVERYONE UNTIL YOU GET BACK!

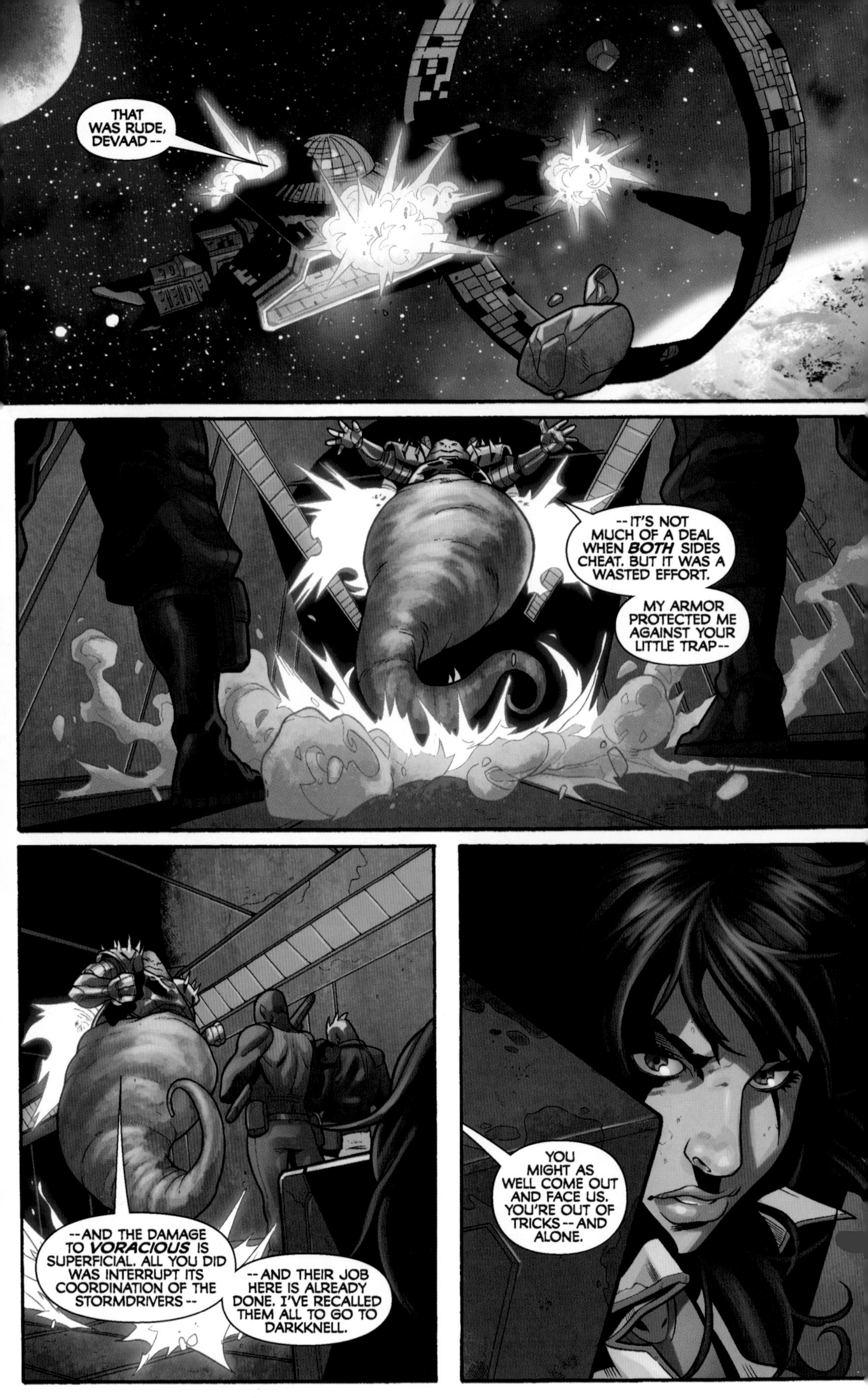
THAT WAS RUDE, DEVAAD --
-- IT'S NOT MUCH OF A DEAL WHEN BOTH SIDES CHEAT. BUT IT WAS A WASTED EFFORT.
MY ARMOR PROTECTED ME AGAINST YOUR LITTLE TRAP--
--AND THE DAMAGE TO VORACIOUS IS SUPERFICIAL. ALL YOU DID WAS INTERRUPT ITS COORDINATION OF THE STORMDRIVERS --
--AND THEIR JOB HERE IS ALREADY DONE. I'VE RECALLED THEM ALL TO GO TO DARKKNELL.
YOU MIGHT AS WELL COME OUT AND FACE US. YOU'RE OUT OF TRICKS -- AND ALONE.

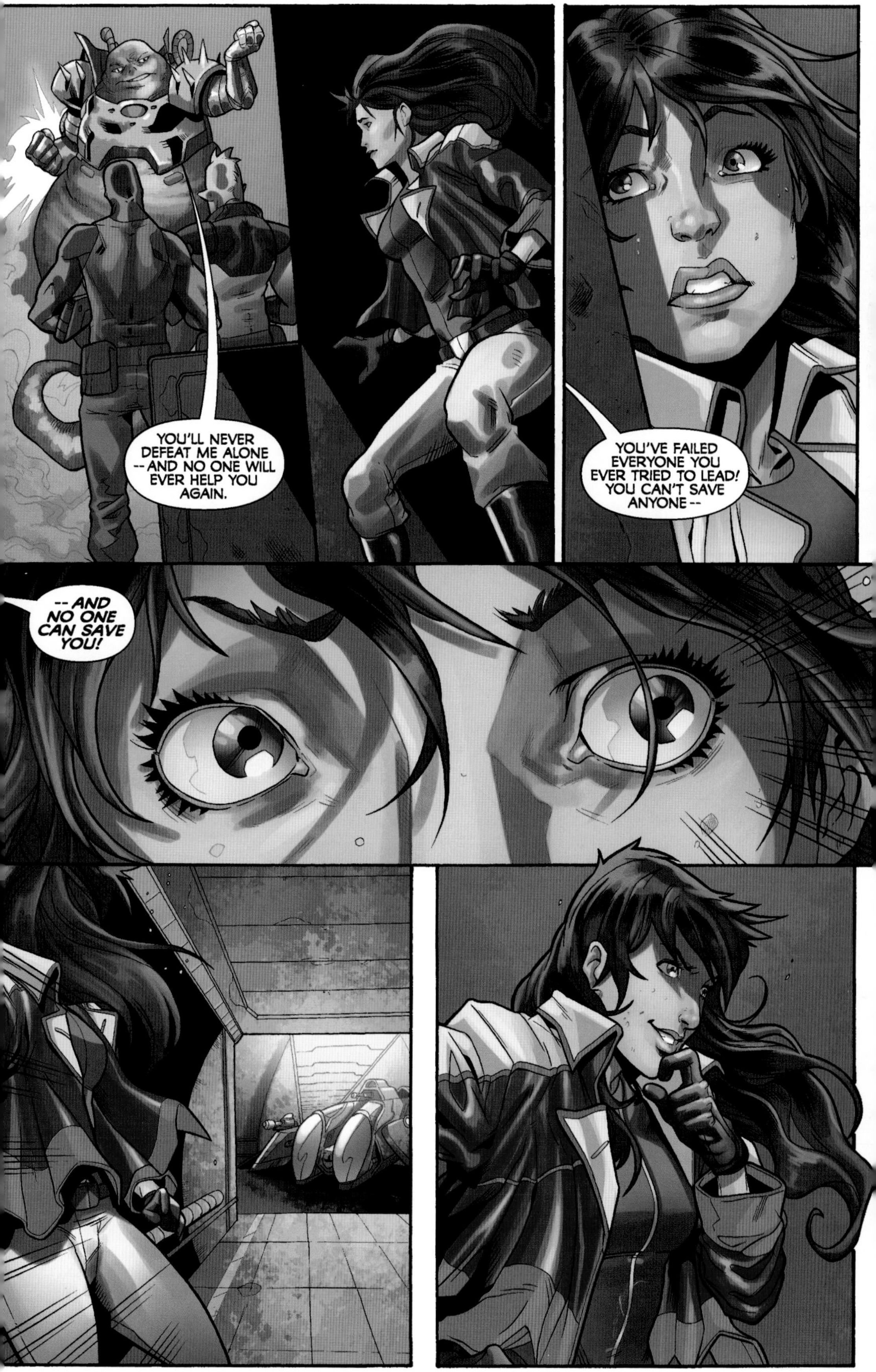
YOU'LL NEVER DEFEAT ME ALONE --AND NO ONE WILL EVER HELP YOU AGAIN.
YOU'VE FAILED EVERYONE YOU EVER TRIED TO LEAD! YOU CAN'T SAVE ANYONE --
--AND NO ONE CAN SAVE YOU!

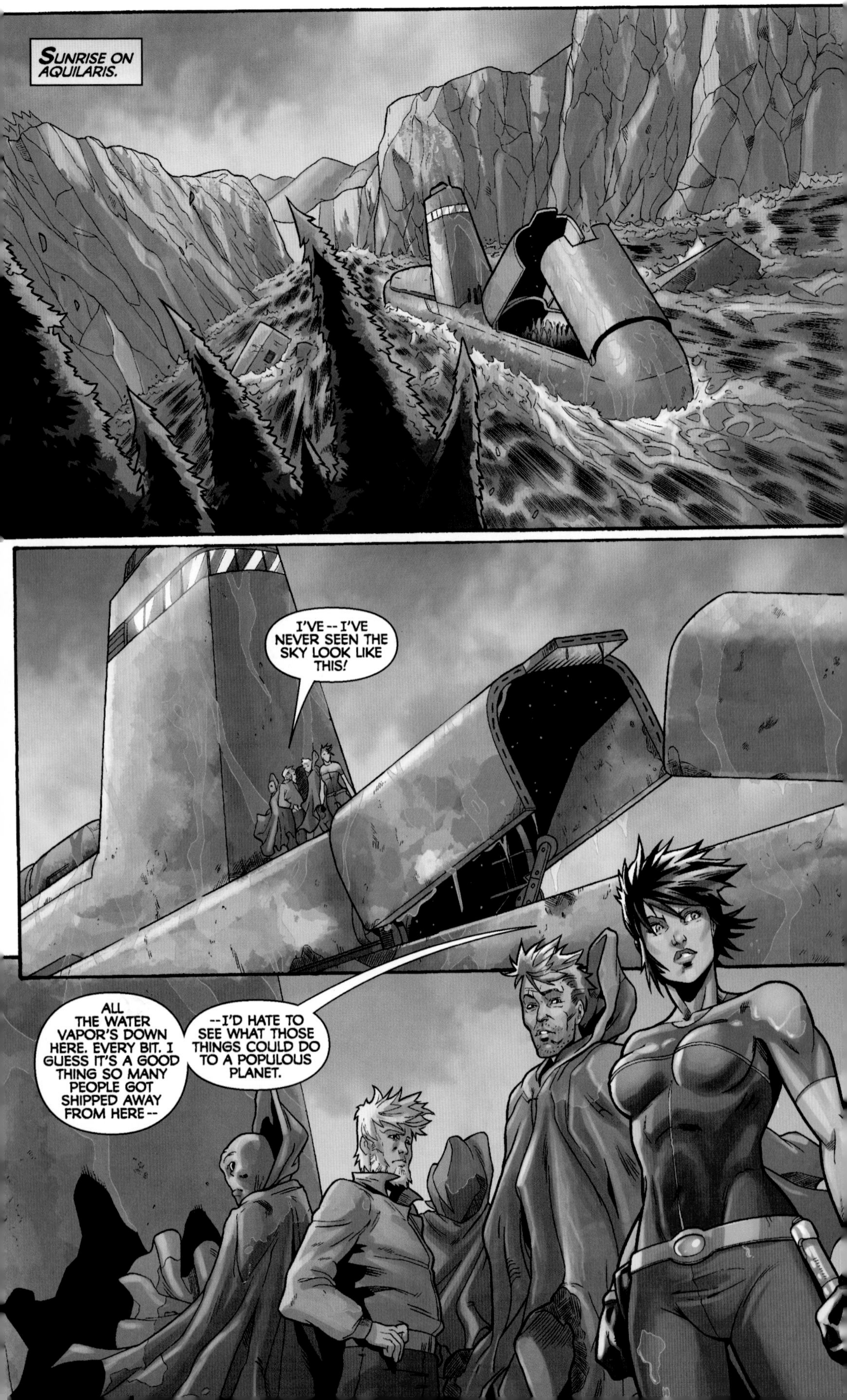
SUNRISE ON AQUILARIS.
I'VE -- I'VE NEVER SEEN THE SKY LOOK LIKE THIS!
ALL THE WATER VAPOR'S DOWN HERE. EVERY BIT. I GUESS IT'S A GOOD THING SO MANY PEOPLE GOT SHIPPED AWAY FROM HERE --
--I'D HATE TO SEE WHAT THOSE THINGS COULD DO TO A POPULOUS PLANET.

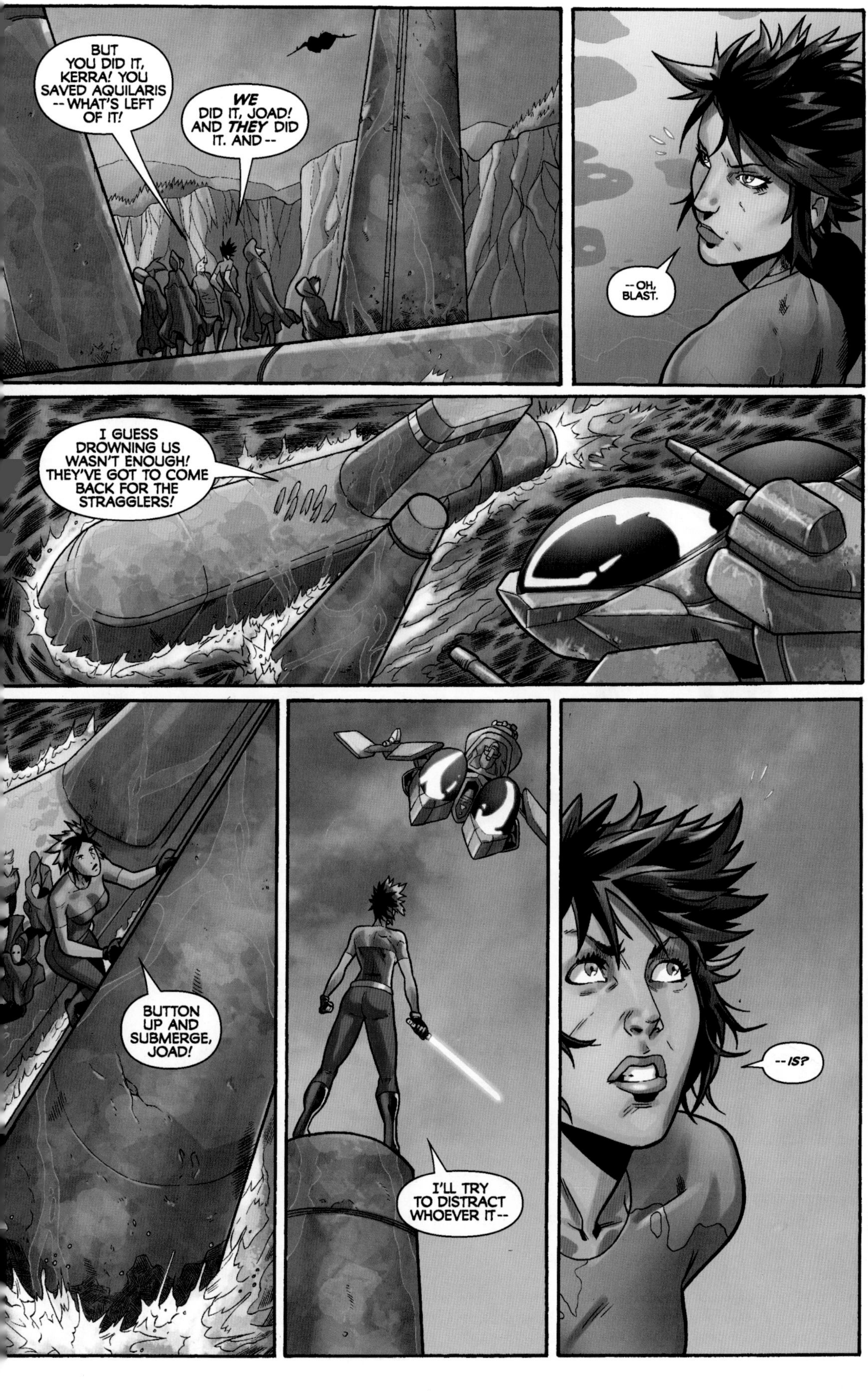
BUT YOU DID IT, KERRA! YOU SAVED AQUILARIS --WHAT'S LEFT OF IT!
WE DID IT, JOAD! AND THEY DID IT. AND --
--OH, BLAST.
I GUESS DROWNING US WASN'T ENOUGH! THEY'VE GOT TO COME BACK FOR THE STRAGGLERS!
BUTTON UP AND SUBMERGE, JOAD!
I'LL TRY TO DISTRACT WHOEVER IT--
--IS?

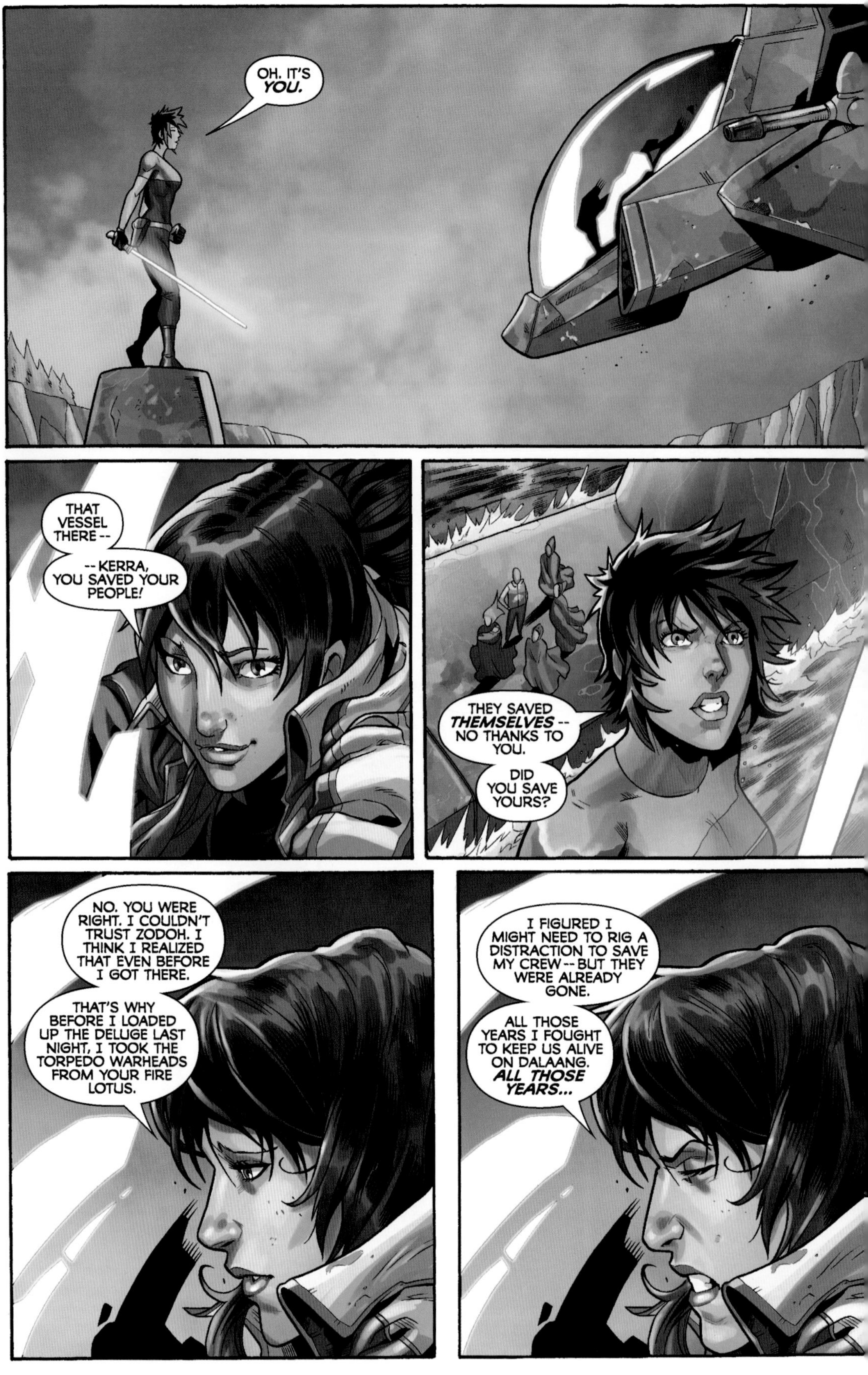
OH. IT'S *YOU.*
THAT VESSEL THERE --
-- KERRA, YOU SAVED YOUR PEOPLE!
THEY SAVED *THEMSELVES* -- NO THANKS TO YOU.
DID YOU SAVE YOURS?
NO. YOU WERE RIGHT. I COULDN'T TRUST ZODOH. I THINK I REALIZED THAT EVEN BEFORE I GOT THERE.
THAT'S WHY BEFORE I LOADED UP THE DELUGE LAST NIGHT, I TOOK THE TORPEDO WARHEADS FROM YOUR FIRE LOTUS.
I FIGURED I MIGHT NEED TO RIG A DISTRACTION TO SAVE MY CREW -- BUT THEY WERE ALREADY GONE.
ALL THOSE YEARS I FOUGHT TO KEEP US ALIVE ON DALAANG. *ALL THOSE YEARS...*

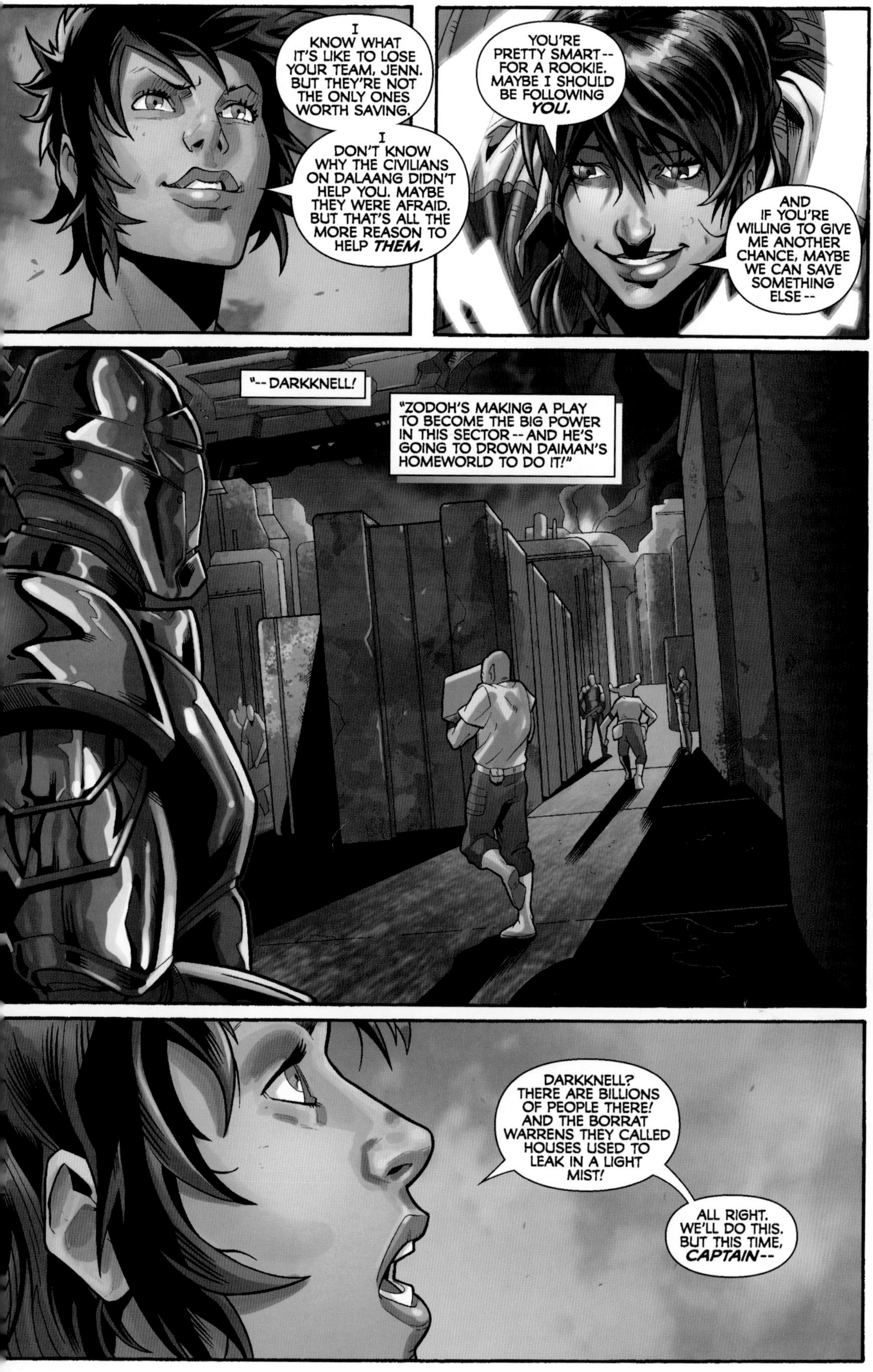

I KNOW WHAT IT'S LIKE TO LOSE YOUR TEAM, JENN. BUT THEY'RE NOT THE ONLY ONES WORTH SAVING.
I DON'T KNOW WHY THE CIVILIANS ON DALAANG DIDN'T HELP YOU. MAYBE THEY WERE AFRAID. BUT THAT'S ALL THE MORE REASON TO HELP *THEM.*
YOU'RE PRETTY SMART-- FOR A ROOKIE. MAYBE I SHOULD BE FOLLOWING *YOU.*
AND IF YOU'RE WILLING TO GIVE ME ANOTHER CHANCE, MAYBE WE CAN SAVE SOMETHING ELSE--
"--DARKKNELL!
"ZODOH'S MAKING A PLAY TO BECOME THE BIG POWER IN THIS SECTOR--AND HE'S GOING TO DROWN DAIMAN'S HOMEWORLD TO DO IT!"
DARKKNELL? THERE ARE BILLIONS OF PEOPLE THERE! AND THE BORRAT WARRENS THEY CALLED HOUSES USED TO LEAK IN A LIGHT MIST!
ALL RIGHT. WE'LL DO THIS. BUT THIS TIME, *CAPTAIN*--

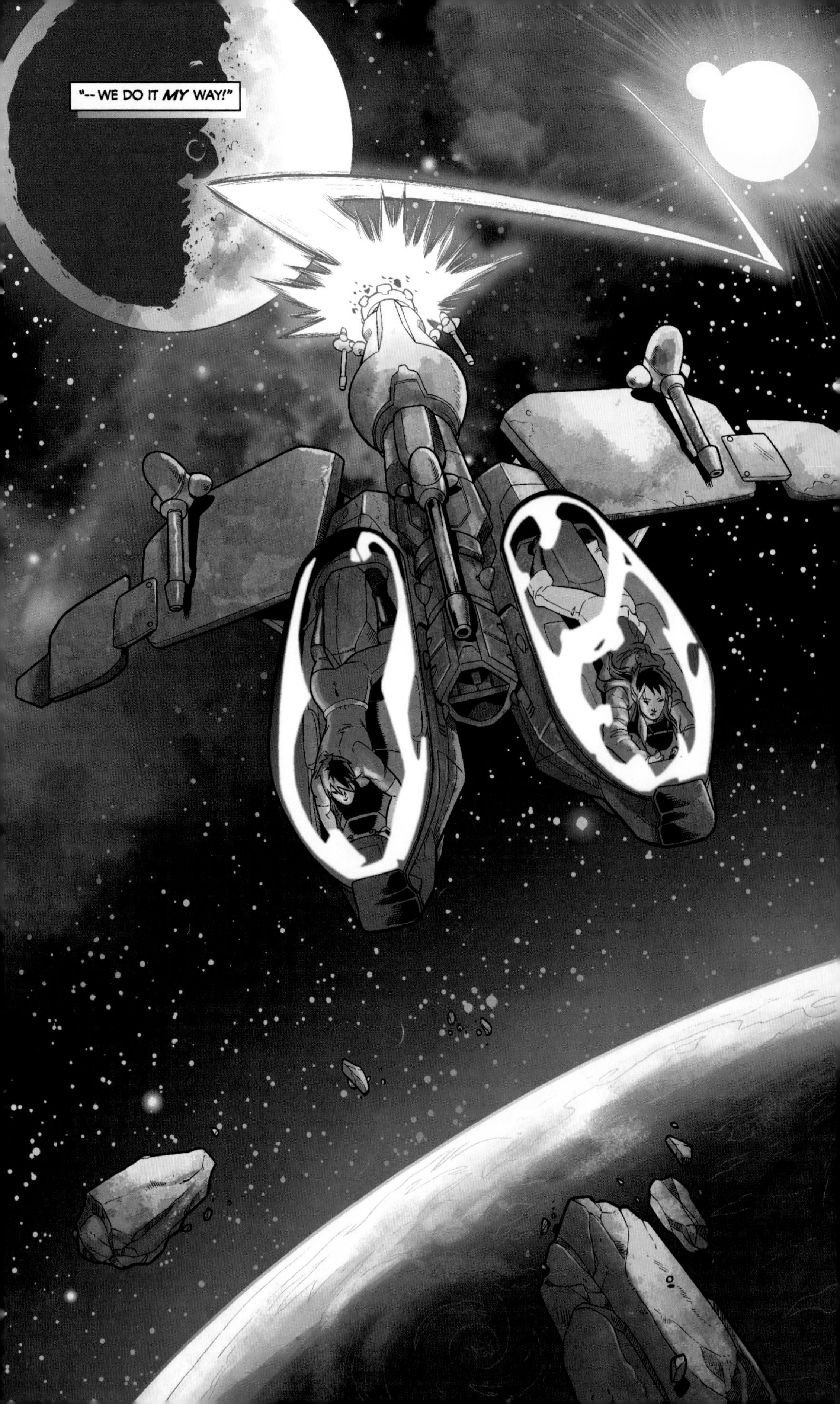
"-- WE DO IT *MY* WAY!"

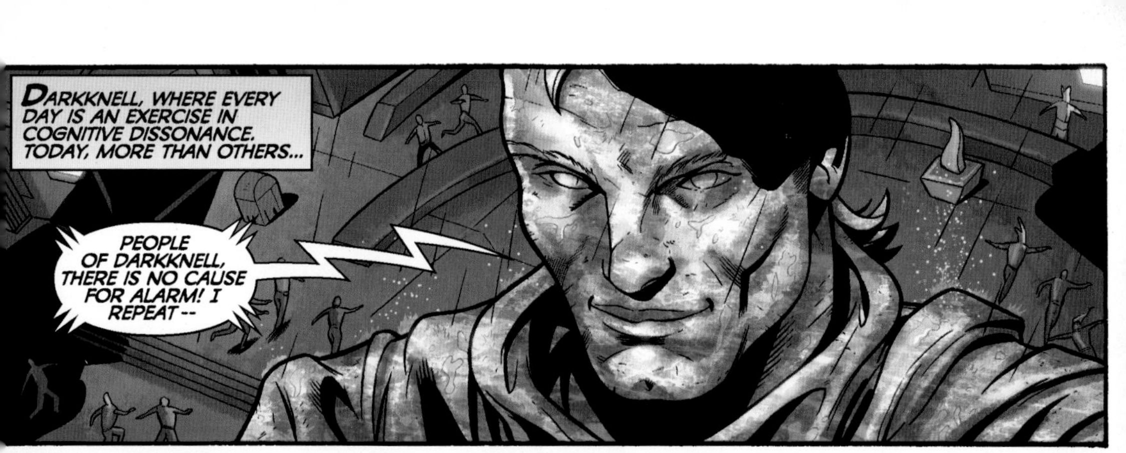
DARKKNELL, WHERE EVERY DAY IS AN EXERCISE IN COGNITIVE DISSONANCE. TODAY, MORE THAN OTHERS...
PEOPLE OF DARKKNELL, THERE IS NO CAUSE FOR ALARM! I REPEAT--

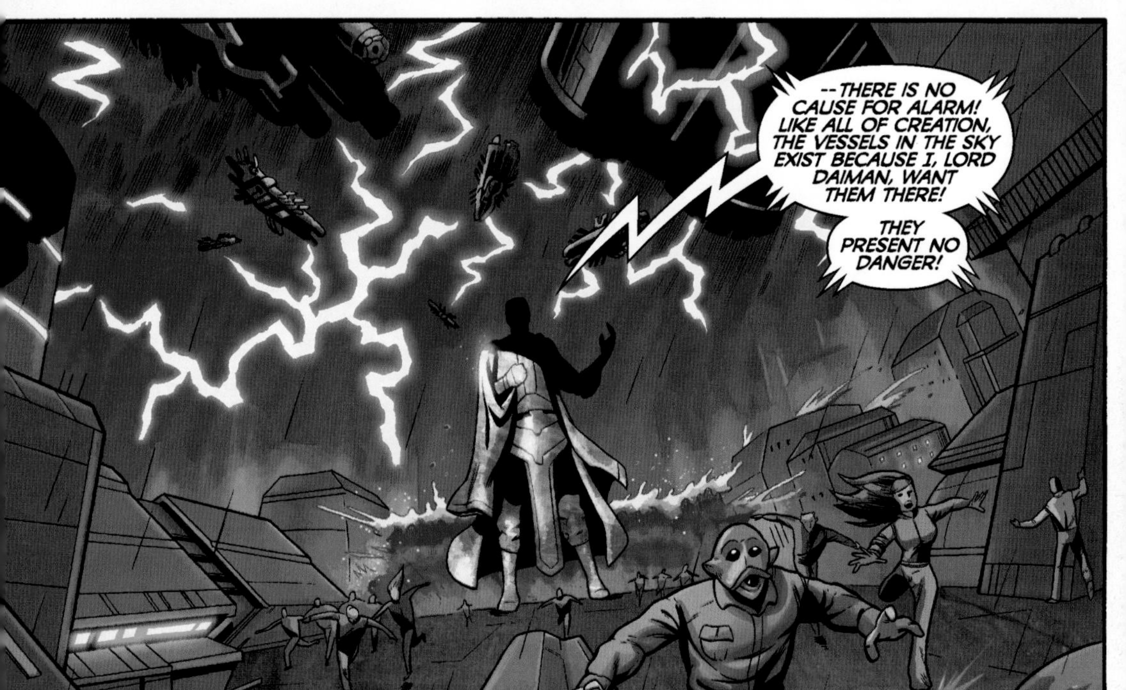
--THERE IS NO CAUSE FOR ALARM! LIKE ALL OF CREATION, THE VESSELS IN THE SKY EXIST BECAUSE I, LORD DAIMAN, WANT THEM THERE!
THEY PRESENT NO DANGER!

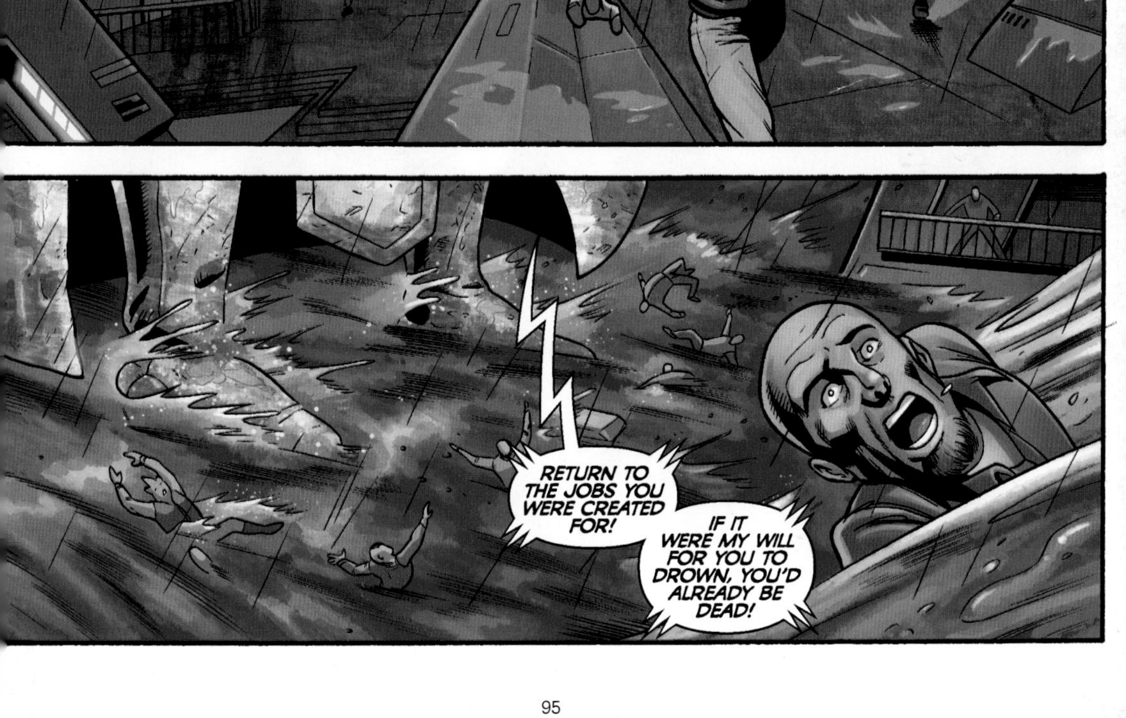
RETURN TO THE JOBS YOU WERE CREATED FOR!
IF IT WERE MY WILL FOR YOU TO DROWN, YOU'D ALREADY BE DEAD!

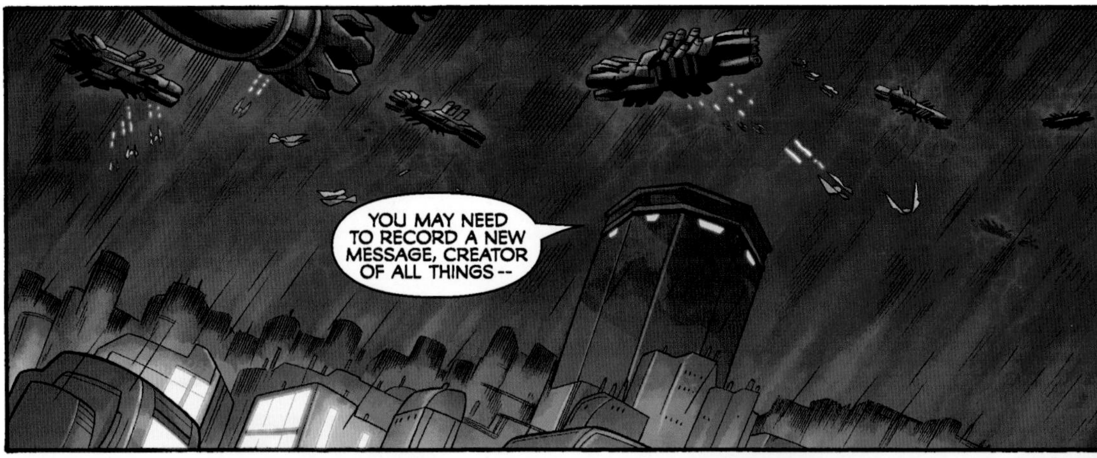
YOU MAY NEED TO RECORD A NEW MESSAGE, CREATOR OF ALL THINGS --

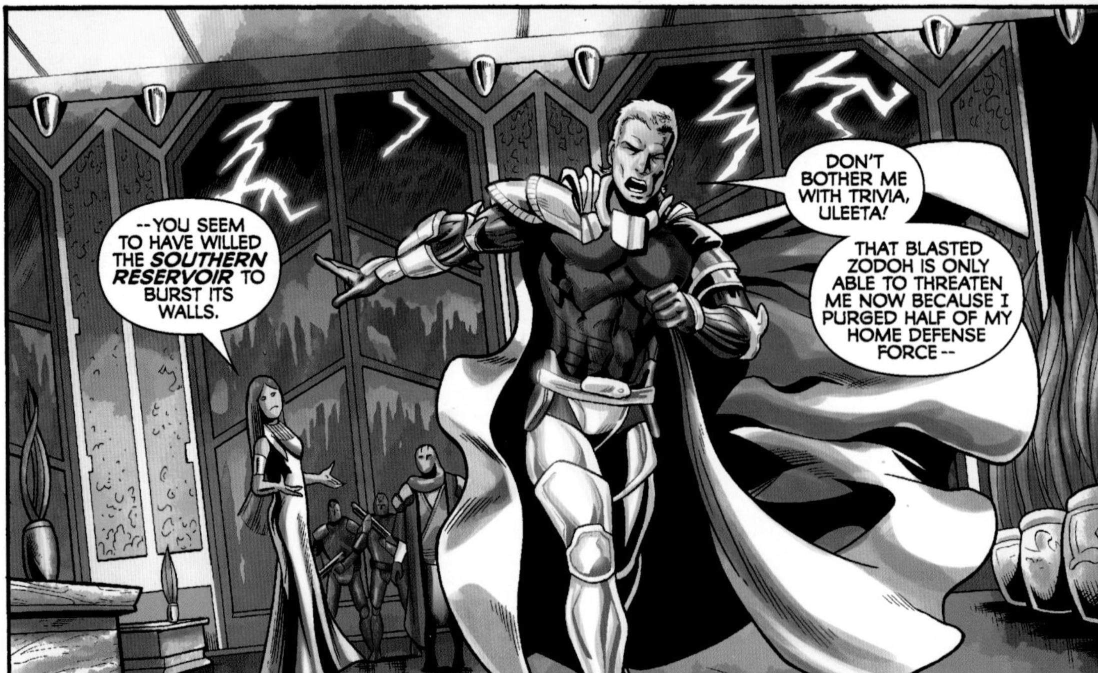
--YOU SEEM TO HAVE WILLED THE ***SOUTHERN RESERVOIR*** TO BURST ITS WALLS.
DON'T BOTHER ME WITH TRIVIA, ULEETA!
THAT BLASTED ZODOH IS ONLY ABLE TO THREATEN ME NOW BECAUSE I PURGED HALF OF MY HOME DEFENSE FORCE --

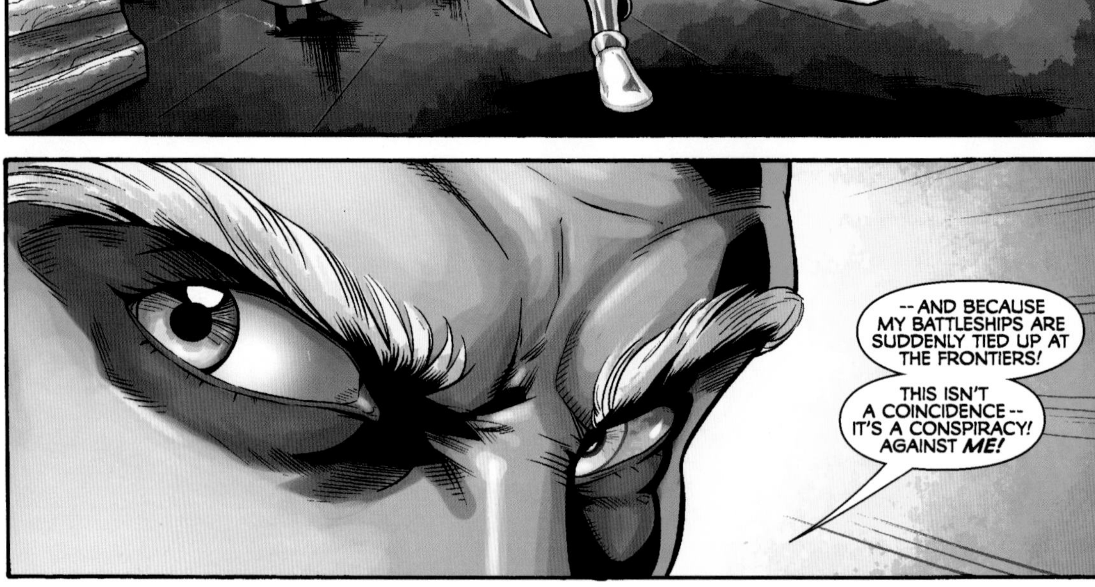
-- AND BECAUSE MY BATTLESHIPS ARE SUDDENLY TIED UP AT THE FRONTIERS!
THIS ISN'T A COINCIDENCE -- IT'S A CONSPIRACY! AGAINST ***ME!***

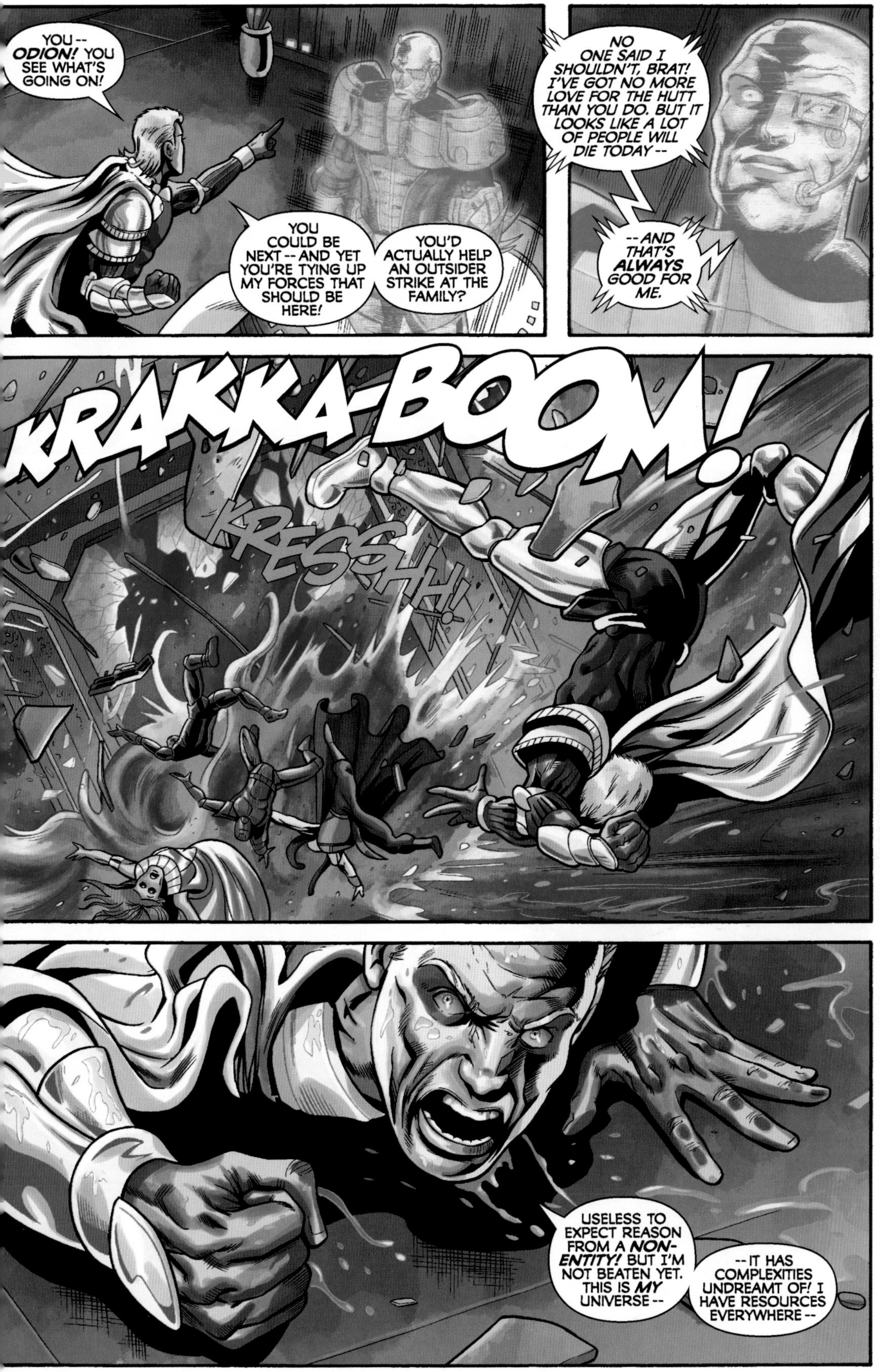
YOU -- ODION! YOU SEE WHAT'S GOING ON!
YOU COULD BE NEXT -- AND YET YOU'RE TYING UP MY FORCES THAT SHOULD BE HERE!
YOU'D ACTUALLY HELP AN OUTSIDER STRIKE AT THE FAMILY?
NO ONE SAID I SHOULDN'T, BRAT! I'VE GOT NO MORE LOVE FOR THE HUTT THAN YOU DO. BUT IT LOOKS LIKE A LOT OF PEOPLE WILL DIE TODAY --
-- AND THAT'S ALWAYS GOOD FOR ME.
KRAKKA-BOOM!
KRESSHH!
USELESS TO EXPECT REASON FROM A NON-ENTITY! BUT I'M NOT BEATEN YET. THIS IS MY UNIVERSE --
-- IT HAS COMPLEXITIES UNDREAMT OF! I HAVE RESOURCES EVERYWHERE --

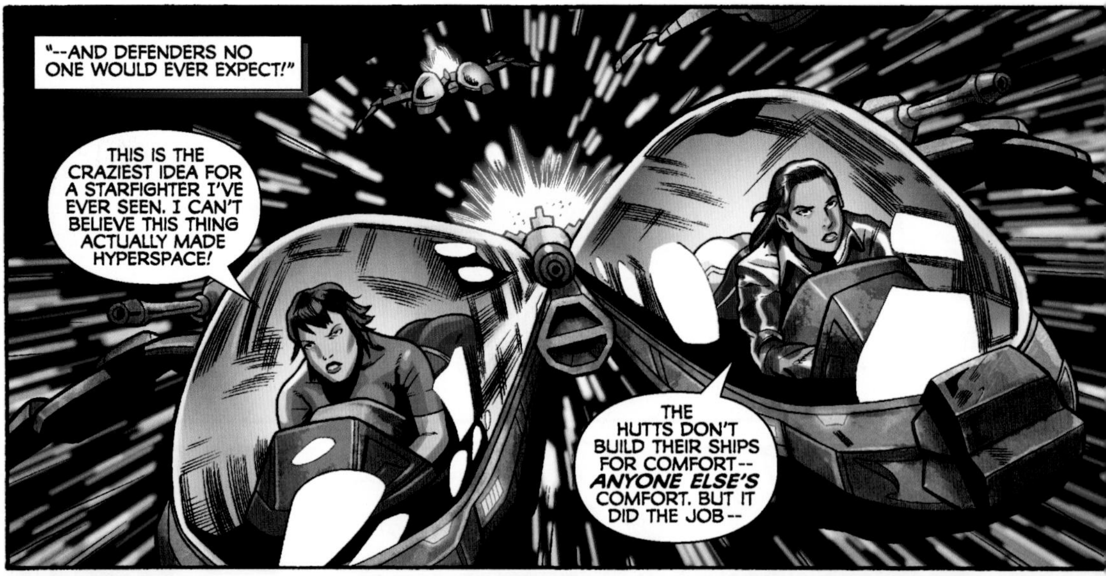
"--AND DEFENDERS NO ONE WOULD EVER EXPECT!"
THIS IS THE CRAZIEST IDEA FOR A STARFIGHTER I'VE EVER SEEN. I CAN'T BELIEVE THIS THING ACTUALLY MADE HYPERSPACE!
THE HUTTS DON'T BUILD THEIR SHIPS FOR COMFORT-- *ANYONE ELSE'S* COMFORT. BUT IT DID THE JOB--

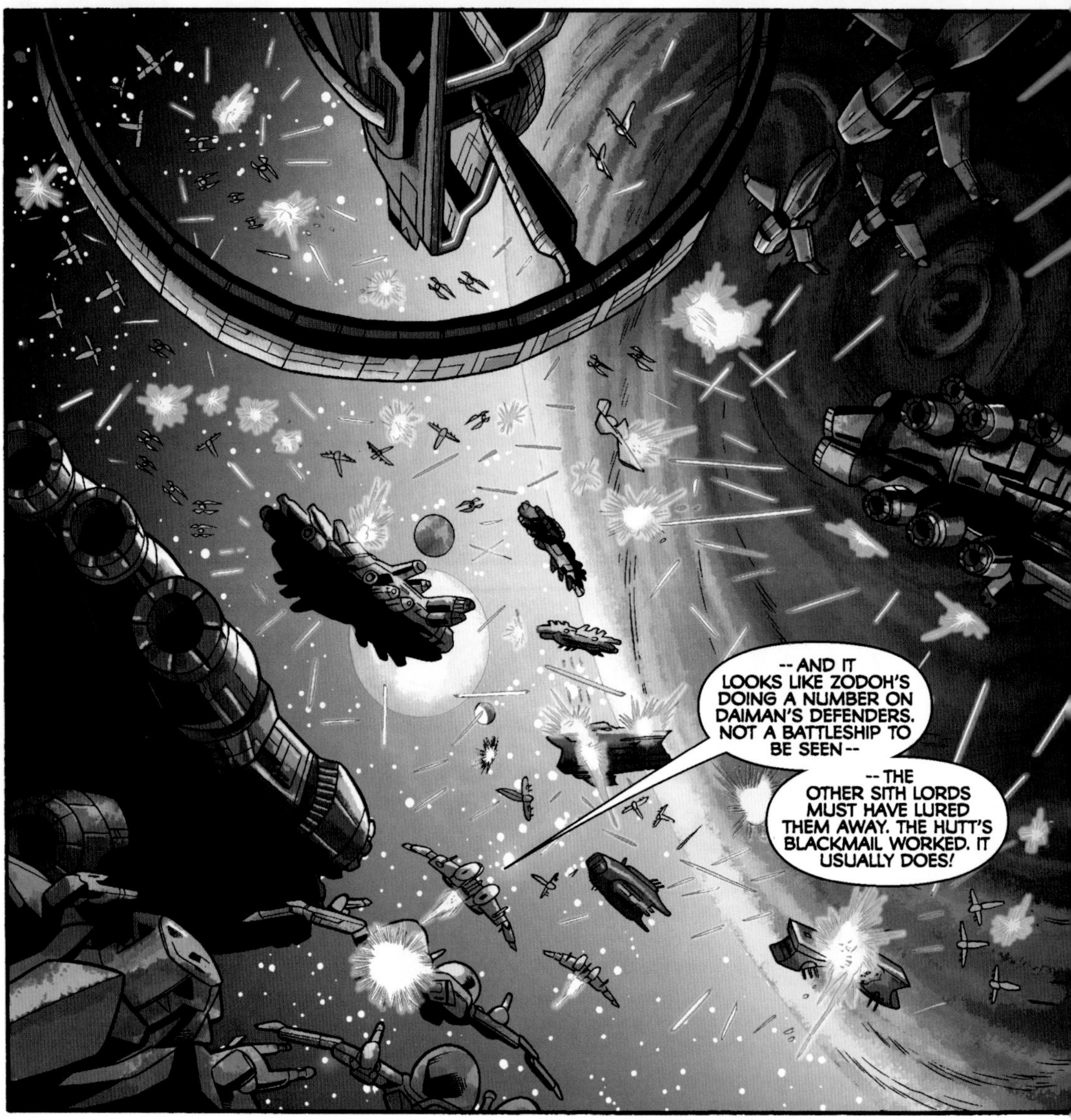
--AND IT LOOKS LIKE ZODOH'S DOING A NUMBER ON DAIMAN'S DEFENDERS. NOT A BATTLESHIP TO BE SEEN--
--THE OTHER SITH LORDS MUST HAVE LURED THEM AWAY. THE HUTT'S BLACKMAIL WORKED. IT USUALLY DOES!

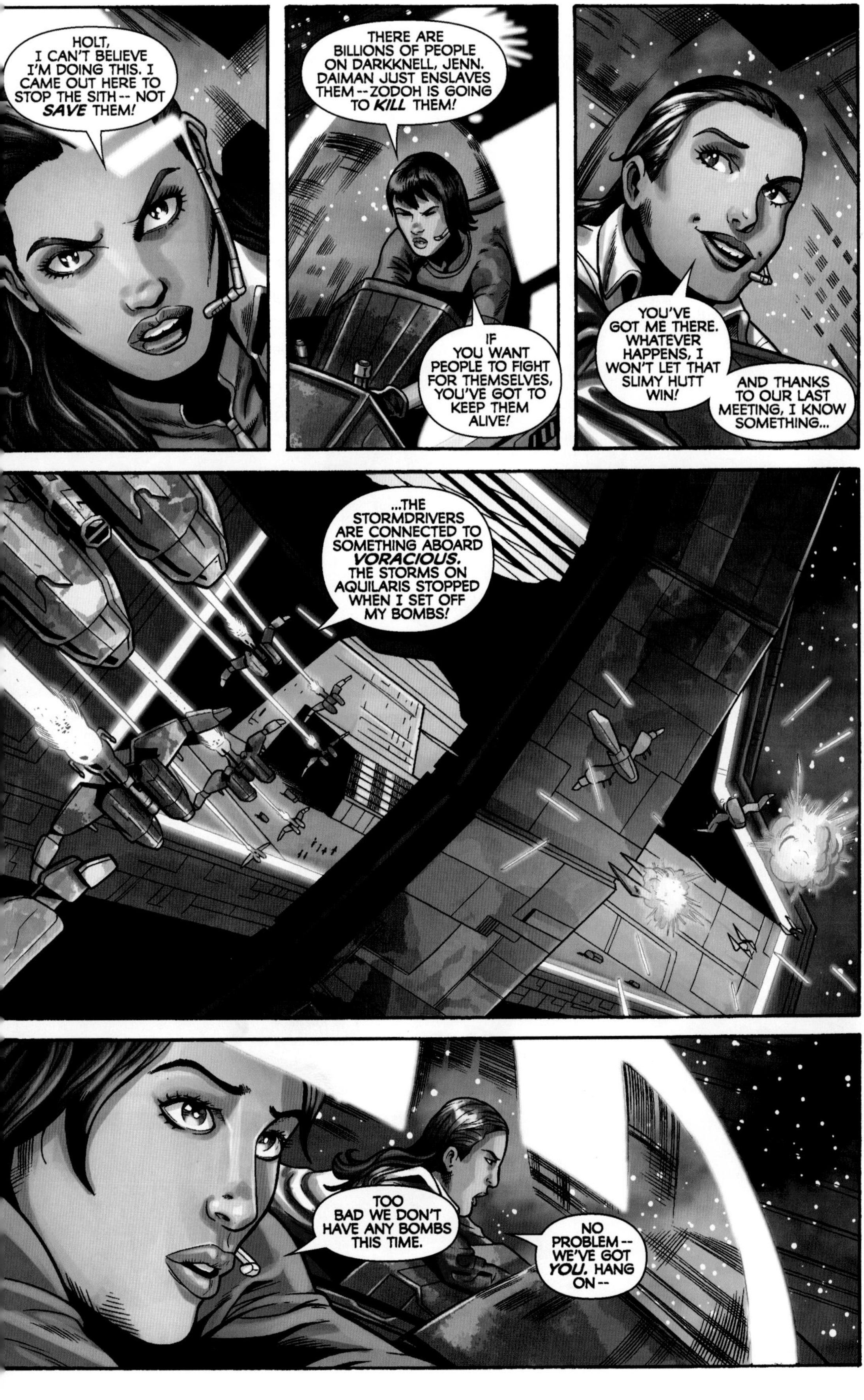
HOLT, I CAN'T BELIEVE I'M DOING THIS. I CAME OUT HERE TO STOP THE SITH -- NOT *SAVE* THEM!
THERE ARE BILLIONS OF PEOPLE ON DARKKNELL, JENN. DAIMAN JUST ENSLAVES THEM -- ZODOH IS GOING TO *KILL* THEM!
IF YOU WANT PEOPLE TO FIGHT FOR THEMSELVES, YOU'VE GOT TO KEEP THEM ALIVE!
YOU'VE GOT ME THERE. WHATEVER HAPPENS, I WON'T LET THAT SLIMY HUTT WIN!
AND THANKS TO OUR LAST MEETING, I KNOW SOMETHING...
...THE STORMDRIVERS ARE CONNECTED TO SOMETHING ABOARD *VORACIOUS.* THE STORMS ON AQUILARIS STOPPED WHEN I SET OFF MY BOMBS!
TOO BAD WE DON'T HAVE ANY BOMBS THIS TIME.
NO PROBLEM -- WE'VE GOT *YOU.* HANG ON --

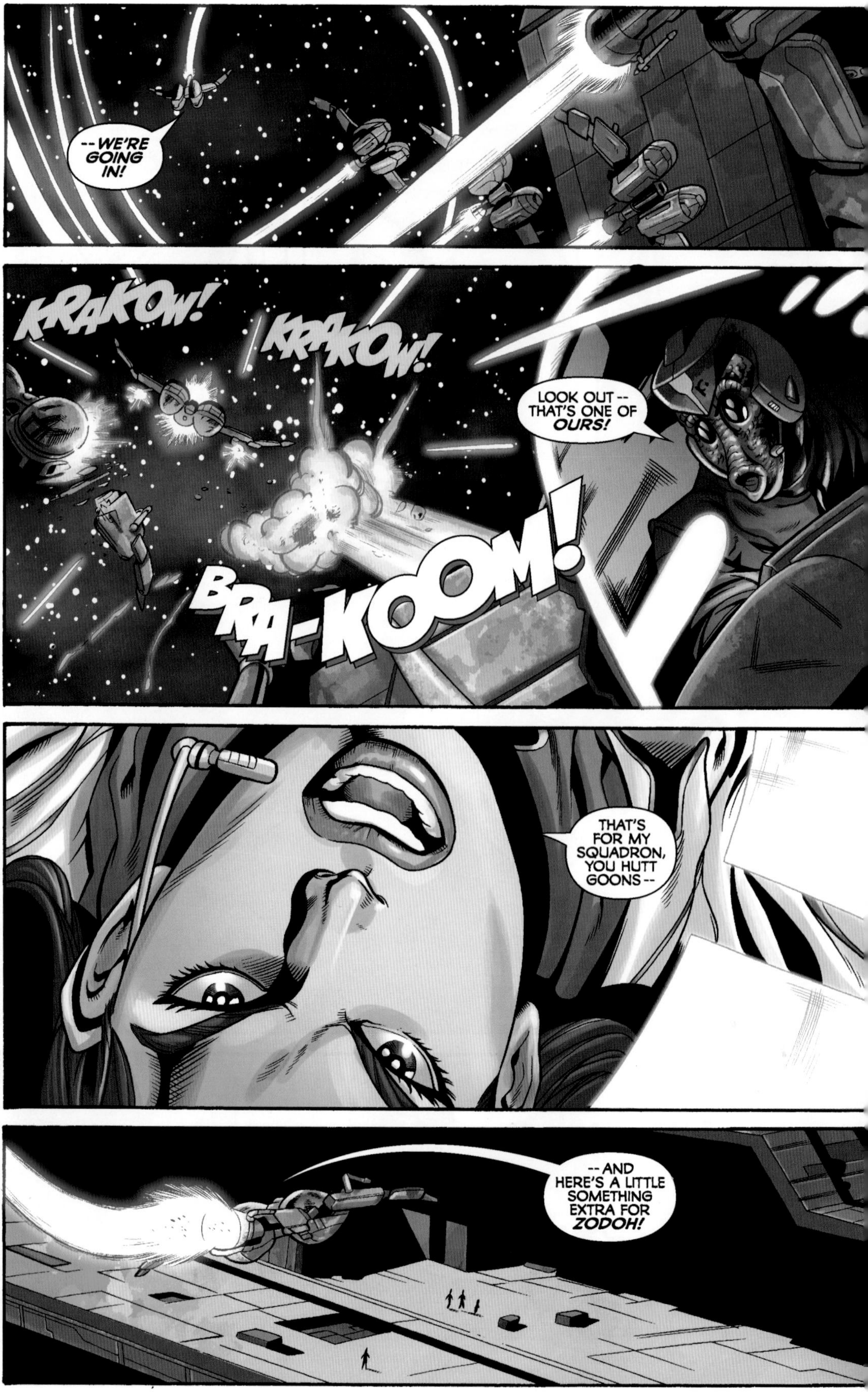
--WE'RE GOING IN!
KRAKOW!
KRAKOW!
LOOK OUT -- THAT'S ONE OF OURS!
BRA-KOOM!
THAT'S FOR MY SQUADRON, YOU HUTT GOONS--
--AND HERE'S A LITTLE SOMETHING EXTRA FOR ZODOH!

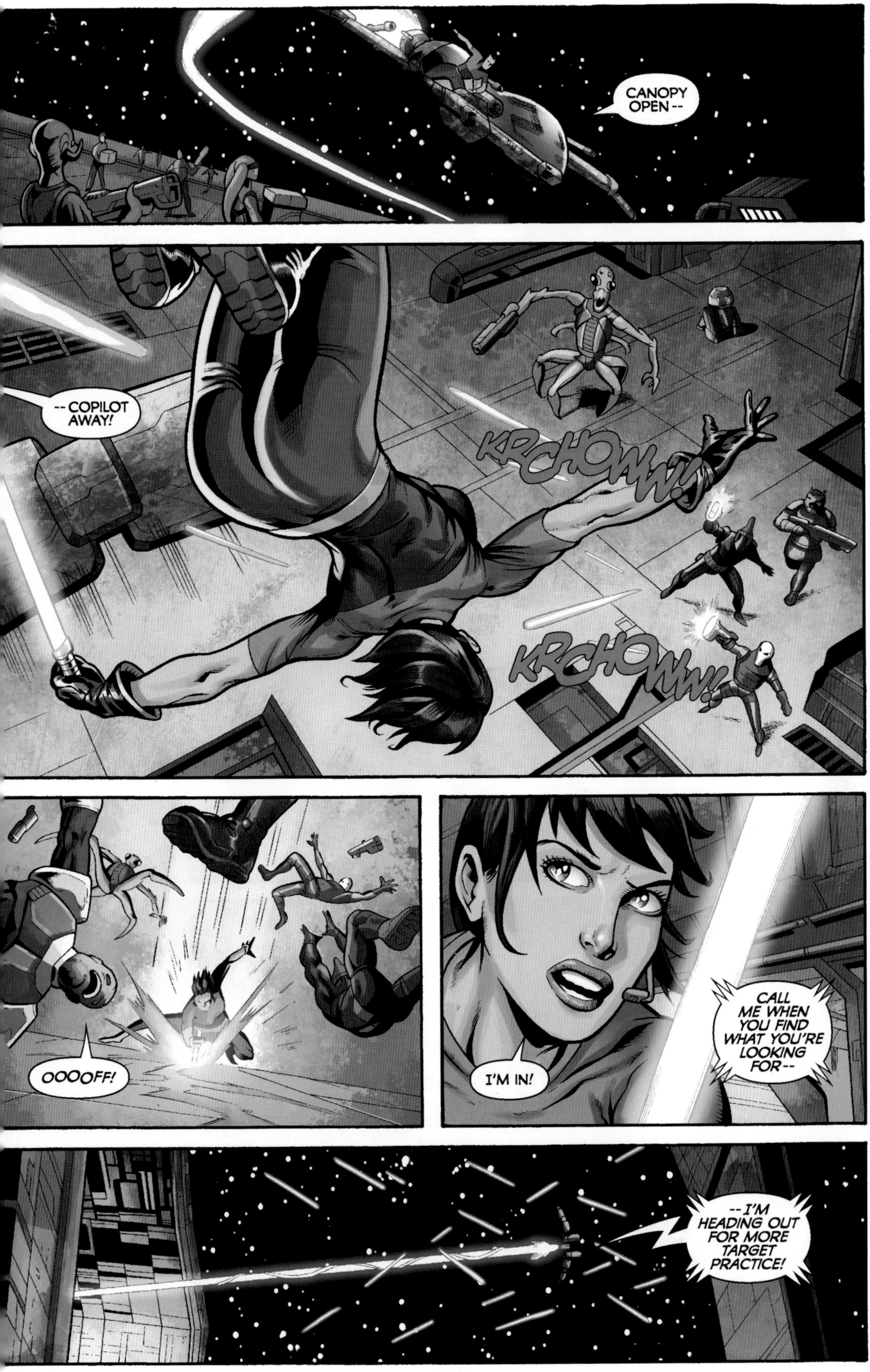
CANOPY OPEN --
-- COPILOT AWAY!
KRCHOWW!
KRCHOWW!
OOOOFF!
I'M IN!
CALL ME WHEN YOU FIND WHAT YOU'RE LOOKING FOR--
-- I'M HEADING OUT FOR MORE TARGET PRACTICE!

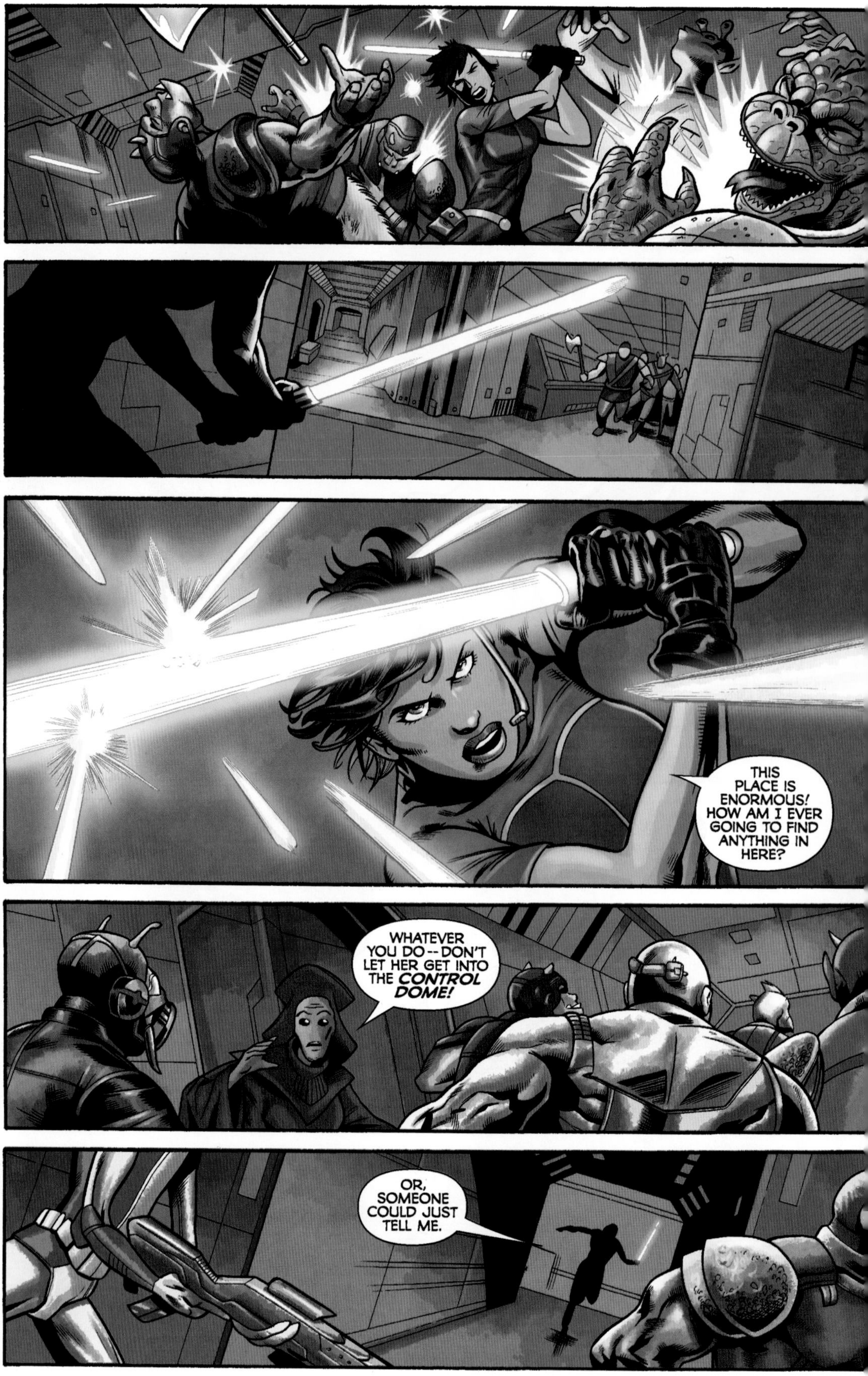
THIS PLACE IS ENORMOUS! HOW AM I EVER GOING TO FIND ANYTHING IN HERE?
WHATEVER YOU DO--DON'T LET HER GET INTO THE *CONTROL DOME!*
OR, SOMEONE COULD JUST TELL ME.

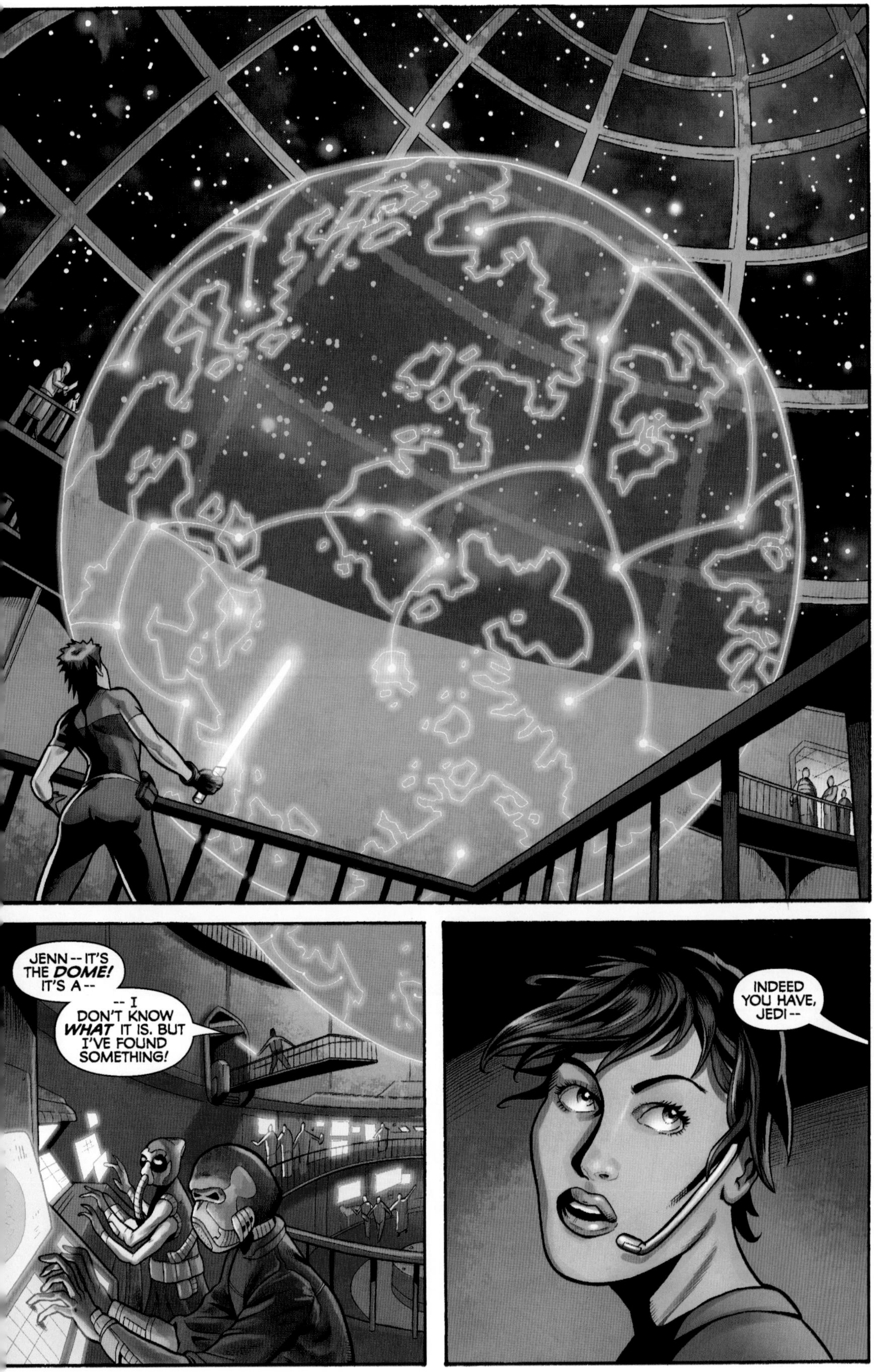

JENN -- IT'S THE **DOME!** IT'S A --
-- I DON'T KNOW ***WHAT*** IT IS. BUT I'VE FOUND SOMETHING!
INDEED YOU HAVE, JEDI --

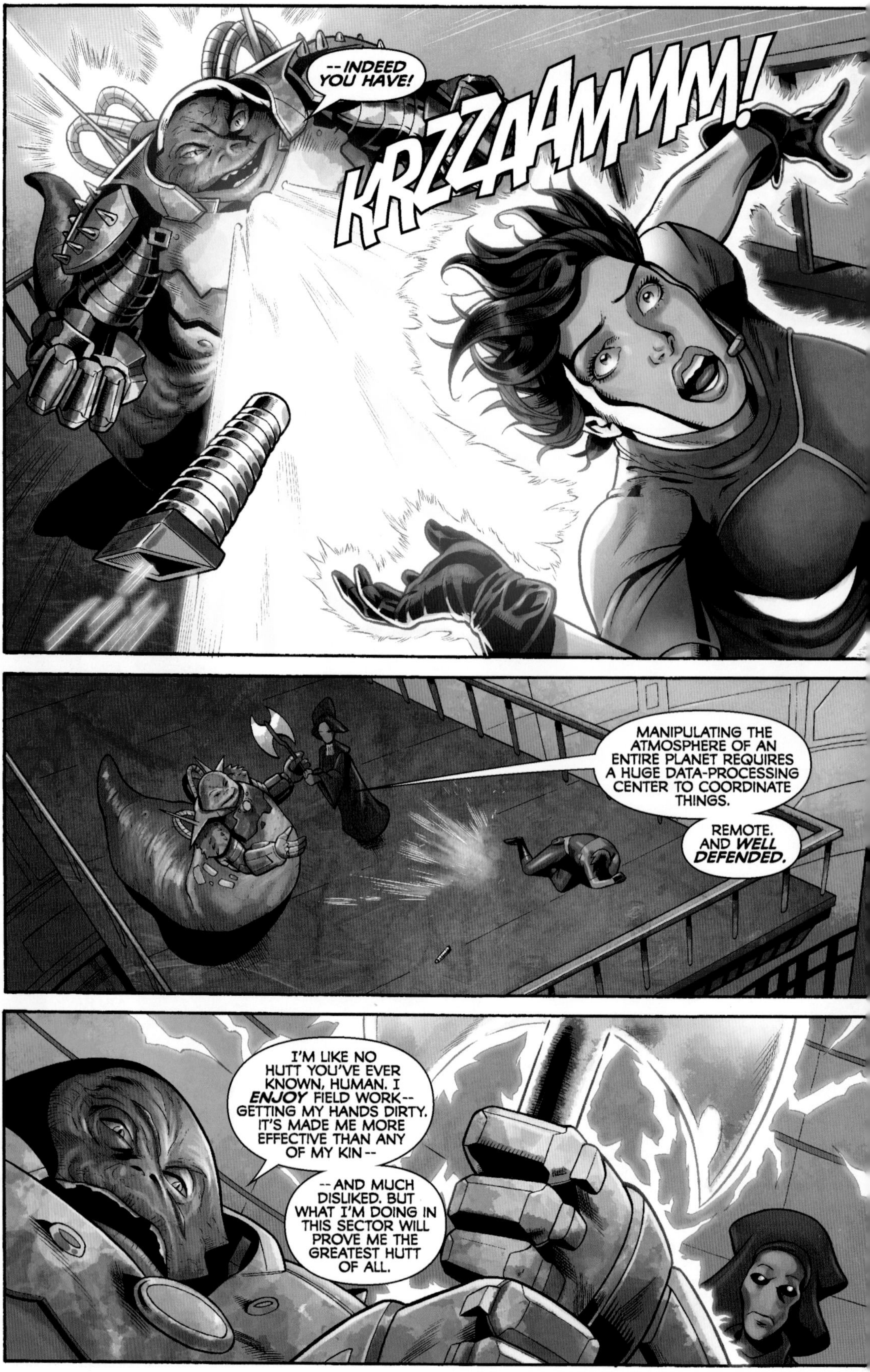
--INDEED YOU HAVE!
KRZZAAMMM!
MANIPULATING THE ATMOSPHERE OF AN ENTIRE PLANET REQUIRES A HUGE DATA-PROCESSING CENTER TO COORDINATE THINGS.
REMOTE. AND WELL DEFENDED.
I'M LIKE NO HUTT YOU'VE EVER KNOWN, HUMAN. I ENJOY FIELD WORK-- GETTING MY HANDS DIRTY. IT'S MADE ME MORE EFFECTIVE THAN ANY OF MY KIN--
--AND MUCH DISLIKED. BUT WHAT I'M DOING IN THIS SECTOR WILL PROVE ME THE GREATEST HUTT OF ALL.

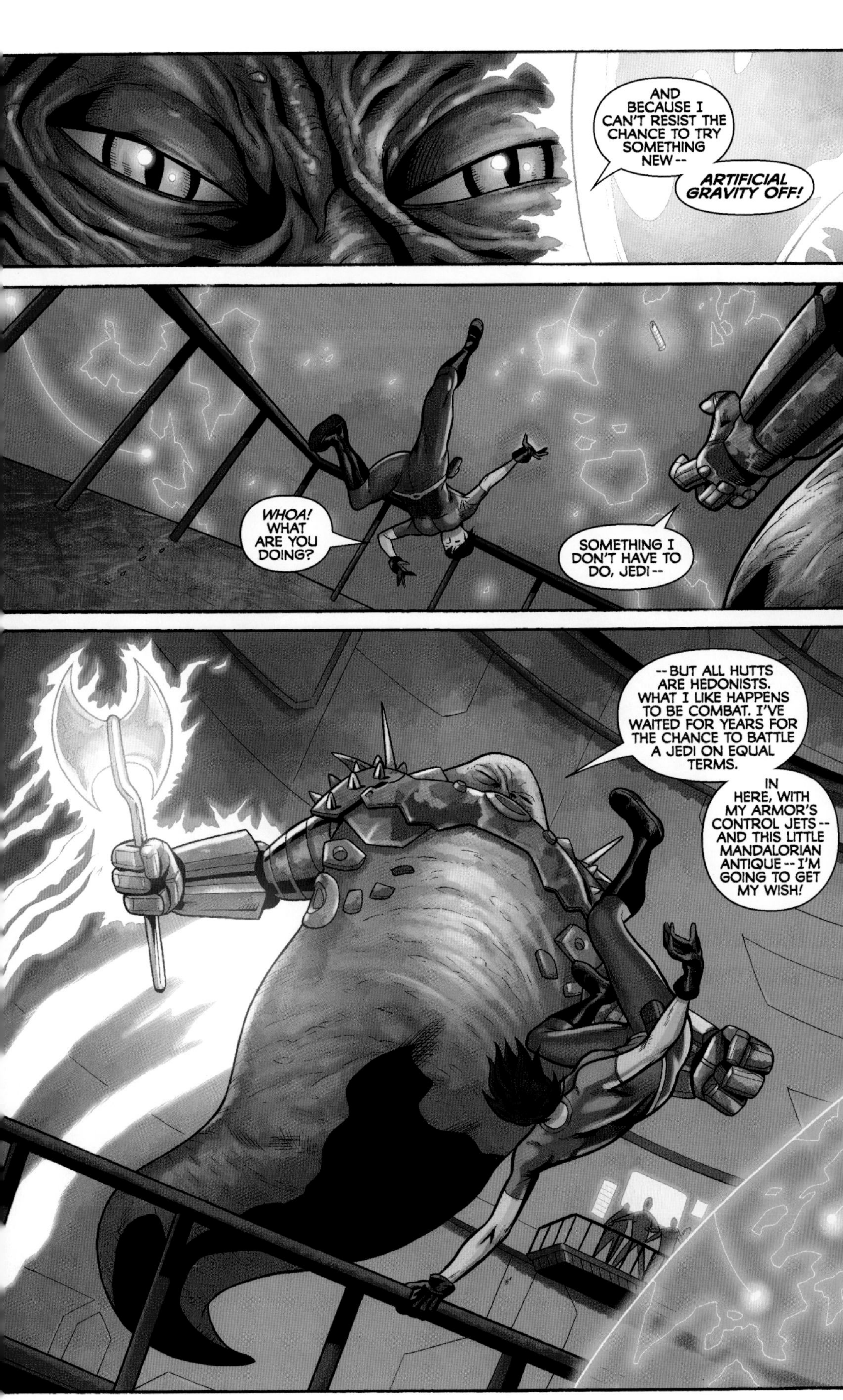
AND BECAUSE I CAN'T RESIST THE CHANCE TO TRY SOMETHING NEW--
ARTIFICIAL GRAVITY OFF!
WHOA! WHAT ARE YOU DOING?
SOMETHING I DON'T HAVE TO DO, JEDI--
--BUT ALL HUTTS ARE HEDONISTS. WHAT I LIKE HAPPENS TO BE COMBAT. I'VE WAITED FOR YEARS FOR THE CHANCE TO BATTLE A JEDI ON EQUAL TERMS.
IN HERE, WITH MY ARMOR'S CONTROL JETS-- AND THIS LITTLE MANDALORIAN ANTIQUE--I'M GOING TO GET MY WISH!

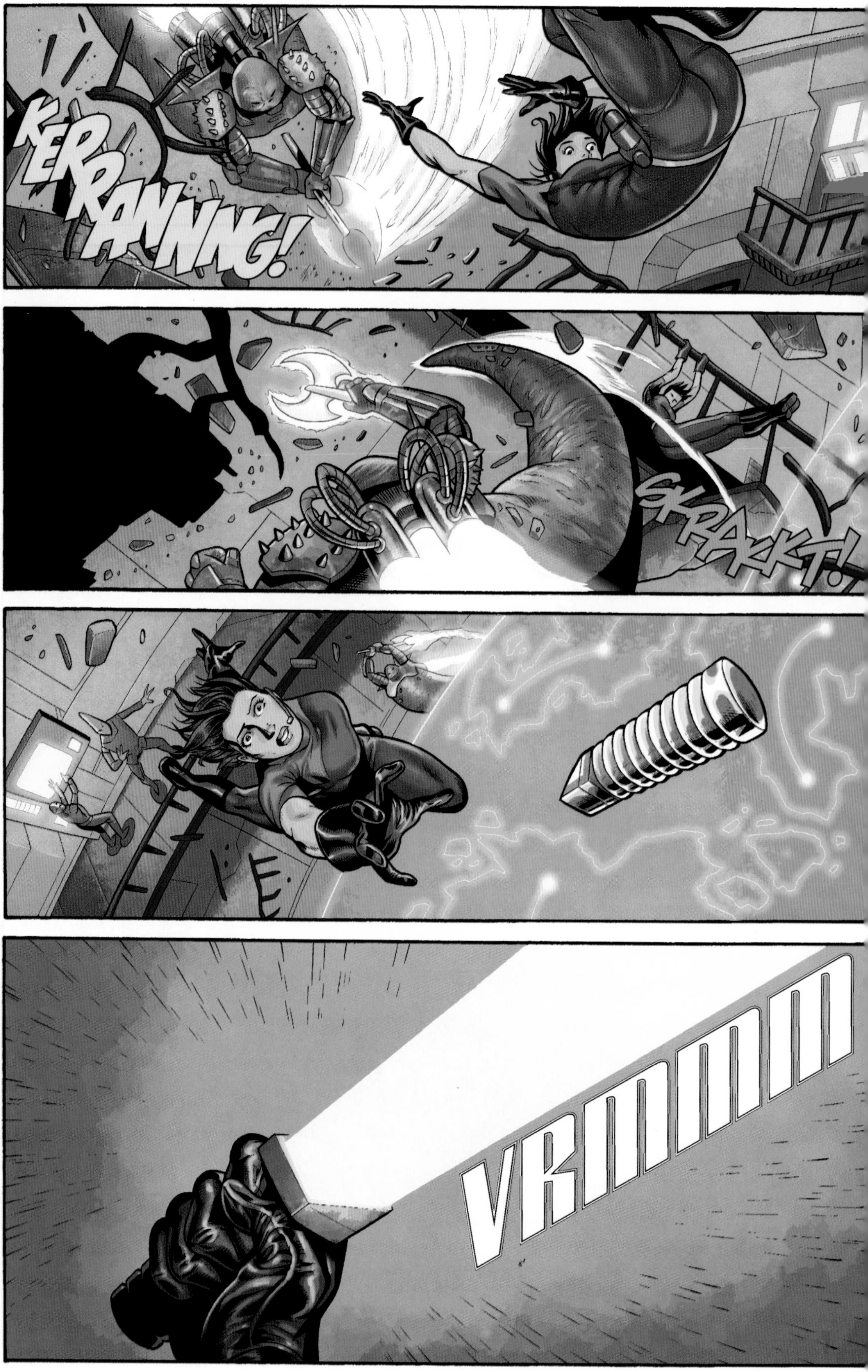
KERRANNNG!
SKRAKT!
VRMMM

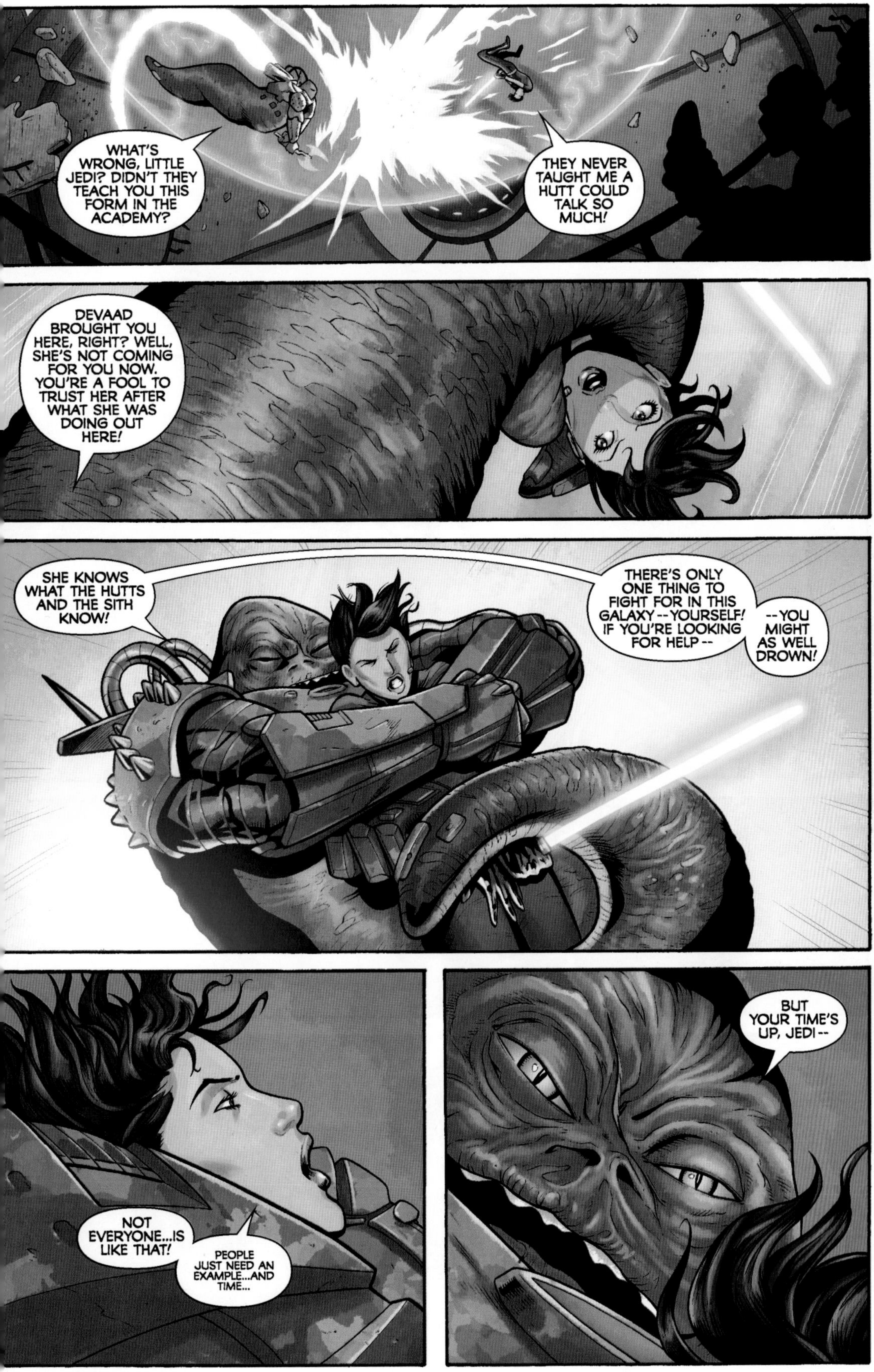
WHAT'S WRONG, LITTLE JEDI? DIDN'T THEY TEACH YOU THIS FORM IN THE ACADEMY?
THEY NEVER TAUGHT ME A HUTT COULD TALK SO MUCH!
DEVAAD BROUGHT YOU HERE, RIGHT? WELL, SHE'S NOT COMING FOR YOU NOW. YOU'RE A FOOL TO TRUST HER AFTER WHAT SHE WAS DOING OUT HERE!
SHE KNOWS WHAT THE HUTTS AND THE SITH KNOW!
THERE'S ONLY ONE THING TO FIGHT FOR IN THIS GALAXY--YOURSELF! IF YOU'RE LOOKING FOR HELP--
--YOU MIGHT AS WELL DROWN!
NOT EVERYONE...IS LIKE THAT!
PEOPLE JUST NEED AN EXAMPLE...AND TIME...
BUT YOUR TIME'S UP, JEDI--

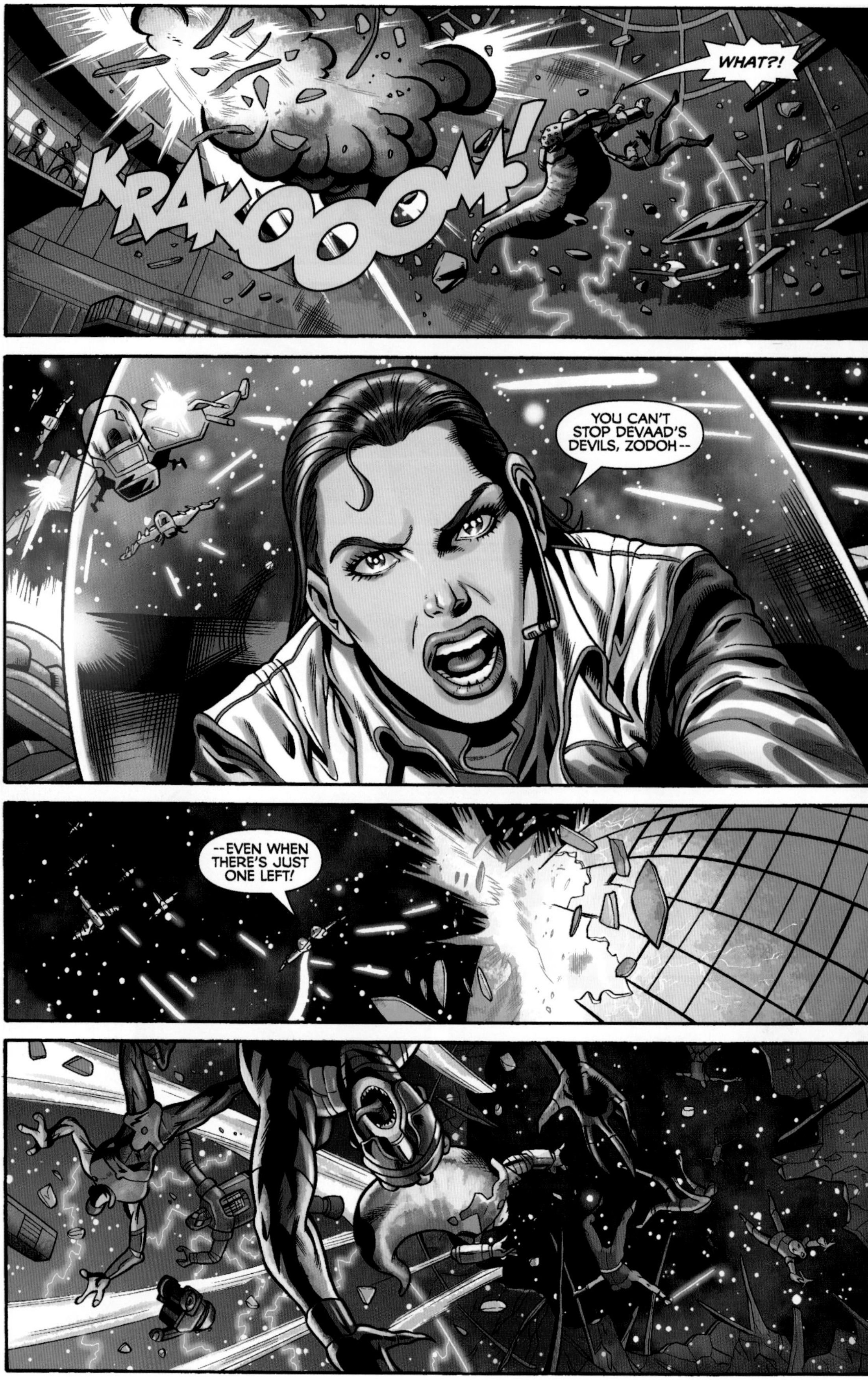
WHAT?!
KRAKOOOM!
YOU CAN'T STOP DEVAAD'S DEVILS, ZODOH--
--EVEN WHEN THERE'S JUST ONE LEFT!

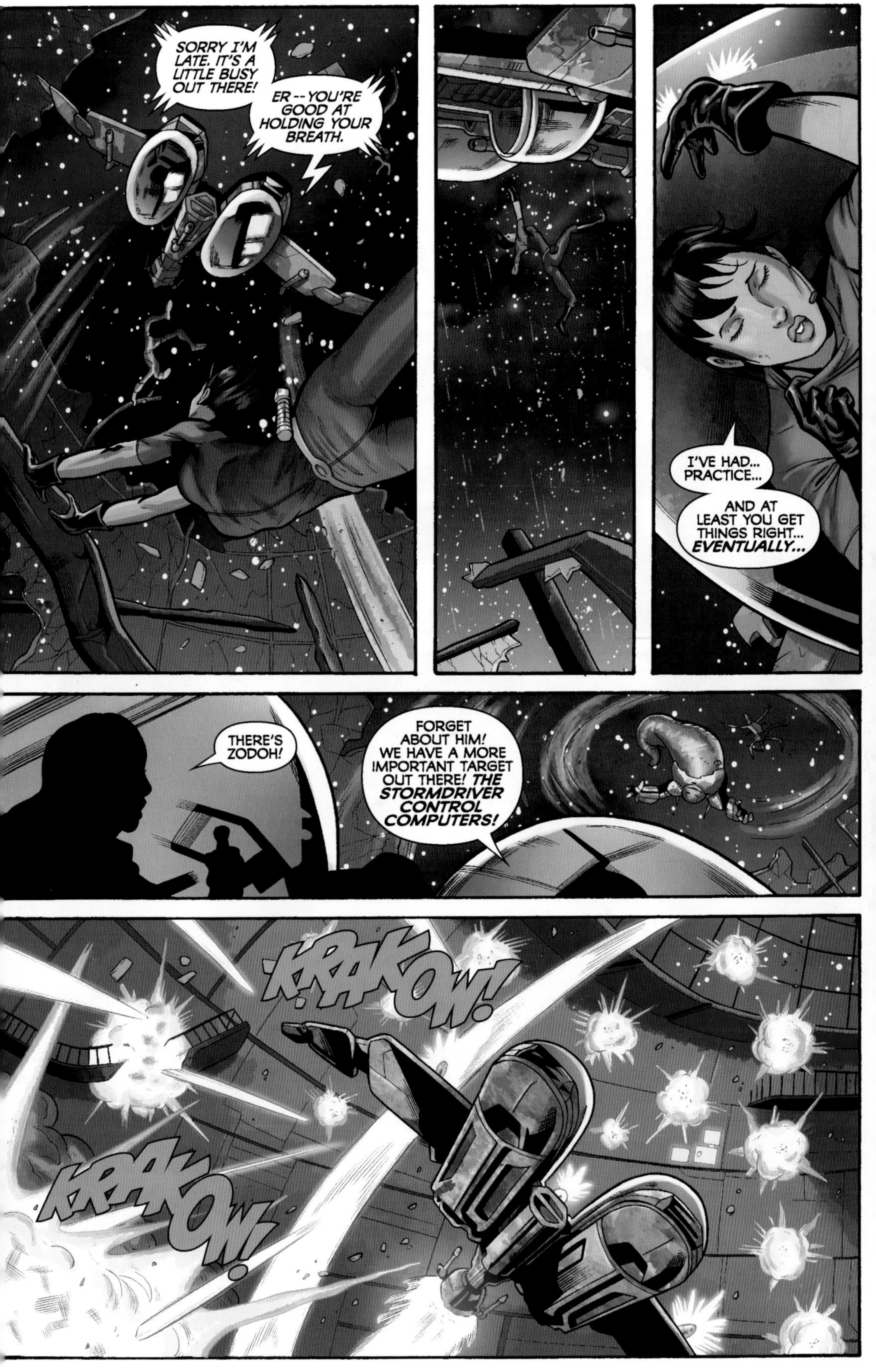
SORRY I'M LATE. IT'S A LITTLE BUSY OUT THERE!
ER -- YOU'RE GOOD AT HOLDING YOUR BREATH.
I'VE HAD... PRACTICE...
AND AT LEAST YOU GET THINGS RIGHT... EVENTUALLY...
THERE'S ZODOH!
FORGET ABOUT HIM! WE HAVE A MORE IMPORTANT TARGET OUT THERE! THE STORMDRIVER CONTROL COMPUTERS!
KRAKOW!
KRAKOW!

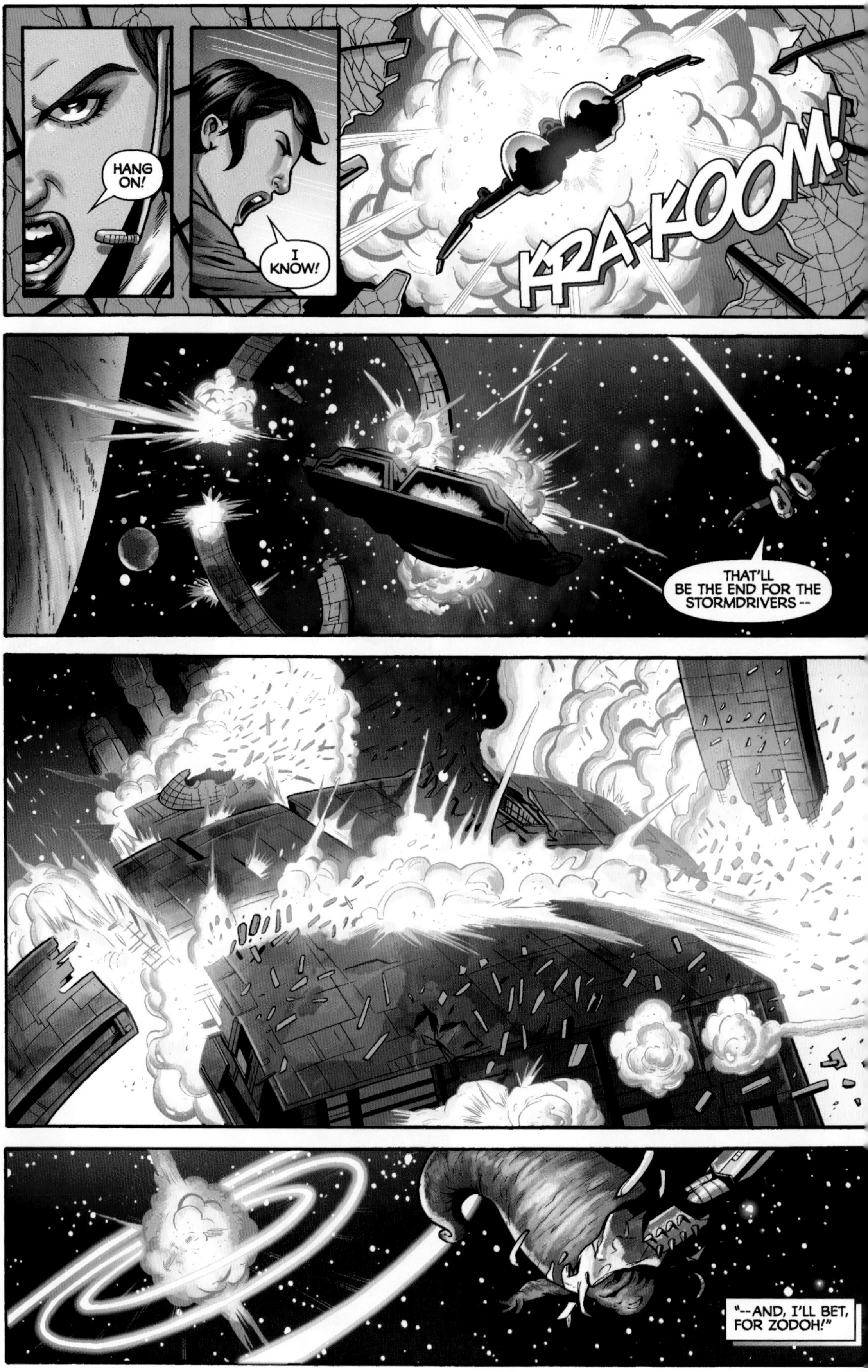
HANG ON!
I KNOW!
KRA-KOOM!
THAT'LL BE THE END FOR THE STORMDRIVERS --
"--AND, I'LL BET, FOR ZODOH!"

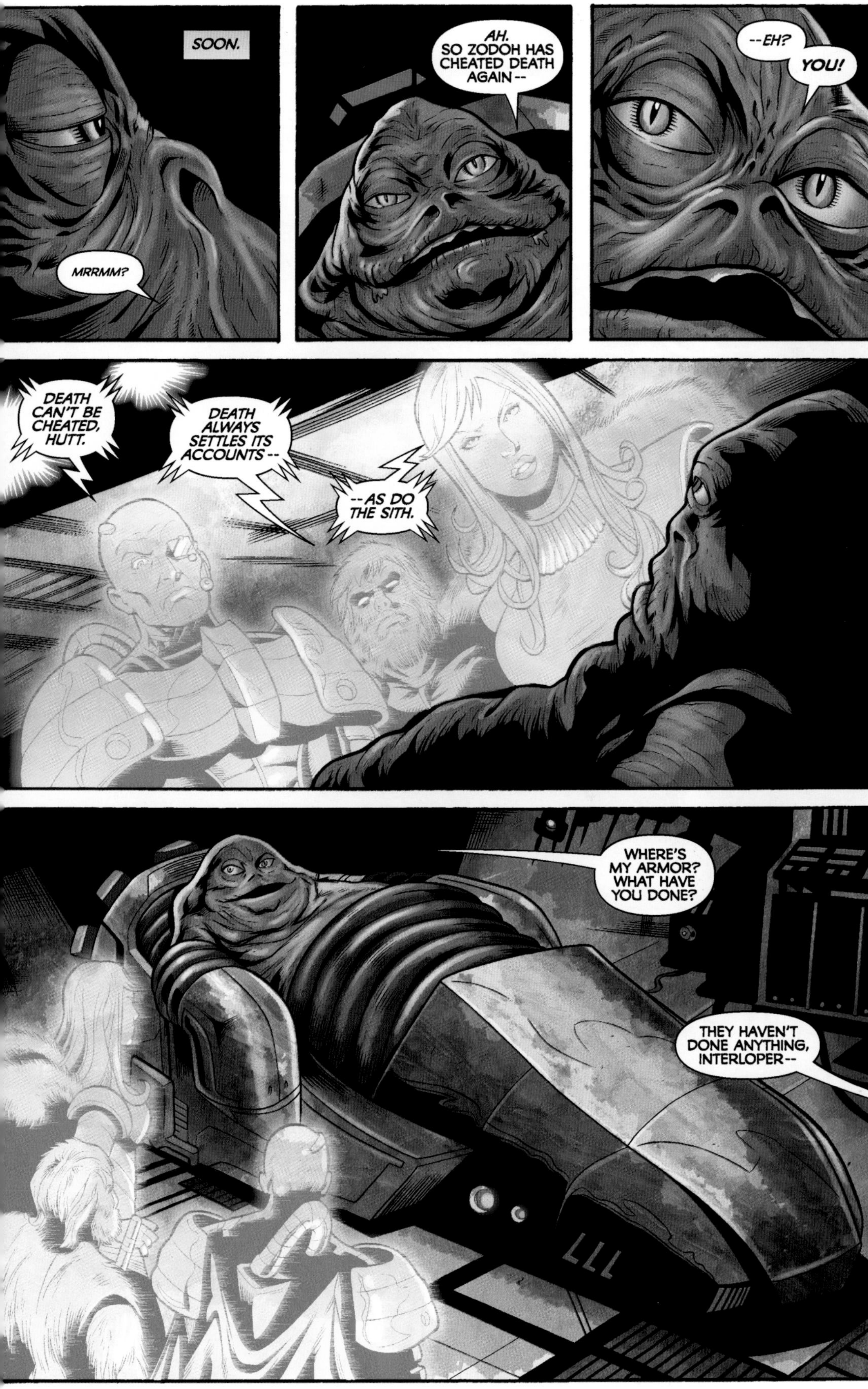
SOON.
MRRMM?
AH. SO ZODOH HAS CHEATED DEATH AGAIN--
--EH?
YOU!
DEATH CAN'T BE CHEATED, HUTT.
DEATH ALWAYS SETTLES ITS ACCOUNTS--
--AS DO THE SITH.
WHERE'S MY ARMOR? WHAT HAVE YOU DONE?
THEY HAVEN'T DONE ANYTHING, INTERLOPER--

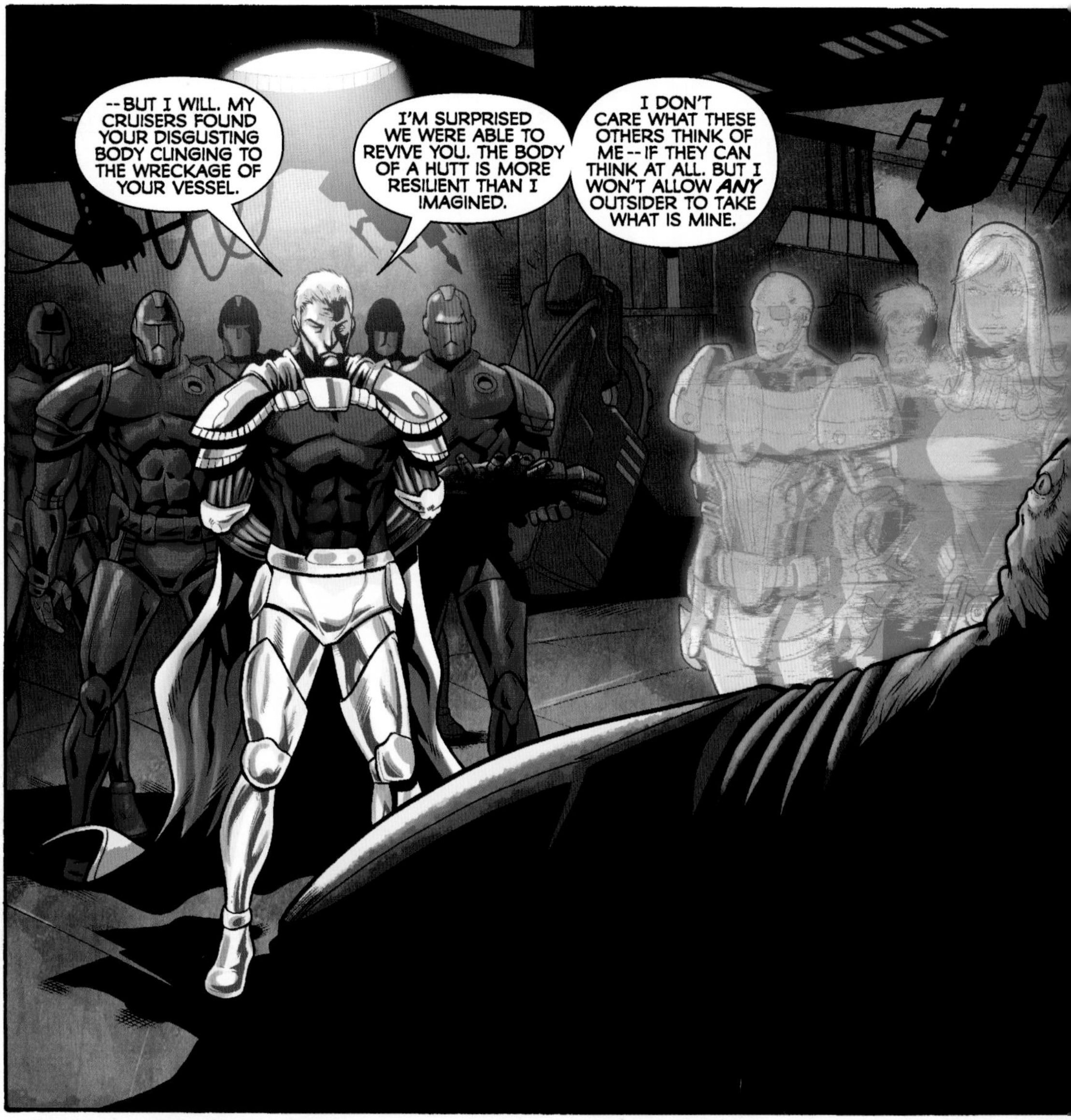
--BUT I WILL. MY CRUISERS FOUND YOUR DISGUSTING BODY CLINGING TO THE WRECKAGE OF YOUR VESSEL.
I'M SURPRISED WE WERE ABLE TO REVIVE YOU. THE BODY OF A HUTT IS MORE RESILIENT THAN I IMAGINED.
I DON'T CARE WHAT THESE OTHERS THINK OF ME--IF THEY CAN THINK AT ALL. BUT I WON'T ALLOW *ANY* OUTSIDER TO TAKE WHAT IS MINE.

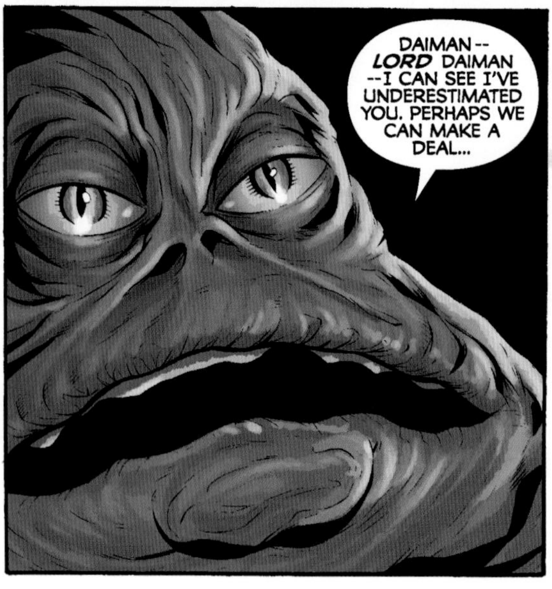
DAIMAN--*LORD* DAIMAN--I CAN SEE I'VE UNDERESTIMATED YOU. PERHAPS WE CAN MAKE A DEAL...

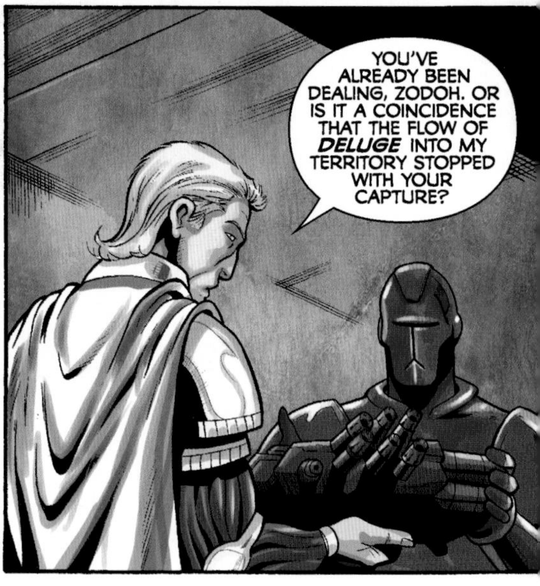
YOU'VE ALREADY BEEN DEALING, ZODOH. OR IS IT A COINCIDENCE THAT THE FLOW OF *DELUGE* INTO MY TERRITORY STOPPED WITH YOUR CAPTURE?

THAT -- THAT WASN'T ME, MY LORD! THAT WAS --

I'VE BEEN STUDYING THEM.

ON A PLANETARY SCALE, YOUR TECHNOLOGY IS IMPRACTICAL, FLAWED BY THE NEED FOR A MASSIVE DATA PROCESSOR --

SAVE IT. I'M NOT IMPRESSED BY YOUR WARES, MERCHANT -- NOR EVEN YOUR VAUNTED *STORMDRIVERS*.

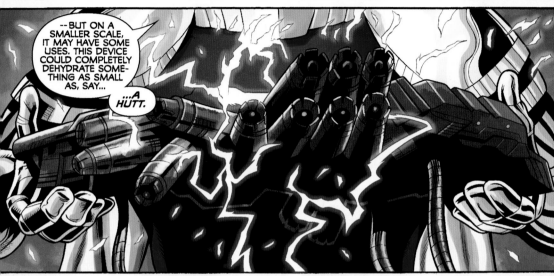

-- BUT ON A SMALLER SCALE, IT MAY HAVE SOME USES. THIS DEVICE COULD COMPLETELY DEHYDRATE SOME-THING AS SMALL AS, SAY...

*...A HUTT.*

W-WHAT?

OH, I KNOW. THERE'S NOTHING SMALL ABOUT A HUTT -- OR PRETTY. EVEN A PERFECT CREATOR CAN MAKE MISTAKES.

BUT I ALWAYS TAKE CARE OF MY MISTAKES.

TAKE CARE OF MY CAPE. THIS COULD GET MESSY.

NNNOOOOO!!!!!

AQUILARIS.

KERRA, I CAN'T BELIEVE DAIMAN'S PEOPLE DIDN'T FOLLOW YOU HERE!

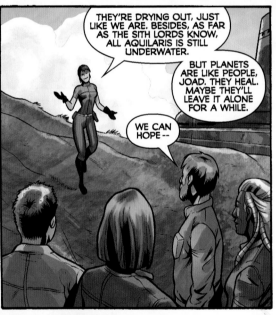

THEY'RE DRYING OUT, JUST LIKE WE ARE. BESIDES, AS FAR AS THE SITH LORDS KNOW, ALL AQUILARIS IS STILL UNDERWATER.

BUT PLANETS ARE LIKE PEOPLE, JOAD. THEY HEAL. MAYBE THEY'LL LEAVE IT ALONE FOR A WHILE.

WE CAN HOPE --

-- AND IF NOT, THE OLD UNDERWATER HARVESTING FACILITIES LOOK SALVAGEABLE. IT HELPS TO HAVE SOMEONE WHO KNOWS HIS WAY AROUND!

YOU CALLIN' ME OLD, KID?

YOU LOOK -- MORE LIKE I REMEMBER, JOAD.

I *FEEL* LIKE I REMEMBER. IT'S GOOD TO *WANT* SOMETHING AGAIN.

NICE FOR ALL OF US TO HAVE A REASON TO GET UP IN THE MORNING.

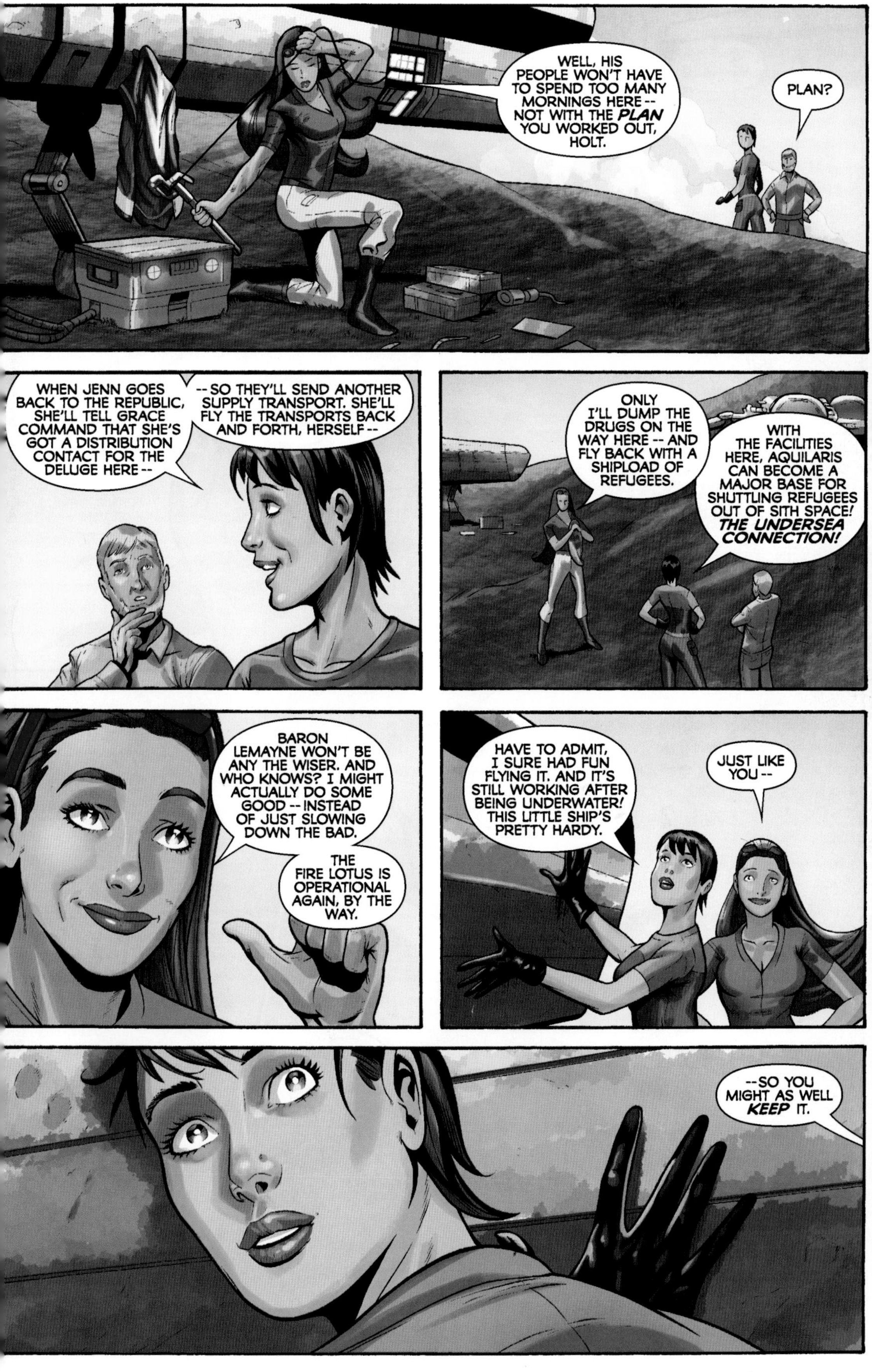

WELL, HIS PEOPLE WON'T HAVE TO SPEND TOO MANY MORNINGS HERE -- NOT WITH THE *PLAN* YOU WORKED OUT, HOLT.
PLAN?
WHEN JENN GOES BACK TO THE REPUBLIC, SHE'LL TELL GRACE COMMAND THAT SHE'S GOT A DISTRIBUTION CONTACT FOR THE DELUGE HERE --
-- SO THEY'LL SEND ANOTHER SUPPLY TRANSPORT. SHE'LL FLY THE TRANSPORTS BACK AND FORTH, HERSELF --
ONLY I'LL DUMP THE DRUGS ON THE WAY HERE -- AND FLY BACK WITH A SHIPLOAD OF REFUGEES.
WITH THE FACILITIES HERE, AQUILARIS CAN BECOME A MAJOR BASE FOR SHUTTLING REFUGEES OUT OF SITH SPACE! ***THE UNDERSEA CONNECTION!***
BARON LEMAYNE WON'T BE ANY THE WISER. AND WHO KNOWS? I MIGHT ACTUALLY DO SOME GOOD -- INSTEAD OF JUST SLOWING DOWN THE BAD.
THE FIRE LOTUS IS OPERATIONAL AGAIN, BY THE WAY.
HAVE TO ADMIT, I SURE HAD FUN FLYING IT. AND IT'S STILL WORKING AFTER BEING UNDERWATER! THIS LITTLE SHIP'S PRETTY HARDY.
JUST LIKE YOU --
-- SO YOU MIGHT AS WELL ***KEEP*** IT.

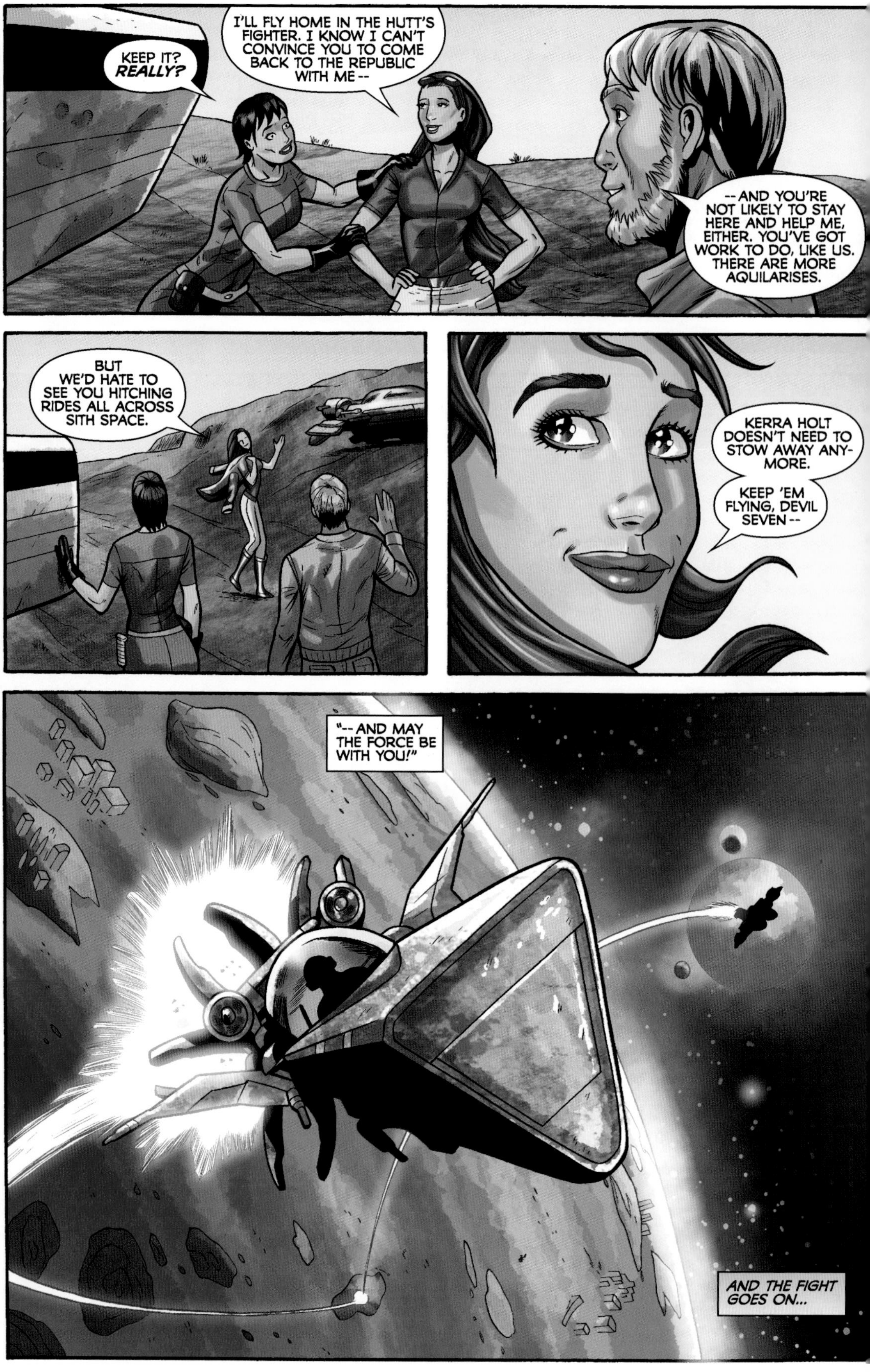
KEEP IT? *REALLY?*
I'LL FLY HOME IN THE HUTT'S FIGHTER. I KNOW I CAN'T CONVINCE YOU TO COME BACK TO THE REPUBLIC WITH ME --
-- AND YOU'RE NOT LIKELY TO STAY HERE AND HELP ME, EITHER. YOU'VE GOT WORK TO DO, LIKE US. THERE ARE MORE AQUILARISES.
BUT WE'D HATE TO SEE YOU HITCHING RIDES ALL ACROSS SITH SPACE.
KERRA HOLT DOESN'T NEED TO STOW AWAY ANY-MORE.
KEEP 'EM FLYING, DEVIL SEVEN --
"-- AND MAY THE FORCE BE WITH YOU!"
*AND THE FIGHT GOES ON...*

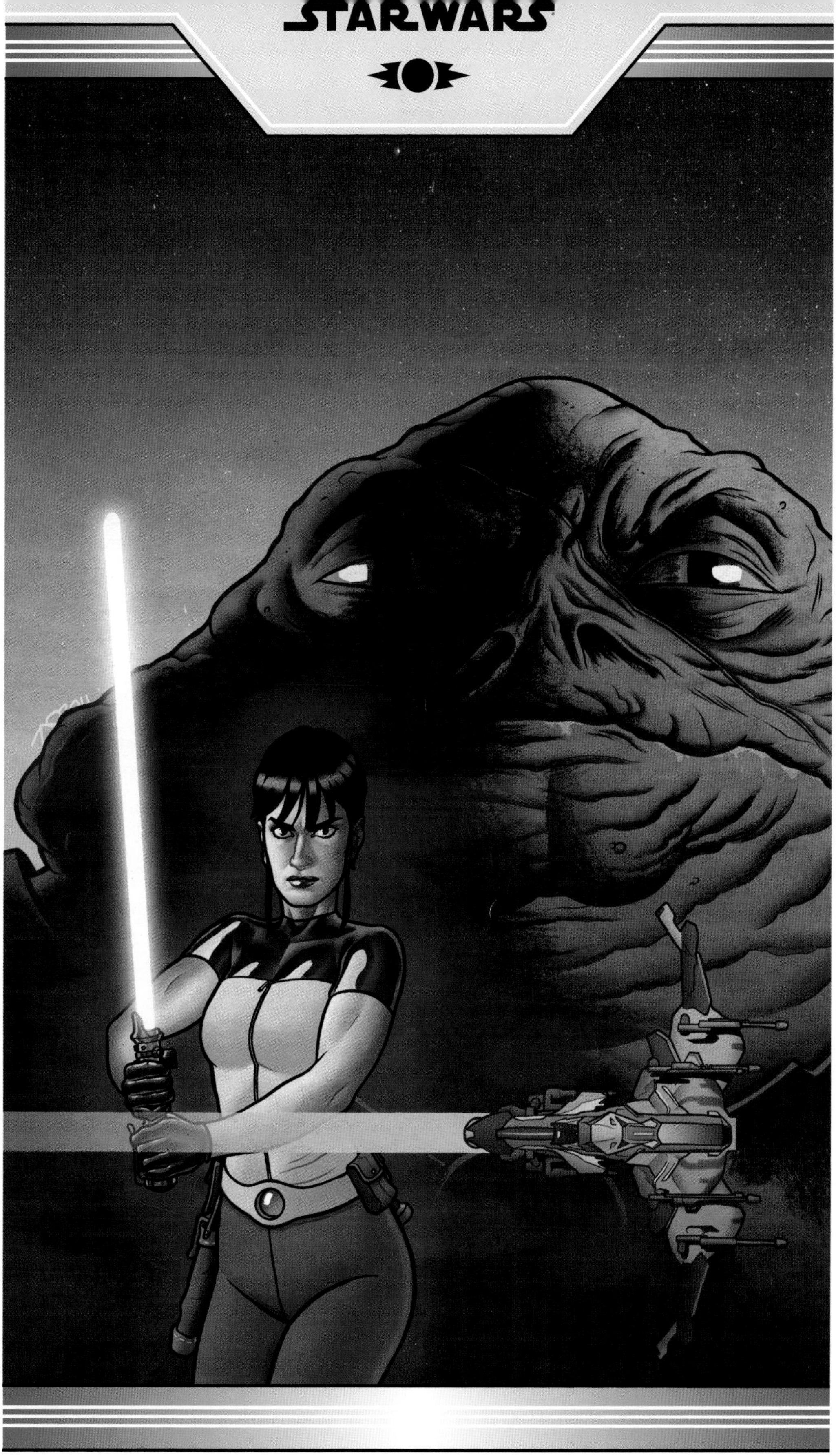
STAR WARS

ILLUSTRATION BY JOE QUINONES

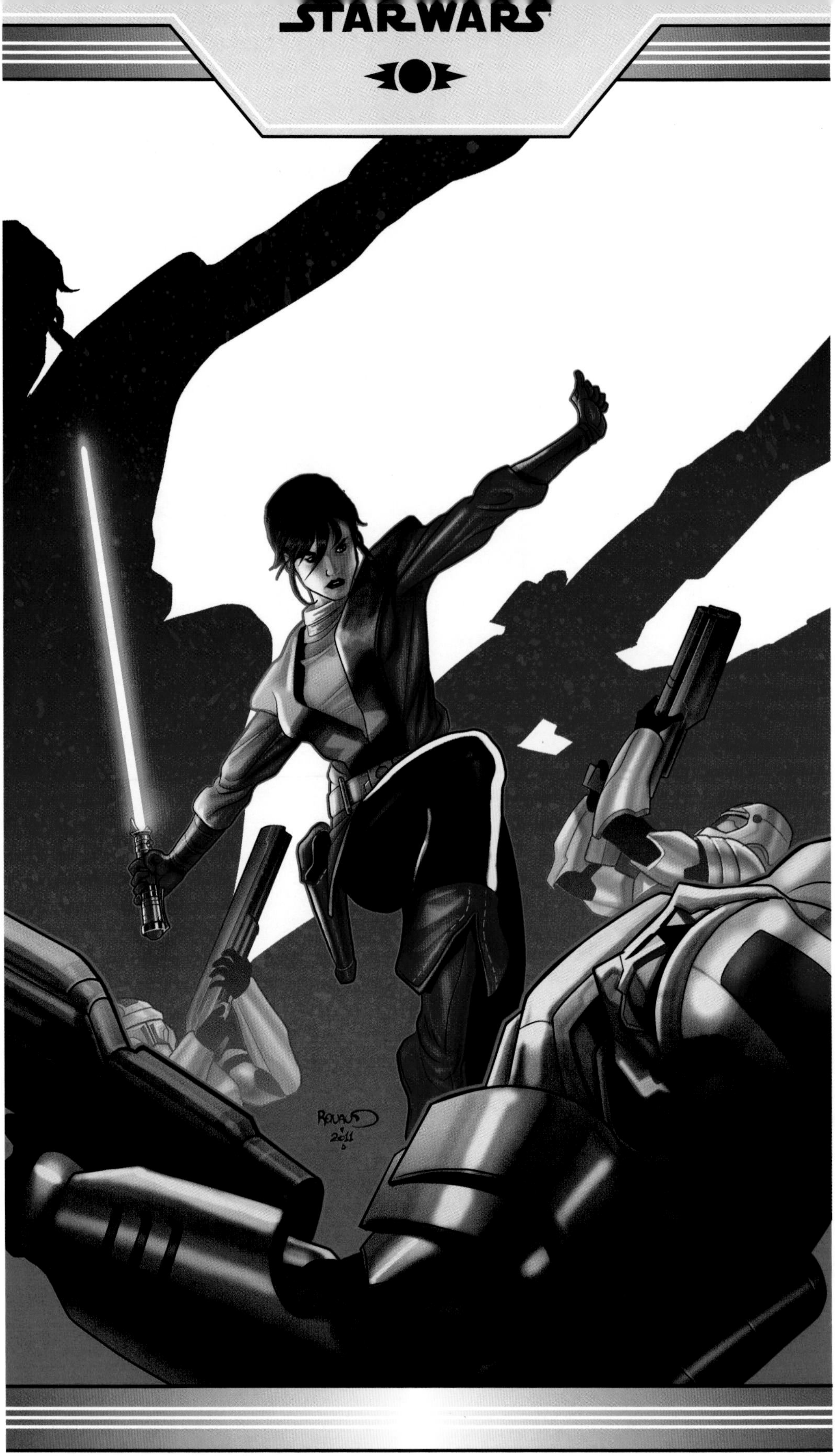

ILLUSTRATION BY PAUL RENAUD

# STAR WARS OMNIBUS COLLECTIONS

STAR WARS
OMNIBUS
TALES OF THE JEDI

## STAR WARS: TALES OF THE JEDI

Including the *Tales of the Jedi* stories "The Golden Age of the Sith," "The Freedon Nadd Uprising," and "Knights of the Old Republic," these huge omnibus editions are the ultimate introduction to the ancient history of the *Star Wars* universe!

**Volume 1 ISBN 978-1-59307-830-0 | $24.99**
**Volume 2 ISBN 978-1-59307-911-6 | $24.99**

STAR WARS
OMNIBUS
RISE OF THE SITH

## STAR WARS: RISE OF THE SITH

Before the name of Skywalker–or Vader–achieved fame across the galaxy, the Jedi Knights had long preserved peace and justice . . . as well as preventing the return of the Sith. These thrilling tales illustrate the events leading up to *The Phantom Menace*.

**ISBN 978-1-59582-228-4 | $24.99**

STAR WARS
OMNIBUS
EMISSARIES & ASSASSINS

## STAR WARS: EMISSARIES AND ASSASSINS

Discover more stories featuring Anakin Skywalker, Amidala, Obi-Wan, and Qui-Gon set during the time of *Episode I: The Phantom Menace* in this mega collection!

**ISBN 978-1-59582-229-1 | $24.99**

STAR WARS
OMNIBUS
MENACE REVEALED

## STAR WARS: MENACE REVEALED

This is our largest omnibus of never-before-collected and out-of-print *Star Wars* stories. Included here are one-shot adventures, short story arcs, specialty issues, and early *Dark Horse Extra* comic strips! All of these tales take place after *Episode I: The Phantom Menace*, and lead up to *Episode II: Attack of the Clones*.

**ISBN 978-1-59582-273-4 | $24.99**

STAR WARS
OMNIBUS
QUINLAN VOS—JEDI IN DARKNESS

## STAR WARS: QUINLAN VOS—JEDI IN DARKNESS

From his first appearance as a mind-wiped amnesiac to his triumphant passage to the rank of Jedi Master, few Jedi had more brushes with the powers of the dark side and the evil of the underworld than Quinlan Vos.

**ISBN 978-1-59582-555-1 | $24.99**

STAR WARS
OMNIBUS
THE COMPLETE SAGA

## STAR WARS: THE COMPLETE SAGA—EPISODES I THROUGH VI

The comics adaptations of the complete *Star Wars* film saga—in one volume! From Qui-Gon Jinn and Obi-Wan Kenobi's fateful encounter with Darth Maul to Luke Skywalker's victory over the Sith and Darth Vader's redemption, it's all here.

**ISBN 978-1-59582-832-3 | $24.99**

STAR WARS
OMNIBUS
DROIDS

## STAR WARS: DROIDS

Before the fateful day Luke Skywalker met Artoo and Threepio, those troublesome droids had some amazing adventures all their own—and they stick together in a dangerous galaxy where anything can happen!

**ISBN 978-1-59307-955-0 | $24.99**

**AVAILABLE AT YOUR LOCAL COMICS SHOP OR BOOKSTORE!**

To find a comics shop in your area, call 1-888-266-4226

For more information or to order direct: • On the web: DarkHorse.com • E-mail: mailorder@darkhorse.com • Phone: 1-800-862-0052 Mon.–Fri. 9 AM to 5 PM Pacific Time

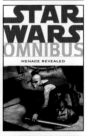

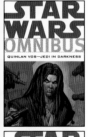

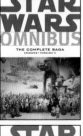

# STAR WARS GRAPHIC NOVEL TIMELINE (IN YEARS

Omnibus: Tales of the Jedi—5,000–3,986 BSW4

Knights of the Old Republic—3,964–3,963 BSW4

The Old Republic—3653, 3678 BSW4

Knight Errant—1,032 BSW4

Jedi vs. Sith—1,000 BSW4

Omnibus: Rise of the Sith—33 BSW4

Episode I: The Phantom Menace—32 BSW4

Omnibus: Emissaries and Assassins—32 BSW4

Omnibus: Quinlan Vos—Jedi in Darkness—31–30 BSW4

Omnibus: Menace Revealed—31–22 BSW4

Honor and Duty—22 BSW4

Blood Ties—22 BSW4

Episode II: Attack of the Clones—22 BSW4

Clone Wars—22–19 BSW4

Clone Wars Adventures—22–19 BSW4

General Grievous—22–19 BSW4

Episode III: Revenge of the Sith—19 BSW4

Dark Times—19 BSW4

Omnibus: Droids—5.5 BSW4

Omnibus: Boba Fett—3 BSW4–10 ASW4

Underworld—1 BSW4

Episode IV: A New Hope—SW4

Classic Star Wars—0–3 ASW4

Omnibus: A Long Time Ago . . . —0–4 ASW4

Omnibus: At War with the Empire—0 ASW4

Omnibus: The Other Sons of Tattooine—0 ASW4

Omnibus: Early Victories—0–3 ASW4

Jabba the Hutt: The Art of the Deal—1 ASW4

Episode V: The Empire Strikes Back—3 ASW4

Omnibus: Shadows of the Empire—3.5–4.5 ASW4

Episode VI: Return of the Jedi—4 ASW4

Omnibus: X-Wing Rogue Squadron—4–5 ASW4

Heir to the Empire—9 ASW4

Dark Force Rising—9 ASW4

The Last Command—9 ASW4

Dark Empire—10 ASW4

Crimson Empire—11 ASW4

Jedi Academy: Leviathan—12 ASW4

Union—19 ASW4

Chewbacca—25 ASW4

Invasion—25 ASW4

Legacy—130–137 ASW4

**Old Republic Era**
25,000 – 1000 years before
Star Wars: A New Hope

**Rise of the Empire Era**
1000 – 0 years before
Star Wars: A New Hope

**Rebellion Era**
0 – 5 years after
Star Wars: A New Hope

**New Republic Era**
5 – 25 years after
Star Wars: A New Hope

**New Jedi Order Era**
25+ years after
Star Wars: A New Hope

**Legacy Era**
130+ years after
Star Wars: A New Hope

**Vector**
Crosses four eras in the timeline

**Volume 1 contains:**
Knights of the Old Republic Volume 5
Dark Times Volume 3
**Volume 2 contains:**
Rebellion Volume 4
Legacy Volume 6

BSW4 = before *Episode IV: A New Hope*. ASW4 = after *Episode IV: A New Hope*.